本书系成都理工大学优秀创新团队培育计划"文化价值观译介团队项目（10912-KYTD201508）"成果之一

编委会

主　　编　段成　董勋

英文校阅　Fatima Pirbhai-lllich（加拿大）

副 主 编　易舫　文斌

编写人员　费比　孟嵊　李瑾　彭莹　肖海

　　　　　　周毅　肖凯　舒舟　景芳

A CULTURAL VOYAGE IN THE LAND OF ABUNDANCE

A Bilingual Reader of the Cultures of Ancient Towns in Sichuan Province

天府文化之旅

四川古镇文化双语读本

段成　董勋·主编

ZHEJIANG UNIVERSITY PRESS
浙江大学出版社

前　言

　　近年来,如何进一步提升中国文化的国际影响力,并有效推动中国文化走出去已成为重要的时代命题之一。然而,中国文化博大精深,遴选哪一方面的文化进行译介,即译什么,引起了广泛热议。随着研究的深入,我们发现古镇文化作为中国文化遗产的有机组成部分之一值得关注。拥有百年以上历史的古镇,承载了当地建筑、民俗、历史等文化内涵。在中国文化外宣话语体系的构建中,讲好古镇文化故事符合当前的时代命题与诉求,可更好地推动中国区域文化的外宣工作;同时,也有助于坚定文化自信心。此外,古镇文化也是民心相通的重要文化载体之一。让蕴含其中的中华优秀传统以日常叙事的形式得以再现,可更好地走进普通民众心中,促进人文交流。

　　四川古镇文化历史悠久,是四川区域文化最直观、生动的写照。其主要通过三种叙事形态得以彰显:(1)物质文化叙事的四川古镇文化,包括建筑文化、自然及人文景观文化遗迹。(2)精神文化叙事的四川古镇文化,包括价值观念、风俗习惯、道德规范等。(3)口头文学叙事的古镇文化,包括民间传说、传奇故事等。本书基于讲好中国故事的时代命题与诉求,精选20座知名的四川古镇,涵盖四川东、南、西、北等不同的方位,对具有鲜明地域特征的四川古镇文化素材进行编译,旨在通过对四川古镇文化三种叙事形态的考察,挖掘古镇背后的文化故事,展现蕴藏其中的历史文化内涵、民风民俗、价值观念等。

　　本书采用统一体例编译,力图为读者展现独具特色的四川古镇文化。每个古镇包括古镇简介、传奇故事、民俗文化、主要景点串游四部分。本书的主要特点如下:

1. 着眼古镇文化故事

　　有别于古镇旅行指南读物,本书除对20座古镇进行整体概述外,最大的亮点在于讲述古镇背后的文化故事,直观生动地再现蕴藏其中的价值观念、风俗习惯、道德规范等。比如,通过对街子古镇背后文化故事的讲述,展示了中国古代文人修身养性、淡泊名利的道德品质。

2. 凸显当地文化特色

　　根据民俗专家乌丙安先生对民俗文化的归类,本书从社会、经济、信仰、游艺的民俗等四方面对四川古镇的民俗文化进行译介,凸显了当地的文化特色。如:洛带古镇的饮食文化、黄龙溪古镇的龙文化、平落古镇的瓷胎竹编、阆中古城的傩戏文化、磨西古镇的婚嫁习俗等。

3. 详细注释，扫清文化障碍

在编译过程中，采取外宣翻译三贴近的原则，即贴近中国发展的实际、贴近国外受众对中国信息的需求、贴近国外受众的思维习惯，对中文内容进行英译。在此翻译理念的指导下，编者还特别邀请英语为母语的国外专家对英文稿进行阅读，并根据他们的阅读反馈，对术语、文化负载词等相关文化信息采用脚注或文内说明的方式进行详细注释。根据英语为母语者的认知阅读习惯，对叙述逻辑进行了适当调整，力求采用简单明了的语言，让文本更加通俗易懂，为英语读者所接受。

4. 双语读本，推动文化外宣

本书编写的语言为汉英双语，英语部分特别请国外专家审校、把关。因此，本书既可作为文化读本，适合对中国文化感兴趣的国内外读者，也可作为英语学习的语言素材，适合各类英语爱好者和自学者学习之用。

我们希望这样的双语读物能帮助读者对四川古镇文化形成直观、感性的认知，更好地走入四川古镇文化深处，体会中华民族伟大的民间智慧、创造力和想象力，感受中国人生生不息的精神和文化内涵。此外，还期盼在中国区域文化外译传播中，本书能发挥抛砖引玉的作用，引出更多诸如中国古镇文化、民俗文化研究、民俗文化语料库建设等相关研究及作品，进一步推动中国文化走出去。

本书编写得到成都理工大学优秀创新团队培育计划"文化价值观译介团队项目（10912-KYTD201508）"的大力资助。全书审校、修订、统稿及校译等工作主要由段成、董勋负责完成，参与本书编写的人员有董勋、易舫、文斌、费比、孟嵘、李瑾、彭莹、肖海、周毅、肖凯、舒舟、景芳等项目组成员。此外，成都理工大学外国语学院教师钟蔚及研究生李曦、巨少华、常富丽、秦琦、张翌博、张艳霞、谭妮等对本书初稿的中文内容进行了部分修订。加拿大里贾纳大学博士生导师Fatima Pirbhai-Illich教授对本书终稿英文内容进行了校读。

书中涉及大量的人物、事件、时间等历史性材料，尽管编写人员做了大量核查、校正工作，但难免有所疏漏，不妥之处恳请读者批评与指正。

文化价值观译介团队
2018年8月8日　成都

Preface

In recent years, how to further enhance the international influence of Chinese culture and effectively promote the going-global of Chinese culture has become one of the most important propositions of the times. However, Chinese culture is so profound that what specific aspect we should concern has aroused widespread debates, in other words, what to translate. With the further research, we find that the culture of ancient town, one of the important parts of Chinese cultural heritage is worthy of our attention. Ancient towns refer to those towns with the history of more than 100 years. They often demonstrate the cultural connotations of local architecture, folklore and history. In the construction of the Chinese culture discourse, telling the cultural stories of the ancient towns is in line with the current propositions and demands of the times, which can better promote the overseas publicity of Chinese regional culture. Meanwhile, it also helps to strengthen cultural self-confidence. In addition, the culture of ancient town serves as an important cultural bridge between Chinese people and their counterparts across the world. In this way, the outstanding Chinese traditions could be reproduced through the daily narratives, which can better expose ordinary people to the cultural essence and greatly promote cultural exchanges.

With a long history, the culture of Sichuan ancient towns is the most intuitive and vivid portrayal of Sichuan regional culture. It is mainly manifested through three narrative forms: (1) The narrative of the material culture in Sichuan ancient towns, including architectural culture, natural landscape and historical cultural relics. (2) The narrative of spiritual culture in Sichuan ancient towns, including values, folklore, ethics and so on. (3) The narrative of oral literary culture in Sichuan ancient towns, including folk legends, legendary stories, etc. Based on the propositions and demands of telling Chinese stories, this book selects 20 well-known Sichuan ancient towns, covering different geographic positions such as the east, south, west and north parts of Sichuan Province. The cultural materials with distinctive regional characteristics of Sichuan ancient towns are carefully compiled, aiming at investigating the three narrative forms of the ancient town culture in Sichuan and revealing the historical and cultural connotations, folk customs and values through the narration of the cultural stories embedded in the culture of ancient towns.

This book is compiled in a unified way, trying to show the unique cultures of Sichuan ancient towns to the readers. Each ancient town includes four parts: a brief introduction to the

ancient town, the legendary story, folk culture, and the main tourist attractions. The main features of this book are as follows:

1. Focusing on Cultural Stories of Ancient Towns

Different from the travel guide books of ancient towns, this book not only gives an overview of the 20 ancient towns, but also highlights their cultural stories, which vividly demonstrate the values, customs, ethics of these towns. For example, the narration of the cultural story of Jiezi shows the morality of ancient Chinese literati who emphasized a lot on self-cultivation and showed indifference to fame and fortune.

2. Highlighting Local Cultural Characteristics

According to the classification of folk culture by Wu Bing'an, a folk expert, this book translates the folk culture of Sichuan ancient towns from the following four aspects: society, economy, belief, and entertainment folklore. We attempt to highlight the local cultural characteristics, such as the food culture of Luodai, the dragon culture of Huanglongxi, the craft of Citaizhubian of Pingluo which is a kind of porcelain-bodied bamboo ware, Nuo Opera of Langzhong which was performed to eradicate diseases and devils, the wedding customs of Moxi and so on.

3. Clearing Cultural Barriers with Detailed Notes

In translation, the three-closeness principle for the overseas publicity-oriented translations is adopted, that is, close to the reality of China's development, close to the information needs of target-language readers, close to the thinking habits of target-language readers. Under the guidance of this translation principle, we invite native English speakers to read the English version of this book, and then footnotes or in-text explanations on terminology, culturally-loaded words and other related cultural information are added based on their reading feedback. In addition, according to the cognitive reading habits of native English speakers, the narrative logic has been appropriately adjusted, and simpler and clearer words or sentences have been used to make the text more understandable and acceptable to English readers.

4. Promoting the Overseas Publicity of Chinese Culture with a Bilingual Reader

The book is written in both Chinese and English. The English part is proofread by foreign experts. Thus, this book can be used not only as a cultural reader, suitable for domestic and overseas readers who are interested in Chinese culture, but also as the language material for English learning, suitable for all kinds of English lovers and learners.

We hope that such a bilingual reading can not only help readers to gain intuitive and perceptual cognition of Sichuan ancient town culture, but also better understand the essence of this culture. In this way, the great folk wisdom, creativity and imagination of the Chinese nation as well as Chinese cultural connotations could be felt. In addition, we also hope that in the translation of Chinese regional culture, this book can play a role in inspiring more researches and works in this field, such as Chinese ancient town culture research, folk culture research, folk culture corpus construction and so on. Through this way, we really expect the further promotion of the going-global of Chinese culture.

This book has been funded by Chengdu University of Technology's Outstanding Innovation Team Development Program: "The Translation and Research Team of Cultural Values (10912-KYTD201508)". The review, revision and translation proof-reading of the whole book were mainly completed by Duan Cheng and Dong Xun. Participants in the book include Dong Xun, Yi Fang, Wen Bin, Fei Bi, Meng Sheng, Li Jin, Peng Ying, Xiao Hai, Zhou Yi, Xiao Kai, Shu Zhou, Jing Fang. In addition, a teacher, Zhong Wei and some graduate students including Li Xi, Ju Shaohua, Chang Fuli, Qin Qi, Zhang Yibo, Zhang Yanxia, and Tan Ni at the College of Foreign Languages and Cultures of Chengdu University of Technology have partially revised the Chinese version of the first draft. Professor Fatima Pirbhai-Illich, a doctoral tutor at the University of Regina, Canada, read the English version of the final draft.

This book involves a large number of historical materials such as characters, events, and time. Although authors have done a lot of work on verification and correction, we know it is impossible to gain the perfection. We are ready to take suggestions on misprints and errors from all readers so that we can make improvements next time.

The Translation and Research Team of Cultural Values

Chengdu, Aug. 8th, 2018

目 录

CONTENTS

1. 崇州街子古镇

Jiezi Ancient Town, Chongzhou County

崇州街子古镇简介

　　街子古镇坐落于崇州城西北25千米的凤栖山下，毗邻青城后山和九龙山。东北与都江堰接壤，西距成都约50千米。街子古镇自建成至今已有1000多年的历史，古时候也被称为"横渠镇"，因横于味江河上而得名。古镇地势平缓，水系发达，地下水极其丰富，岷江的支

流也流经此处。镇上石板路两侧及居民屋院后，常年清水不断，因而有"川西水乡"之名。街子镇依山傍水，山清水秀，有"青城后花园"之美称。古镇自然资源丰富，历史文化深厚，孕育了"诗、史、禅、茶、非遗"五朵文化奇葩，是当代中国儒、释、道文化共存的川西小镇典范。古镇气候宜人，全年均适宜旅游。2012年被评为国家4A级旅游景区。

——传奇故事——

宁静致远：古刹秘史

　　街子古镇旁的凤栖山上有一古寺，始建于晋代，原名常乐庵。后来，明朝永乐年间，为

A Brief Introduction to Jiezi Ancient Town

Jiezi Ancient Town is located at the foot of Fengqi Mountain which is in an area 25 kilometers northwest of Chongzhou City, adjacent to Qingcheng Back Mountain and Jiulong Mountain in Sichuan Province. It is bounded by Dujiangyan Water Conservancy Project in the northeast, which is about 50 kilometers west from Chengdu City. With a history of more than one thousand years, the ancient town of Jiezi was known as "Hengqu Town" because it stretches over the Weijiang River. Jiezi is located on a flat terrain and has abundant river systems and groundwater. A tributary of the Minjiang River also flows through here. Jiezi has earned the title "a water town of western Sichuan" on account of the continuous clear streams which flow through both sides of the stone road and houses throughout the year. With picturesque scenery, Jiezi, which is situated at the foot of a mountain and beside a river, enjoys the reputation of being "the back garden of Qingcheng Mountain". With rich natural resources as well as rich historical and cultural heritages, this ancient town in western Sichuan Province is also famous for five cultural treasures, namely, poetry, history, Zen (Chan Buddhism), tea and intangible cultural tradition and heritage, which demonstrates the combination of Confucian, Buddhist, and Taoist cultures. With a pleasant climate, it is suitable for traveling all year round. Jiezi was rated as a national AAAA-grade tourist attraction in 2012.

—Legendary Stories—

Still Water Runs Deep: A Secret History of the Ancient Temple

There is an ancient temple on Fengqi Mountain which is next to Jiezi Ancient Town. The temple was built during the Jin Dynasty (265—420) with the original name of Changle[1] Monastery. During the Yongle period[2] of the Ming Dynasty (1368—1644), to show the respect

---

① Changle means being happy all the time in Chinese.

② Yongle period (1403—1424) refers to the reign of Zhu Di, the third emperor of the Ming Dynasty.

避免"乐"字之讳，蜀献王朱椿奏请皇上敕赐寺名"光严禅院"。古寺因有《初刻南藏》（又名《洪武南藏》）、贝叶梵文、御赐极品三件宝物而驰名天下，被喻为"西川第一天"。

古寺远近闻名，国内外游客、僧人远道而来，竭诚膜拜。它与明朝廷有着一段秘闻。据说明太祖朱元璋叔父朱五六在此出家。朱元璋叔父朱五六，人称悟空禅师，法号"法仁"。他曾云游印度等地，取回真经后，在街子古镇的古寺担任住持方丈。侄儿朱元璋当皇帝后，他不为所动，仍坚持在深山修禅。悟空禅师在这里扩建寺院，传播佛学，建树颇丰。圆寂后肉身完好，于是古寺僧人建灵塔，其肉身保存了600余年，不幸在20世纪50年代被毁。后人在佛塔门柱题联曰："从今日回头大悟，是浮云过眼皆空"。联尾藏"悟""空"二字，意指悟空禅师淡泊名利，潜心修行。

另据民间传说，朱元璋孙子建文帝朱允炆也在此出家。因皇叔朱棣篡位，朱允炆被大火围困宫中，走投无路之时，打开爷爷朱元璋当年传给他的一只铁箱，试图找到锦囊妙计，结果发现箱内装着一身和尚的行头。箱内还有一封书信，信中详细描述了通往宫外的秘道。聪慧的朱允炆立即化装成和尚，从秘道逃出，投奔了他的叔曾祖父悟空禅师。从此，他便在这座深山的古寺里潜心向佛，远离红尘，淡泊名利。

淡泊明志："一瓢诗人"

街子场外有条江，江上有座铁索桥，桥边原有座唐公祠。祠内不供神，只供一尊清奇古貌的文人像，此人就是"一瓢诗人"唐求。

唐求是唐代末期蜀州人，人称"唐隐居"，曾经当过青城县令，后来隐居于山清水秀的

for the emperor, Zhu Chun, King Xian of Shu①, suggested that the emperor give a new name to the temple, for "le" in the name of the temple was similar to the title of the emperor's reign. From then on, this temple was called "Guangyan Temple". This ancient temple was famous throughout the world for *Chu Ke Nan Zang*② (also called *Hong Wu Nan Zang*), Pattra-leaf scripture, and gifts③ bestowed by the emperor. It has the nickname "Di Yi Tian of Xichuan", which means the first wonderland for the God of Buddhism in western Sichuan.

The ancient temple, which is widely known, attracts tourists both from home and abroad and monks come from afar to worship there. It has a secret history related to the imperial court of the Ming Dynasty. It is said that Zhu Wuliu, one of Zhu Yuanzhang's④ uncles, became a monk here. Zhu Wuliu, called Wukong Buddhist Master, adopted the religious name of Fa Ren⑤. He once travelled around India and brought back scriptures and later became the Buddhist abbot of the ancient temple in Jiezi. Even though his nephew became the emperor, the Buddhist Master insisted in practicing Buddhism on the mountain. He made a great contribution to this ancient temple including extending the temple and spreading Buddhism. When the Buddhist Master Wukong passed away, the monks built a stupa⑥ to preserve his body. Thus, his body was kept intact. The body was preserved for more than 600 years. Unfortunately, it was destroyed in the 1950s. A Chinese couplet was found on the doorposts of the stupa. The couplet reads as follows: "Awakening soul comes from reflecting on history; floating clouds becomes void after drifting across the eyes". The last Chinese characters include the words "Wu"⑦ and "Kong"⑧, which refer to the Buddhist Master's pursuit of a simple life and dedication in practicing Buddhism.

According to folklore, Zhu Yunwen (grandson of Zhu Yuanzhang), Emperor Jianwen, also took his vows to become a monk at this temple. It is said that Zhu Yunwen was deliberately trapped by fire in the imperial palace, because his uncle Zhu Di planned to usurp his throne.

---

① Shu, also called Shu Han (221—263), was one of the three major states that competed for supremacy over China in the Three Kingdoms Period (220—280). The state was based in the area around present-day Sichuan and Chongqing. It was founded by Liu Bei, who had named his state "Han", as he considered it the legitimate successor to the Han Dynasty (206 BC—AD220), while "Shu" is added as a geographical prefix to show the differences.

② *Chu Ke Nan Zang* refers to the original official version of Buddhist scriptures in the Ming Dynasty.

③ Here the gifts consist of one royal sedan chair with four chair-carriers, four royal flags embroidered with a design of dragon and phoenix, five glazed tiles and two cooking pots.

④ Zhu Yuanzhang was the first emperor of the Ming Dynasty.

⑤ Fa Ren is a religious name in Buddhism with the meaning of benevolence.

⑥ Stupa is a kind of pagoda which is used to preserve Buddha's relics.

⑦ The Chinese Character "Wu" (悟) means the understanding of life.

⑧ The Chinese Character "Kong" (空) means void or non-existence.

味江边，也就是今天的街子古镇。当时的蜀国将军王建，听闻唐求才华出众，想要聘请他为参谋，但唐求对此无意，可又不好直接拒绝王将军的邀约，于是就以醉酒来回避王建派来的使者，以此表明婉拒之心。使者一来他就喝酒，喝得烂醉如泥，无法待客。有时，他躲在青城山的道观里，听道长讲经论道，避而不见。最后，王建也明白了唐求之意，便不再强人所难。

在长期的隐居生活中，唐求专注于写诗、吟诗，以诗会友。唐求写诗与众不同，他只要想起一句或一联，不管长短，都随手记在纸上，等凑成篇了，就把一首完整的诗稿搓成纸团，丢进一个大葫芦瓢中。因此，大家送他一个美称——"一瓢诗人"。

晚年卧病，唐求知道自己在世的时日不多，就把诗瓢投入味江，看着装满诗作的诗瓢越漂越远，他跪在河边祈祷说："上苍保佑，这个诗瓢若不沉没，捡到的人便知我唐求一生的苦心追求！"后来这个诗瓢漂到新渠镇，有个老头子看见了，觉得有些稀奇，赶忙撑船去把它捞上来。打开一看，原来是唐求的诗瓢，可惜只剩下30多首了。消息传开后，远近的人们都来传抄。后人编《全唐诗》时，将他的诗全部收了进去，自成一卷。"一瓢诗人"唐求的诗这才流传下来。

—民俗文化—

建筑文化

街子古镇的建筑和民居集中反映了四川西南部独特的自然风光；古街区现存以江城街

Whilst trying to escape, he found an iron case that was handed to him from his grandfather Zhu Yuanzhang. He opened the case hoping to find some wise counsel about his uncle's betrayal. Surprisingly, in that iron case he only found a monk robe and a letter in which a secret passage that led to the outside of the imperial palace was described. Smart Zhu Yunwen disguised himself as a monk and escaped through the secret passage. He went to the Buddhist Master Wukong, the uncle of his grandfather, for shelter. Since that time, he practiced Buddhism diligently, stayed away from society and became indifferent to fame and wealth.

Showing High Ideals by Simple Living: "Poet of the Gourd Ladle"

Outside Jiezi is a river, above which there is an iron cable bridge, where there is a temple called Tanggong Temple. Although no gods are worshipped in this temple, there is a statue of a scholar named Tang Qiu, known as "poet of the gourd ladle".

Tang Qiu was born in Sichuan Province in the late Tang Dynasty (618—907) and was popularly known as Mr. Tang Hermit. He was a magistrate of Qingcheng Town and later became a hermit, living beside the wonderful Weijiang River, in the area that we now call Jiezi Ancient Town. At that time, Wang Jian, a general of the Shu kingdom appreciated the talent of Tang Qiu and invited him to be his adviser. Tang Qiu showed no interest in this, but as a civilian, he couldn't refuse the general's invitation directly. To save the general's face, Tang Qiu came up with a brilliant idea. He pretended to be drunk when he heard about the coming of messengers sent by Wang Jian. As a result, the messengers thought he was too drunk to talk to them. Sometimes, he avoided messengers by deliberately going to the Taoist Temple in Qingcheng Mountain to meet with a Taoist priest. Finally, Wang Jian understood what Tang Qiu longed for and no longer invited him.

While living as a hermit, Tang Qiu spent a lot of time reading and writing poems. He had a special way of writing poems, in which he usually noted down one sentence or two from an inspiration on a piece of paper and then twisted these manuscripts into a roll and threw the roll into a big gourd ladle. Therefore, he won the reputation as "poet of the gourd ladle".

In his later years, he became very ill and was told that he was going to die. Before he died, he decided to throw the gourd ladle full of his poems into the Weijiang River. He knelt beside the river and prayed that God may bless the gourd ladle not to sink in the river and that those who picked it up would understand his lifelong pursuit. This gourd ladle slowly drifted to Xinqu Town where a senior man noticed it and drew it out of the water. The man opened it and discovered Tang Qiu's poems, but there were only about 30 poems left in it. Some people heard the news and rushed to copy the poems. Finally, these poems were collected in a volume of *Tang Poems*. Since then, Tang Qiu's poems have spread across the country.

为中心的六条街，街道两旁房屋大体根据清朝工部法则建造，以清代中、晚期建筑为主，清末建筑中有欧式装饰的痕迹，街上还有明代所挖的水井。现存的这些建筑朴素、小巧，不失深厚的历史文化底蕴，是反映清代西南小镇风貌的典型实物。

饮食文化

汤长发麻饼，简称汤麻饼，是街子古镇一道著名的小吃。从清乾隆五十一年（1786）起，街子汤氏家族以代代相传的方式将汤麻饼的制作技艺传承下来。据说其手艺只传儿媳不传儿女，怕儿子酒醉泄密，怕女儿出嫁失密。汤麻饼采用上等面粉、白糖、冰糖等原料，手工制作而成，形似馅饼。麻饼微甜、干香，为纯绿色食品，不含添加剂，保鲜时间可达半年以上。汤麻饼与竹编、藤编、棕编被列为成都市首批"非物质文化遗产"。

天主堂鸡片是川菜中的一道凉拌菜，因其创始人聂福轩在天主教堂附近摆摊年久而得名。这道凉菜色、香、味、形俱佳，颇负盛誉，驰名于民国十七年（1928），20世纪70年代入选《四川菜谱》，被称作"崇庆鸡片"。制作时选不足一岁的肥嫩公鸡，蒸熟切片装盘后，沿盘放入窝油，抖上花椒面，淋上芝麻酱和红油，然后撒上白糖，上桌后拌匀即食。1990年，天主堂鸡片被评为成都名小吃。

—Folk Culture—

Architectural Culture

The buildings and houses in Jiezi demonstrate the unique natural scenery of southwest Sichuan. The existing ancient town consists of six streets centering on Jiangcheng Street. The houses on both sides of the street were mainly built on the construction rules issued by the Ministry of Works in Qing Dynasty[①] (1616—1911) and were given priority to the architectural style of middle and late period of Qing Dynasty. There are even traces of European-style decoration and wells that had been dug in the Ming Dynasty. Steeped in history and culture, these simple and compact buildings are typical examples that reflect the architectural features of a southwestern town that flourished during the Qing Dynasty.

Food Culture

Tang's Sesame Pastry, short for Tang Changfa Sesame Pastry, is a famous snack in Jiezi. It was invented by the Tang family in 1786, the 51st year of the Qing Emperor Qianlong's reign (1736—1795), and its recipe and method of cooking have been handed down from generation to generation. It is said that only the daughter-in-law of the Tang family could inherit the recipe and cooking method for fear that their sons might spill the beans if drunk and their daughters may fail to hand down the recipe after they got married. The ingredients of this pastry consist of flour of fine quality, white sugar and rock candy. The pastry is in the shape of a pie and is made by hand. As a local organic food, the pastry, with its light, sweet-smelling fragrance, contains no additives, and can be kept for up to half a year. Together with bamboo, rattan and palm knitting, Jiezi Tang's Sesame Pastry is on the first list of intangible cultural heritage issued by Chengdu Municipal Government.

Tianzhutang[②] Sliced Chicken is a cold dish in Sichuan cuisine. It was named for a story: its creator Nie Fuxuan kept a sliced chicken selling booth near a Catholic church. The famous delicacy enjoys an excellent reputation for its perfect combination of color, aroma, taste and appearance. It won great fame in 1928, the 17th year of the Republic of China (1912—1949), and the recipe was included in *A Cookbook of Sichuan* with the name of Chongqing[③] Sliced Chicken in 1970's. The process of cooking this dish is as follows: first, select a fat chicken less than one year old, and steam it. When cooked, it should be sliced. Finally, season the chicken

---

① The Ministry of Works was in charge of engineering construction in the Qing Dynasty (1616—1911).

② Tianzhutang means a Catholic church in Chinese.

③ Chongqing refers to a county in Chongzhou City of Sichuan Province.

茶文化

街子古镇的茶文化源远流长，与青城山佛道养生文化相互渗融，滋养出街子的怡养文化。据考证，唐宋时，街子周边盛产茶叶，崇州曾是汉藏茶马贸易重要的集散地。崇州的枇杷茶是唐时进贡朝廷的贡茶。近年来，手工茶叶发展迅猛，品茗成为古镇的重要休闲文化活动之一。

兰文化

街子镇也是著名的"兰花之乡"。这里夏无酷暑，冬无严寒，雨量适宜，是种植兰花的好地方。街子的兰花品种多，名贵兰花多，这源于街子人爱兰的习俗。在街子人眼中，兰花不仅是一种商品，更是一种文化，一种积淀了数千年民族精神的兰花文化。正月十九的街子兰花会更是成了与龙泉桃花会、彭州牡丹会、新都桂花会等齐名的成都市著名的"八大花会"之一。

—主要景点串游—

字库塔

街子字库塔建于清咸丰二年（1852），为六角五级攒尖楼阁式，通高20米。外壁浮雕刻

with soybean oil, Sichuan pepper, sesame paste, red chilli oil and sugar before serving. In 1990, it was rated as one of Chengdu's most popular snacks.

Tea Culture

The tea culture in Jiezi, unique for its influence from Buddhism and Taoism, enjoys a long history. Historical records suggest that in the dynasties of Tang and Song, Chongzhou had been a significant distributing center of the Han and Tibetan tea-horse trade. In ancient times, the surrounding areas around Jiezi Town produced abundant quantities of tea. Loquat Tea, one kind of tea in Chongzhou, had been the chosen tea at the imperial court of the Tang Dynasty. In recent years, tea has become very popular and drinking tea has been an important part of the leisure culture of the ancient town.

Orchid Culture

Jiezi, also known as "orchid village", enjoys pleasant weather and regular rainfall, which are suitable for the growing of orchids. In this town, there are a variety of orchids, including some rare species. Local residents enjoy the custom of orchid appreciation. In their opinion, orchids are not a commodity, but a kind of culture symbolizing the national spirit. Every 19th day of the first month of the Chinese New Year, the Jiezi Orchid Festival is held. This has become one of the famous eight flower exhibitions[1] in Chengdu, along with Peach Flower Festival in Longquan, Peony Festival in Pengzhou, and Osmanthus Flower Festival in Xindu, etc.

—Main Tourist Attractions—

Ziku Pagoda

Ziku Pagoda in Jiezi, particularly used for the accumulation and burning of wasted paper, was built in 1852, the 2nd year of Xianfeng (1851—1861) in the Qing Dynasty. This pagoda is 20 meters high with a pavilion-like style of five tiers and six upswept eaves. On the outside structure of this pagoda are carved in relief the "Tale of White Snake", mountains, lakes and flowers. Its hollow masonry structure derives from the style of Buddhist pagodas, becoming one of the last surviving and finest pagodas in western Sichuan Province. The function of the Ziku Pagoda lies in collecting and disposing of wasted paper. In ancient China, a belief was held that

---

① The eight flower exhibitions in Chengdu refer to Peach Flower Festival in Longquan, Pear Flower Festival in Xinjin, Peony Festival in Pengzhou, Tulnip Festival in Pujiang, Lotus Festival in Jintang, Orchid Festival in Jiezi, Osmanthus Flower Festival in Xindu and Camelia Festival in Mountain Tiantai.

绘《白蛇传》片段和山水、花卉。借用佛教塔的基本型制，砖石中空结构，为川西地区仅存的精美字库塔之一。字库是收存和焚烧字纸的专用设施，源自古人"敬惜字纸"之风与"惜字得福"之说。

光严禅院

光严禅院位于凤栖山上，又名"古寺"。始建于晋隋时期。据民间传说，明太祖朱元璋叔父和孙子建文帝均在此出家避难。古寺因拥有《初刻南藏》、贝叶梵文、御赐极品三件宝物而享"西川第一天"之誉。古寺收藏的《初刻南藏》（又名《洪武南藏》）是明代刻造的中国佛门经典三个官版中唯一保留下来的印本，堪称中华佛门之经典。

唐公祠

唐公祠为纪念晚唐诗人唐求而建，原位于御龙桥头，1958年不幸被毁。后来为了纪念唐求，重新修建了一座唐公祠。正殿内有唐求塑像一尊，他手持诗笺，腰间挂一大葫芦，旁有青牛卧伴，形象再现了诗人悠闲自得的隐逸生活。祠堂前广场护栏上，展现了《全唐诗》辑录的35首半唐求诗句，集中体现了街子古镇源远流长的历史文化。

people who cherished words and paper were blessed with good luck.

Guangyan Temple

Guangyan Temple, also named Ancient Temple, located on Fengqi Mountain, is said to have been built during the Jin (266—420) or Sui Dynasty (581—618). According to folklore, Zhu Yuanzhang's uncle and grandson Zhu Yunwen, Emperor Jianwen became monks here to stay away from society and wars. The ancient temple was famous throughout the world for *Chu Ke Nan Zang*, Pattra-leaf scripture, and gifts bestowed by the emperor. It has a nickname "Di Yi Tian of Xichuan", which means the first wonderland for the God of Buddhism in western Sichuan. *Chu Ke Nang Zang* (*Hong Wu Nang Zang*) collected by Guangyan Temple is not only a Buddhist classic in China but also the only existing Buddhist script among the three official versions of the Ming Dynasty.

Tanggong Temple

Tanggong Temple next to Yulong Bridge was built in memory of Tang Qiu, a poet of the late Tang Dynasty. Unfortunately, this temple was destroyed in 1958. However, another temple was built in its place to commemorate this poet. In the main hall stands a statue of Tang Qiu. He is holding a sheet of paper for poem writing in his hand and has a big gourd tied to his waist. Lying next to him is a bull as a companion. The leisure life of Tang Qiu as a hermit is vividly demonstrated by the two statues. Approaching the temple, Tang Qiu's 35 and a half poems which were collected in a volume of *Tang Poems* are all carved on the guardrails of Tang Qiu Square, in which the long history and rich culture of Jiezi Ancient Town are well documented.

2. 龙泉洛带古镇

Luodai Ancient Town, Longquan District

龙泉洛带古镇简介

　　洛带古镇位于成都市东郊龙泉山麓，距成都市区约20千米。三国时建镇，传说因蜀汉后主刘禅的玉带落入镇旁八角井中而得名。洛带是全国首批重点小城镇，中国西部最大的也是唯一的客家古镇，因85%以上的居民为客家移民而享有"中国西部客家第一镇"之称，蕴含深厚的客家文化。其方言"土广东话"音韵依存，被世人称为"世界的洛带、永远的客家"。场镇老街以明清建筑风格为主，呈"一街七巷子"格局，拥有四大客家会馆，是名副其实的"客家名镇、会馆之乡"。2008年被评为第四批中国历史文化名镇。古镇属亚热带季风气候，年平均气温16～17℃，温暖湿润，全年均适宜旅游。

——传奇故事——

太子落带：镇名传说

　　洛带古镇迄今已有1700多年历史，原名甑子场。有关镇名的来历有好几种说法：一说为镇旁有一"洛水"盘绕，形如玉带，故名"洛带"；二说为场镇老街蜿蜒千米，似玉带从天飘落，故名"落带"，后演变为"洛带"；三说与蜀汉后主刘禅玉带落入井中相关，这也是目前得到

A Brief Introduction to Luodai Ancient Town

The Ancient Town of Luodai is located at the foot of the Longquan Mountains, which is 20 kilometers east from downtown of Chengdu. The town was built during the Three Kingdoms Period (220—280). The name of the town is said to derive from a legend when Liu Shan, the king of Shu Han[①] Kingdom (221—263), accidentally dropped his jade belt into one octagonal well of the town. Luodai is not only on the first list of important national towns but also the only and largest Hakka ancient town in western China. As this town has more than 85% of Hakka residents and a strong Hakka culture, the town has earned the title of "the first Hakka town in western China". Here, the local dialect of Cantonese keeps its rhythm and charm. For this reason, it is also called "the international Luodai with eternal Hakka". The main layout of the town is that of one-street-and-seven-lanes incorporating architectural styles of the Ming and Qing dynasties. With four main Hakka Guild Halls, the town is worthy of its title "a famous Hakka town, and the home of guild halls". In 2008, Luodai was included in the list of Famous Historical and Cultural Towns in China (the fourth batch). With subtropical humid climate, the annual average temperature here is 16–17℃, and it is warm and humid. It is suitable for traveling all year round.

—Legendary Stories—

The Falling Belt of the Prince: Stories about the Name of the Town

Luodai was called Zengzi Town for more than 1,700 years. There are several stories about the name of the town. The first story is related to the river around the town. The shape of the river is like a jade belt and thus the town was called Luodai (dai in Chinese means belt). The second associates the name with an old street in the town winding across one kilometer as if a jade belt were falling from the sky. The third and the most widely acknowledged story is related with Liu Shan, the young king of Shu Han, who had accidentally dropped his jade belt into a well of the town.

It's said that there was a pond in Luodai during the period of Three Kingdoms. In the middle of the pond, there was an octagonal well with a water source that originated from the mouth of

---

① See foot note ① on page 5.

普遍认可的一种说法。

  相传，三国时洛带古镇有一池塘，中间造有一口八角井，井水是东海龙王口中吐出来的，味道甘甜，取之不尽。

  民间流传着一种说法，称井里有东海鲤鱼，味道鲜美，可延年益寿。蜀主刘备的儿子刘禅，小名阿斗，居住在甑子场。他年幼贪玩，顽劣异常，听闻此说法后，便择黄道吉日，带着随从们来到了八角井。时值正午，阳光照在井口边，阿斗小心翼翼地趴到井台向里望去，突然看见无数的金色鲤鱼在水井和池塘的石洞间穿梭游动。他一时兴起，便令随从们下水捉鱼，然而捞了半天，随从们皆是空手而归，阿斗气急败坏。

  突然，只听一声"好"，一条大鲤鱼随着一位白发老翁的钓竿甩动，一下子飞出井来。阿斗心生羡慕，想要买下此鱼。白发老翁不愿出售，阿斗收买不成便率领所有随从去抢鱼。鱼在阿斗手中拼命挣扎，由于阿斗年纪尚小，没什么力气，一不小心连人带鱼一起跌进池塘。那鱼儿掉进池塘后，穿过石洞进入八角井，通过"海眼"游回东海去了。阿斗被救上岸后，发现腰间的玉带也不见了踪影。

  此时，老翁已驾鹤离去，只见从空中飘下一条绸帕，写道："不思创业苦，孺子太荒唐；带落八角井，帝运终不昌。"阿斗气得将手帕扔入井中，结果手帕变巨石，阻塞海眼，井水因此变得浑浊苦涩。从此，太子落带的故事就不胫而走，人们因此将甑子场改名为"落带"。后

Dragon King of East Sea. That was why the water in the well tasted sweet and was thought to be inexhaustible.

Another folk legend says that there were delicious carp in the well. The carp were thought to be beneficial to people's health and could prolong their life. Hearing of this legend, Liu Bei's son Liu Shan, a young prince of Shu Han who had a pet name of "Ar Dou" and was very naughty, came to the octagonal well on an auspicious day with his attendants. At noon, whilst the sun shone down, Liu Shan looked cautiously into the well, and saw numerous golden carp swimming inside. He immediately ordered his attendants to jump into the water to catch these carp. Although they tried to catch some carp, they caught nothing. This upset the young naughty king extremely.

Suddenly, they heard someone exclaiming "great". Liu Shan turned around and saw a grey-haired old man catching a big carp with his fishing rod. Liu Shan was jealous and wanted to buy the fish. However, his request was rejected. Liu Shan, together with his attendants snatched the carp away from the old man. The carp struggled so desperately that the young weak prince accidently fell into the pond together with the fish. After falling into the pond, the carp immediately swam away into the well through a hole and then back to the East Sea through the well which was said to be connected to the sea. Rescued ashore, Liu Shan found his jade belt had disappeared.

Whilst this was happening, the old man flew away on his crane, dropping a silk handkerchief from the sky with the words, "You are too naïve to know how hard it is to establish a kingdom. It is doom for you as a king to drop your jade belt into the well". Seeing these words, Liu Shan got so angry that he threw the handkerchief into the well and surprisingly, the handkerchief turned into a huge rock. This rock obstructed the well, making the well water muddy and bitter. Since then, the story of the jade belt dropping into the well has spread far and wide. Hence, people renamed Zengzi Town to Luodai. However, the Chinese character "落"（Luo）sounds unlucky in Chinese, which means to fall, to decline or to take a bad turn, thus the locals finally adopted a homophone " 洛 "（Luo）. That's the folk legend of how the ancient town of Luodai got its name.

True Love in Adversity: The Origin of Water-dragon Dance Festival

Water-dragon Dance is one of the traditional folklore activities in Luodai. This is a type of dance practiced by the local people to pray for rain. There is a touching story about its origin. In the town, lived a beautiful young lady who was admired by a stream of young men. However, no youth in the village could make her heart pound, for she wanted to find a man who was kind, hardworking and who would love her with all his heart.

One day, the young lady contracted a strange disease. Her body was covered with long hair, and her face was dotted with strange sores. Such a beautiful lady suddenly turned into an

来因"落"字不吉利而将其改成了"洛"，"洛带"之名由此而来。

患难真情：水龙节传说

洛带素有舞水龙祈雨的传统，关于其来历，还有一个动人的传说。相传在古代，有一位十分美丽的姑娘，追求者络绎不绝。姑娘想找一位勤劳善良、真心爱她的青年，却始终没能如愿。

有一天，姑娘突然得了一种怪病：全身长出了很长的毛发，脸上、身上也生出怪疮。美丽的姑娘一下子变得又老又丑，爱慕她美貌的男子都躲得远远的。姑娘很伤心，找不到治疗的方法，变得越来越憔悴。有一天，姑娘梦见一位神仙对她说，如果她坚持沐浴九天即可痊愈。梦醒后，姑娘既高兴又失望。高兴的是得到了神仙的指点，有望治好疾病。失望的是沐浴需大量用水。这一年适逢大旱，村民只能到百里外的河里挑水，许多人死于饥渴。此时的水如此宝贵，不知有谁愿意帮她去百里之外取沐浴之水。

不出所料，村里的男青年们听说此事后，都不愿意帮忙。然而，村东有一位男子，得知姑娘生怪病后，下定决心帮助她。原来这位小伙子非常倾慕姑娘，但因家境贫寒一直没敢表达自己的爱意。为了尽快取回水，他几乎天天早出晚归。姑娘用青年背回来的水沐浴后，病情开始好转，皮肤渐渐变白。青年知晓后无论再苦再累都坚持取水。到了第九天，当他把水背到村头时，天已黑，青年因过于疲倦饥渴而晕倒了，桶里的水洒了一地。在村头等待青年的姑娘看到他昏倒在树旁，急忙把桶里仅有的几滴水喂进青年口中。待青年醒来，两人不禁相拥而泣。神仙曾说如果姑娘不能连续沐浴九天，将会前功尽弃。幸运的是，青

old and ugly woman, scaring all the young men away. She was in deep pain and sad every day. Having no idea of how to cure this disease, she was gradually becoming tired. A few days later, the lady dreamed of a fairy, who told her in the dream that if she took a bath for nine days in a row, she could recover. When she woke up the next morning, the young lady felt much happier but was still worried. Using the dream for guidance, she expected to be cured. However, she needed a lot of water for a bath. In that year, a severe drought struck the village and many people died of hunger and thirst. Villagers had to walk a hundred miles to get water from a river. Water was so precious at the time that she was not sure if anyone would be willing to carry water for her from that far.

Unsurprisingly, the young men in the village were not willing to holp her after hearing about the incident. To the east of the village lived a young man, who was also one of her admirers. However, because he was poor, he was not confident enough to express his love for her. When he heard of what had happened to the lady, he was very anxious and determined to help cure her disease. So eager was he to get water for the lady, the young man started off early every morning to fetch water from the river with a bucket and by the time he returned, it was very late at night. Luckily, after bathing with the water that was fetched by the young man, the lady began to recover, and her skin gradually started becoming clear again. Seeing this, the young man persisted in setting off early to fetch water despite his hunger and thirst.

On the ninth day when the young man returned to the village with water on his back, the moon had climbed up to the sky. Tired, hungry and thirsty, he couldn't support himself anymore and fainted under a tree by the roadside. The water in the bucket spilled all over the ground. The anxious lady who was waiting for him at the end of the road hurried to the man and fed him with the last drops of water that were left in the bucket. At last, he woke up slowly. They embraced each other, weeping together. However, if the lady couldn't take the bath for nine days in succession, all the efforts the young man had done would have been in vain. Fortunately, the young man's perseverance and his true love for the young lady moved the Dragon King[①] who was the God in charge of rains. By a miracle, a heavy rain poured down. The lady's skin became as beautiful and charming as she was before she got the disease. Additionally, the severe drought in the village was greatly eased and hundreds of villagers were saved. The young couple got married and lived happily ever after.

Since then, in commemoration of this beautiful and touching love story, people perform the Water-dragon Dance and splash water on that day every year, in the hope of good weather for their crops and a happy life for the people. Passed from generation to generation, the Water-dragon Dance Festival has become a unique folk festival of the Hakka.

---

① In ancient Chinese myth, Dragon King led aquarium and could control clouds and rain.

年坚持不懈的精神和他对这位姑娘真诚的爱最终感动了龙王，下了一场瓢泼大雨。这时，奇迹出现了：姑娘在雨中恢复了以前的美貌，大雨也缓解了旱情，拯救了无数生命。从此，两人相爱相依，过上了幸福美满的生活。

此后，每年的这一天人们都会舞水龙、泼水，以祈求风调雨顺、祈求幸福生活来纪念这个动人的爱情故事。水龙节代代相传，成为客家人独有的民俗节日。

—民俗文化—

建筑文化

古镇呈封闭式布局，"一街七巷子"①和"五馆一园"②最具代表性。入夜时，上下街口和七条小巷栅门关闭，古镇即呈完整而封闭的防御体系，体现了客家独特的围楼建筑。这一封闭式的建筑格局折射出客家人的文化心理。客家人总是四处迁徙，家里的男子又常年在外谋生。出于对家里妇幼老人安全性的考虑，其房屋建筑注重防御功能。因此，客家民居多为单进四合院式围拢屋，正中为堂屋，屋脊上常有"中花"和"鳌尖"等装饰物。冬暖夏凉，通风采光科学。巫氏大夫第是目前古镇上保存最完好的清代典型客家民居。

客家山歌

客家人喜欢唱山歌，内容丰富，唱腔优美。歌词善用比兴，韵脚齐整，极富生活气息。每逢端午节，客家人皆要举行斗山歌比赛，男女对歌更是一大亮点。

舞龙

洛带舞龙以"刘家龙"最负盛名，分为火龙和水龙。火龙七节，每逢伏旱，则大显身手，以祈雨。水龙九节，年初一至元宵节，每日飞舞，以祈福。舞龙高潮是烧火龙，同时会放鞭炮、焰火。居民、游客和舞龙者在龙舞与焰火中攻防进退，非常壮观。

---

① "一街七巷子"指上下街和北巷子、凤仪巷、槐树巷、江西会馆巷、柴市巷、马槽堰巷、糠市巷。
② "五馆一园"指广东会馆、江西会馆、湖广会馆、川北会馆、客家博物馆和客家公园。

—Folk Culture—

Architectural Culture

Luodai has a closed architectural layout, with the representative patterns of one-street-and-seven-lanes and five-guild-halls-and-one-park[①]. At night, all the entrances to the up-and-down-street and seven lanes are closed. Therefore, the town has a complete and enclosed defense system, which represents the special Hakka earthen building. Such an enclosed architectural layout reflects the Hakka's cultural psychology. The Hakka have always been mobile, and men often have to make a living far away from home all year round. For the security of their women, children and the elderly, the citizens of Luodai attached more importance to the defense function of buildings. Hence, Hakka residences are also mostly designed and built in a quadrangle-courtyard style, with only one single entrance. The main house stands in the central part with flowers or turtles carved on the ridge of roof. The houses are warm in the winter and cool in the summer, with fine ventilation and natural lighting. Lord Wu's Residence is the best-preserved typical Hakka house of the Qing Dynasty (1616—1911) in this ancient town.

Hakka Folk Songs

The Hakka people love singing folk songs, and these songs consist of rich content and beautiful arias. The lyrics employ both metaphor and analogy with rhymes and have a strong breath of life. During the Dragon Boat Festival, love song competitions are always the highlight of the folk song competition.

Hakka Dragon Dance

Among the Hakka Dragon Dance teams of Luodai, the most representative one is Liu's Dragons which consist of a water dragon and a fiery dragon. The fiery dragon's body has seven sections and when summer droughts occur, people perform the dance to pray for rain. The water dragon's body has nine sections, and from the 1st to 15th day of the first lunar month, the dance is performed seeking for blessings. The highlight of the fiery dragon dance is the burning of the fiery dragon and the setting off of fireworks. Both tourists and locals dance with the fiery-dragon dancers under the spectacular fireworks.

---

① One-street-and-seven-lanes refers to the Up-and-down Street, North Lane, Phoenix-like Lane, Locust Tree Lane, Jiangxi Guild Hall Lane, Firewood Lane, Manager Lane and Bran-market Lane. Five-guild-halls-and-one-park refers to Guangdong Guild Hall. Jiangxi Guild Hall, Huguang Guild Hall and Chuanbei Guild Hall, Hakka Museum and Hakka Park.

饮食文化

豆腐干是客家著名的"八大干"之一，是客家人为适应迁徙生活而制造出来的一种特殊食品，便于携带、保存，一般可保存两至三个月。其大小约二寸[①]半见方，薄如纸，呈金黄色，嚼起来略带咸味。

酿豆腐也是客家人生活中常见的小吃，据说与北方饺子有关。客家先民原居住在中原地区，当地盛产小麦，常用面粉做饺子。后因战乱等原因，客家先民迁徙至南方生活，南方多产大米，少产小麦，面粉很少，酿豆腐则成为替代饺子的食物。其制作方法为：将油炸豆腐或白豆腐切成小块，在每小块豆腐中央挖一个小洞，将香菇、碎肉、葱蒜等佐料填补进去，然后用砂锅小火烹煮，食时再配酱油、胡椒等调料即可。

伤心凉粉是洛带知名小吃之一。其名来源有两种说法：一为客家人初来四川，每当夜深人静制作家乡凉粉时就会思念家乡，故取名客家伤心凉粉；另一种说法是该凉粉很辣，吃后会辣出眼泪，被误认为伤心，故得此名。

除此以外，客家菜最出名的还有九斗碗、盐卤鸡、油烫鹅、面片汤。

—主要景点串游—

广东会馆

广东会馆为洛带镇的标志性建筑，又名"南华宫"。它由广东籍客家人出资，始建于清乾隆十一年（1746）。主体建筑由戏台、乐楼、耳楼及前中后三殿组成，呈中轴线对称排列，复四合院式结构，主体建筑面积3310平方米。其风火墙建筑结构在四川绝无仅有，是目前全国保存最完好、规模最宏大的会馆之一。

---

① 1寸≈3.33厘米。

Food Culture

Dried Tofu is one of the Hakka's famous eight dried foods. This food is easy to carry and could be stored two to three months for convenience because of the men's mobile life style. Dried Tofu, a golden-brown cube with the size of around two cuns[①] and a half is as thin as a sheet and it tastes salty.

Yong Tau Foo[②] or Hakka-style Stuffed Tofu, is also a common Hakka snack, which is said to be related to Jiaozi, a type of food in northern China. Hakka ancestors lived in the central part of China where there was an abundance of wheat. Thus, Jiaozi is one of the daily foods for Hakka. However, due to wars and fights, the Hakka migrated to southern China where there was abundance of rice rather than wheat. Thus, Yong Tau Foo became a substitute for Jiaozi. The process of cooking is as follows: first, cut the fried tofu or soft tofu into cubes and then scoop out a teaspoon of tofu in the middle to make room for some minced meat, mushrooms, garlic and spices. Finally, stew them in a casserole on low heat and season with soybean oil, pepper and spices according to taste before serving.

Sad Bean Jelly is a famous snack in Luodai. There are two stories about the origin of this snack. The first one is about how the Hakka people missed their hometown when making jelly, one of their hometown foods. That's how the food got its name. The other version is that the jelly is so spicy that people often burst into tears when tasting it, seeming they are sad.

Besides Bean Jelly, there are other famous dishes such as Hakka Jiudouwan[③], salted pot-stewed chicken, fire-cured goose and noodle soup.

——Main Tourist Attractions——

Guangdong Guild Hall

Guangdong Guild Hall is also called Nanhua Hall, which is one of the representative buildings in the town of Luodai. Donated by a Hakka native from Guangdong, this guild hall was built in 1746, the 11th year of the reign of Emperor Qianlong (1736—1795). Covering an area of 3,310 square meters, the main part consists of a drama stage, a music stage, subsidiary halls, and three other halls respectively in the front, middle and rear of the guild hall. All the buildings are symmetrically laid along an axis, in the double quadrangle-

---

① Cun ("寸") is a unit of length which equals to 3.33 centimeter.

② Yong Tau Foo belongs to traditional Chinese Hakka cuisine, which is mainly made by tofu stuffed with minced meat.

③ Jiudouwan refers to nine steamed dishes. "Dou" means a big container in Sichuan dialect. Here, Jiudouwan shows that there are so many dishes.

湖广会馆

湖广会馆因供奉大禹，又称"禹王宫"，清乾隆十一年（1746）由湖广籍移民捐资修建。依中轴线对称排列，由牌坊、戏台、耳楼、中后殿及左右厢房构成，建筑面积2771平方米。无论下多大雨，该处都不会被淌水淹没。现馆内设有"客家博物馆"，较完整地反映了湖广移民的艰苦创业和社会生活。其内的"睡观音"据说是全国最大的卧式观音像。

江西会馆

江西会馆，又名"万寿宫"，由江西籍客家人于清乾隆十八年（1753）捐资兴建而成，位于洛带镇老街中街。会馆坐北向南，由戏台、

courtyard style. The fire wall[1] construction of this guild hall is unique and rare in Sichuan Province. Guangdong Guild Hall is one of the best-preserved and largest guild halls in China.

Huguang Guild Hall

Huguang[2] Guild Hall is also called King Yu's Palace, for it enshrines Yu the Great[3]. Funded by Huguang migrants, it was built in 1746, the 11th year of the reign of Emperor Qianlong. The guild hall, covering an area of 2,771 square meters, consists of a paifang (a memorial archway), a drama stage, subsidiary halls, middle hall, real hall and wing rooms on the left and right sides. All the buildings are symmetrical along an axis. The guild hall has never flooded no matter how heavy the rainfall. Today, there is a Hakka museum in the guild hall, fully demonstrating the social life and hardships when Huguang migrants started their business in the early days. There is also a Sleeping Guanyin[4] inside it, which is said to be the largest reclining Guanyin statue in China.

Jiangxi Guild Hall

Jiangxi Guild Hall, also known as "Wanshou[5] Hall", was built in 1753, the 18th year of Qianlong's reign with the money donated by the Hakka people from Jiangxi Province. It is located at the center of the old street, facing south and covers an area of 1,185 square meters. It consists of a drama stage, a paifang, wing rooms on both sides, the front, middle and rear halls and a small drama stage. Such a double quadrangle courtyard is valuable for its overall layout and architectural aesthetics. Its small drama stage is especially unique and unprecedented among the styles of Hakka guild halls in Sichuan Province. It has become a frequent site these days for filming.

Randeng Temple

Randeng Temple[6] was built during the reign of the first emperor in the Sui Dynasty (581—

[1] Fire wall, also called horse-head wall, refers to a kind of wall that has been built in a traditional Chinese architectural style, especially applied in Anhui and Jiangxi architectural buildings. Its function is to stop the fire from spreading to other parts of the buildings.

[2] Huguang was a Province in Yuan Dynasty (1271—1368). In Qing Dynasty, it was divided into two parts. The north part was called Hubei Province, and the south part was called Hunan Province.

[3] Yu the Great (c.2200 BC—2100 BC) was a legendary ruler in China's prehistoric times, famous for his introduction to curbing floods.

[4] Guanyin is the abbreviation for Guanshiyin. It means Merciful Buddha or Avalokitesvara, which was translated from Kumārajīva. Guanyin is popular in China, for it symbolizes compassion and wisdom.

[5] Wanshou means longevity.

[6] Randeng Temple enshrines Dipankara. Randeng means lamp lighting in Chinese.

牌坊、左右厢房、前中后三殿及一个小戏台构成，为复四合院式，建筑面积1185平方米，在整体布局和建筑美学方面都颇有价值。其小戏台构思独特，为四川客家会馆中前所未有的建筑风格，因而经常被影视界选为拍片场所。

燃灯寺

燃灯寺建于隋开皇年间（581—600）。清嘉庆年间（1796—1820）因其殿上奉有燃灯铁佛，故得名"燃灯寺"。传说善男信女燃其灯而病自怯，甚是灵验。

600）. It got the current name Randeng Temple during the reign of Jiaqing（1796—1820）in the Qing Dynasty, for Dipankara Buddha[①] was enshrined there. It is believed that if believers light the candle in the temple, they will efficaciously recover from their illness.

---

① Dipankara Buddha, meaning a lamp bearer, is a buddha of the past. He is said to have lived on Earth one hundred thousand years ago. Buddhists believe that there has been a succession of many Buddhas in the distant past and that many more will appear in the future. Dipankara, Gautama, and Maitreya are "the Buddhas of Three Times".

3. 金堂五凤溪古镇
Wufengxi Ancient Town, Jintang County

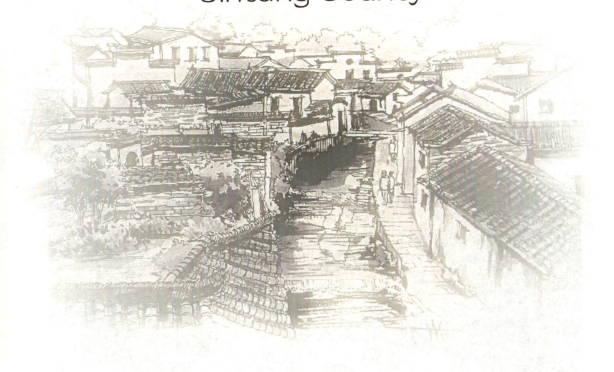

五凤溪古镇简介

　　五凤溪古镇位于龙泉山脉中段的沱江之畔，属成都市金堂县，距成都市48千米，离县城赵镇45千米。古镇建于清朝康熙年间（1662—1722），是成都市十大古镇中唯一的山地古镇。自古以来，五凤溪山清水秀，镇周五座山岗，翘首企天，树木郁郁葱葱，酷似冲霄之凤。镇中金凤、玉凤、青凤、白凤、小凤五条主要街道布局有致。其地貌地形，天然雕琢，地理位置更似凤凰展翅。黄水河穿镇而过，交汇于沱江，地理条件得天独厚，故名"五凤溪"。2004年6月，五凤溪镇被成都市政府列为首个市级历史文化名镇。

—传奇故事—

五仙忘返：镇名传说

　　关于五凤溪名字得来的传说有很多。一说为该地五山聚集，远远看像五只冲上云霄的凤凰，故此得名。1921年编修的《金堂县续志》卷一对此有详细解说，"石城寺山，又名小

A Brief Introduction to Wufengxi Ancient Town

The Ancient Town of Wufengxi is located near Tuojiang River, adjacent to the middle part of Longquan Mountains. It is 48 kilometers from Chengdu City, and 45 kilometers from Zhao Town of Jintang County. Built during the reign of Emperor Kangxi (1662—1722) of the Qing Dynasty (1616—1911), it is the only mountain town among the ten famous ancient towns of Chengdu City. Since ancient times, with picturesque scenery, it has been surrounded by five luxuriantly green mountains which look as if they have raised their heads in expectation, exactly like phoenixes rushing up into the sky. Thus, there are five main streets named after the five mountains, called Jinfeng, Yufeng, Qingfeng, Baifeng and Xiaofeng, all of which are arranged orderly in the town. The landforms of the town seem as if they have been carved naturally. And its geographic position looks more like phoenixes spreading wings. Huangshui River runs through the town and merges into the Tuojiang River. Favorably endowed geographically, it was named Wufengxi, which means Five Phoenixes Stream in Chinese. In June 2004, Wufengxi Town was listed as the first Municipal Historical and Cultural Town by Chengdu Municipal Government.

—Legendary Stories—

Five Fairies' Reluctance to Leave: Stories about the Name of the Town

There are many legends about the name of the town, one of which is that five mountains gathered here. From afar they look like five phoenixes rushing up into the sky breaking out over the clouds, hence the name. There is a detailed narration in Volume One of *Jintang County Continued Annals* compiled in 1921, which states that "Shichengsi Mountain which is also called Little Yunding Mountain winds its way from Heifeng Temple, from north to south and east all the way round forty to fifty miles with sharp and thin crests. Looking from afar, it is like five phoenixes that are rushing up into the sky and breaking out over the clouds. The five mountains are so steep that the predecessors named their streams Wufengxi, meaning Five Phoenixes Stream in Chinese".

Another legend is that, five daughters of the Queen Mother of the West[1] secretly descended

---

[1] The Queen Mother of the West is a goddess in Chinese religion and mythology.

云顶山，自黑风寺下，山极屈曲，自北而南而东，周转四五十里，一路尖峰拔列，瘦削逼人，遥望之若冲霄之五凤，破空而出，其峰之尖且高者有五，前人名其溪曰五凤，殆由于此"。

另据传说称，西王母有五个女儿，偷偷下凡来，对该地山水流连忘返，便化作五座山峰永留于此。在这五座山间蜿蜒的小溪被美称为"五凤溪"。后来，镇中的街道都以凤字命名，有金凤、青凤、小凤、白凤、玉凤五条主要街道，布局错落有致，被人们戏称为"金青小白玉"。

千帆齐聚：码头趣闻

五凤溪古镇背靠龙泉山，面临沱江水。有渣浮渡、鸣阳渡、金牛渡、罗坝渡四个渡口，是沱江水系进入成都的必经之路。在清代中叶，五凤溪也是川西第一水陆码头。

五凤溪当地流传着一首民谣："五凤溪一张帆，要装成都半城盐。五凤溪一摇桨，要装成都半城糖。"虽然有些夸张，但也道出了五凤溪当年"门泊万里船，千帆竞待发"的繁盛景象。大江南北的商贾聚集此地，孕育了发达的码头文化。在这里，重庆的洋货、宜宾的水果、自贡的井盐、内江的白糖，沿着沱江运到五凤，再从这里上岸，由脚夫转运至成都。高峰时，每天有100多条船在五凤码头装卸货物。

小镇骄傲：哲学巨擘贺麟

五凤溪依山傍水，在这里诞生了一位世界级的哲学大师：贺麟（1902—1992）。贺麟出生于五凤溪镇杨柳沟村的一个士绅家庭。17岁考入清华大学，成为梁启超的学生。贺麟深受梁启超、梁漱溟、吴宓等名师影响，后来留学美国、德国。对斯宾诺莎和德国古典哲学深

to earth. The five fairies were so enchanted by the mountains and rivers of this area that they were unwilling to leave. Thus, they turned themselves into the five mountains. The stream winding between the mountains got the name Five Phoenixes Stream. Later, all the streets in the town included the name with Feng, meaning Phoenix. Jinfeng, Qingfeng, Xiaofeng, Baifeng and Yufeng are the five main streets in the town and they have a well-proportioned lay-out. This is jokingly called "Jin Qing Xiao Bai Yu[①]".

The Gathering of Thousands of Sails: Wharf Anecdote

Backing on to the Longquan Mountains and facing the Tuojiang River, the Ancient Town of Wufengxi has four feries, namely Zhafu, Mingyang, Jinniu and Luoba Ferries. Taking a ferry on the Tuojiang River is the only way to get to Chengdu. Hence it has gained the title "the number one land ferry of western Sichuan" since the middle of the Qing Dynasty.

"One sail in Wufengxi can be loaded with twice the salt of one from Chengdu. One oar in Wufengxi can be loaded with twice the sugar of one from Chengdu." This is a folk song from Wufengxi. Exaggerated as it is, this folk song really portrays the prosperity of the town at that time. Merchants across the country gathered there as it nurtured a wharf culture. Foods such as fruit, well salt and sugar from different provinces and cities such as Chongqing, Yibin, Zigong and Neijiang were shipped to this town along the Tuojiang River. These merchants landed ashore, and then transported these goods to Chengdu by porters. In the past, during the busy rush hours of seasons, there were over 100 boats being loaded and unloaded onto the Wufeng Wharf.

The Pride of the Town: He Lin, a Master of Philosophy

In a small village of Wufengxi, a place with green mountains and clear rivers, He Lin, a master of philosophy was born. He was from a noble family in Yangliugou Village and was admitted to Tsing hua University at the age of 17. Learning from Liang Qichao, one of the most influential historical figures of China in the 20th century, he was also deeply influenced by other famous scholars like Liang Shuming, Wu Mi, and so on. Later he went to America and Germany to study classical philosophy especially philosophers such as Spinoza and German classical philosophy. He Lin obtained a thorough knowledge of both Western and Chinese learning and was hailed as the "oriental Hegel" in the translation field of Western classics. Moreover, he had very high attainments in Chinese philosophy. As early as the 1940s, He Lin came up with the "New Philosophy of Mind", different from New Rationalistic Confucian Philosophy of Feng Youlan[②].

---

① It refers to the acronym of five streets. Jin means the golden color. Qin means green. Xiao means small. Bai means white. Yu is the color of jade.

② Feng Youlan (1895—1990) was a Chinese philosopher and founded New Rationalistic Confucian Philosophy.

有所得。贺麟学贯中西，不仅在译介西方经典著作方面被誉为"东方黑格尔"，而且在中国哲学方面也有极高的造诣。早在20世纪40年代，贺麟就创立了与冯友兰"新理学"相对的"新心学"思想体系，被尊为现代新儒学八大家之一。

现在，五凤溪古镇修复重建了贺麟故居。故居原为土木结构，始建于清咸丰年间（1851—1861）。推开大门，走过通道，祠堂门上方有一旧匾："诗书传家"。贺麟出生书香门第，曾祖父为清道光贡生，祖父为咸丰朝监生，父亲贺松云为晚清秀才，当过当地学董。贺麟生于贺氏，长于五凤。授业北大，哲育中国。当地有人作诗："五凤溪边引兴长，春花秋实沁心香；青山绿水偏多意，此地有人添国光。"贺麟是继李劼人、巴金之后又一位为中国当代文化做出杰出贡献的成都籍大师级人物，也是成都文化的又一标杆。

—民俗文化—

建筑文化

五凤溪古镇是成都平原唯一的山地古镇，其建筑颇具特色，五条主要街道都顺山势、顺河道而建，弯弯曲曲，高低错落，宽处两排房，窄处一排房，俗称"半边街"。镇上还有一种房屋，临河而建，墙在河边，房在水上，俗称"吊脚楼"。

五凤溪的三圣宫、南岸关圣宫、北岸南华宫均依地势而建，布局选址上注意平衡，十分讲究。而在建筑材料上也都就地取材，以土筑墙，以石铺路。房屋、桥梁基本上为土木、土石、木石结构，显得非常和谐。

在古镇民居建筑上，我们可以发现中国古代传统哲学的影子。古宅大多建于高台之上，从侧顺势布梯，拾阶而上。譬如有民国时期的一座宅子，主人是民国时五凤乡乡长。该房依山势而建，前低后高，中西合璧，每个部分各具功用，无不体现出和谐的气息。

He was thus greatly honored as one of the eight masters of Modern Neo-Confucianism.①

Recently, He Lin's former residence in Wufengxi Ancient Town was restored. Built in the reign of Emperor Xianfeng (1851—1861) of the Qing Dynasty, the former residence was made from a combination of earth and wood. When one enters the house and walks along the passage, an old tablet over the door of the ancestral hall comes into view. It reads "Poetry and literature are handed down from generation to generation in this family". He Lin was from a literary family. His great-grandfather was a senior licentiate in the reign of Emperor Daoguang (1821—1850) of the Qing Dynasty. His grandfather was a student of Imperial College in the reign of Emperor Xianfeng. His father, He Songyun, was a Xiucai② in the late Qing Dynasty and once was the president of the local school. He Lin was born and grew up in Wufengxi. He taught in Peking University and spread his philosophical ideas across China. There is a poem written by the locals in his hometown, "Interest is aroused on the bank of Wufengxi; glorious flowers in spring and solid fruits in autumn refresh people; green mountains and rivers are affectionate; someone here wins honors for the motherland." In addition to Li Jieren and Ba Jin③, He Lin was another great master from Chengdu who has made great contribution to the modern Chinese culture and was regarded as another representative of Chengdu culture.

—Folk Culture—

Architectural Culture

Wufengxi is the only mountain town on the Chengdu plain, so its architecture has special characteristics. The five main streets in this town were built making full use of the twists and turns of the mountains and rivers which are scattered at high and low altitudes. There are two rows of houses in the wide areas and one row of houses in the narrow areas, known as Banbian④ Street (also called Half Street). Houses have also been built on the bank of the river and even over water. These houses are called Stilted Houses.

Sansheng Hall⑤ or Hall of Three Saints, Guansheng⑥ Hall on the south bank and Nanhua

---

① Modern Neo-Confucianism was a school of philosophy, founded by Feng Youlan.

② Xiucai refers to the scholar who passed the imperial examination at the county level in the Ming and Qing dynasties.

③ Li Jieren and Ba Jin are great writers from Sichuan Province.

④ Banbian means half in Chinese.

⑤ Sansheng means three saints in Chinese. King Yu of the Xia Dynasty (c. 2070 BC—1600 BC), King Tang of the Shang Dynasty (1600 BC—1046 BC) and King Wen of the Zhou Dynasty (1046 BC—256 BC).

⑥ Guansheng refers to Guan Yu, also called Guandi; it is respected as a war god in China. In Chinese, di means king or emperor. When people call Guan Yu Guansheng or Guandi, it shows their respect and admiration for him.

饮食文化

五凤钵钵鸡，其中的钵钵指瓦罐，钵身外通常画有红黄相间的瓷质龙纹。钵内盛放麻辣为主的佐料。菜品经特殊加工后用竹签串制，晾冷浸于各种口味的佐料中。食用时自取自食，除味道悠长外，更添盎然情趣。

五凤陈烧腊因其香味悠长闻名方圆百里。当地流传着这样几句顺口溜："陈烧腊，摆上摊，小街上下香气窜，花钱买个鸡爪爪，翻来覆去啃半天。"

—主要景点串游—

南华宫

南华宫建于清雍正年间（1723—1735），距今200多年历史，占地约6500平方米，建筑面积约3500平方米，为木结构四合院布局。南华宫祀奉南华老祖，是旧时广东移民聚会谈生意之处。南华宫隐藏在丛林中，步入宫门，头顶为木雕装饰的戏楼。据说每逢佳节，道会道教武士将会上楼表演道术。上台阶后，有一宽敞的院坝。两旁是一个个单独的房间，这

Hall in the north of Wufengxi River were all built based on topography of the land, and balance has been considered in both the layout and location. Construction materials for these halls were obtained locally. The walls were built with soil and the roads were paved with stones. Houses and bridges have soil-wood, soil-stone and wood-stone structures that are in harmony with each other.

Chinese ancient traditional philosophy can be found in the architecture of these ancient civil residences. Most of the ancient houses were built on high platforms, with steps along the side. There was one ancient house, whose owner was the Wufeng Township Chief during the period of the Republic of China (1912—1949). This house was built in harmony with the mountain and combined both Chinese and Western features. One of the features of the house is that it is low in the front and high in the back, each part having its own function, demonstrating the philosophy of harmony.

Food Culture

The word Benben in Wufeng Benben Chicken, also pronounced BoBo, refers to a pot with red and yellow porcelain dragon patterns on its exterior. A spicy sauce is placed in the pot. Cooked skewers of cold slices of chicken or vegetables are served in this earthenware vessel after the food has undergone special processing and has been soaked in chili sauce with different flavors. This type of food is served in a buffet style, adding more pleasure to the meal.

Wufeng Chen Roasted Meat is famous for its scent that can be smelt from far away. Some jingles are sung in the ancient town, "Chen Roasted Meat, on a market stall. Aroma pervades the air in the street. If you buy a chicken paw, you can't help biting it all."

——Main Tourist Attractions——

Nanhua Hall

Nanhua Hall was built around the reign of the Emperor Yongzheng (1723—1735) during the Qing Dynasty, with more than 200 years of history. It covers an area of 6,500 square meters and the buildings cover 3,500 square meters in area. It was built with wood in the form of courtyard houses. Nanhua Hall was where the ancester of Nanhua[1] was worshipped and Guangdong migrants gathered to talk about business in the old days. Nanhua Hall was hidden in the jungle. In the hall, there was a drama stage decorated with wood carvings overhead. It was said that whenever there was a festival, Taoist warriors would be performing Taoist magic arts on the stage. There was a spacious yard up the steps and a separate room on both sides, which was a place for Hakka people to get together and talk business. Behind the left-wing hall, some

---

[1] Here Nanhua refers to Zhuangzi, a respectful name for Zhuang Zhou, who was a famous philosopher and a representative of Taoism.

是客家人聚会谈生意的地方。左偏殿后建有殿堂布局以外的附属庭舍、粮仓、古井等。

移民广场

五凤溪是个名副其实的移民古镇。自康熙年间，陆续有移民从江西、两湖、两广迁徙到五凤溪，耕田造屋，置地经商，繁衍后代，造就了五凤溪古镇。这里留存的绝大部分古迹都与移民有关。移民广场的景观体现了五凤溪独特的移民文化。其中，"逆水溯源"是景观精髓所在，它象征着踏遍了30余个县市的移民足迹，形象地再现了"湖广填川"的移民历史。

基督教堂

美国循道宗教徒于1920年租下江西馆并在此兴办教会活动。新福音堂在旧址基础上进行了重修和扩建。

buildings including subsidary houses, barns and ancient wells were built in addition to the main hall.

Migrant Square

Wufengxi is worthy of the name of "an ancient migrant town". Since the reign of Emperor Kangxi, people migrated from Jiangxi, Hunan and Hubei, Guangdong and Guangxi in succession. They cultivated the fields and built houses, bought land, engaged in business, and produced offspring, and in this way Wufengxi Ancient Town was establised. Most historical sites preserved here are related to migrants. The scenes of Migrant Square reflect the unique migrant culture of Wufengxi. Among them, the man-made scenery of Nishuisuyuan, which means to take a boat against the current in order to trace the source of the water, is the essence of all scenes. It symbolizes migrants' footprints that covered more than 30 cities and counties and vividly reproduces the migrant history of people from Hunan, Hubei, Guangdong and Guangxi to Sichuan.

Christian Church

The American Methodists rented Jiangxi Guild Hall in 1920 and founded a church here. The new gospel church was restored and extended based on the old site.

4. 大邑平落古镇

Pingluo Ancient Town, Dayi County

平落古镇简介

　　平落古镇位于成都市西南93千米，邛崃市西南18千米处，迄今已有2000多年的历史。史前蜀王开明氏时期，平落这块四面环山的平坦绿色小盆地因"修水利、兴农桑而起聚落"得名。平落镇以"秦汉文化·川西水乡"风情著称，有"一平二固三夹关"[①]的美誉。古镇有三绝：古街、古榕和乐善古桥，还有"九古"历史遗迹：古街、古寺、古桥、古树、古堰、古坊、古道、古风、古歌，以及镇外之景：芦沟自然风景区、金华山风景区、花楸山风景区和秦汉古驿道风景区。平落瓷胎竹编历史悠久，远销东南亚和欧美。古茶树、农夫手工茶、根雕、木刻和古镇特色名小吃享有盛名。古代造纸作坊也是古镇一大看点。平落在2004年被列为全国重点镇、全国环境优美镇及成都市区域发展重点镇。2005年被评为成都市"十大魅力城镇"，同年被列为第二批中国历史文化名镇。

---

　　① 在秦灭蜀以前的古蜀，临邛有三大古镇，分别为平落镇、固驿镇和夹关镇。

A Brief Introduction to Pingluo Ancient Town

The Ancient Town of Pingluo is 93 kilometers southwest of Chengdu and 18 kilometers southwest of Qionglai City, and has a history of over 2,000 years. In the reign of Kaimingshi (c. 666 BC—316 BC) who was said to be a king of the ancient Shu Kingdom, Pingluo, the small flat basin surrounded by green mountains, developed into a village because of the construction of a water irrigation system and flourishing agriculture, hence the name. The town, famous for its Qin-Han culture[1] and water-abundant style of the western Sichuan, is regarded as the number one ancient town in this area, followed by Guyi Town and Jiaguan Town.

The town boasts three wonders: an ancient street, an ancient banyan tree and an ancient bridge named Leshan. Besides, there are also nine historical features: ancient street, ancient temple, ancient bridge, ancient tree, ancient weir, ancient paper making workshop, ancient path, ancient custom and ancient folk song. Four tourist attractions include Lugou Natural Landscape Spot, Jinhua Mountain Scenic Spot, Huaqiu Mountain Scenic Spot and Ancient Qin-Han Path. These places have attracted many tourists. Citaizhubian, a kind of porcelain-bodied bambooware is a historical craft that has found its market in southeast Asia and Europe; ancient tea tree, peasant-handmade tea, bamboo-root carving, wood carving and local snacks of this ancient town have earned it a good reputation. Additionally, ancient paper making workshops are also considered a main attraction of the town. Pingluo has gained many titles, such as a National Key Town, a National-level Town of Beautiful Environment. It was considered as one of The Key Regional Development Towns of Chengdu in 2004. In 2005, it was listed among The Top Ten Attractive Towns of Chengdu and became one of The Most Famous Historical and Cultural Towns in China (the second batch).

——Legendary Stories——

Love at First Sight: The Story of Elopement

Two thousand years ago, there was a man named Sima Xiangru who was a follower of Liu

---

[1] Many tourist attractions in Pingluo like Ancient Qin-Han Path, possess the cultural characteristics of Qin-Han period (221 BC—AD 220), which gains it the title of Qin-Han culture.

—传奇故事—

一见钟情：私奔传说

2000多年前，梁孝王死后，司马相如没了依靠，只得回到成都故里，投靠临邛县令。在此期间发生了一段为人津津乐道的爱情故事：琴挑文君。司马相如有些名气，县令每日必访，这在小县城属一大新闻。有个靠炼铁暴富的大富豪卓王孙，对这位县令的座上宾大感好奇，于是也附庸风雅，在家大摆宴席款待司马相如。司马相如到了宴席上，其风采立即让在场的宾客为之一震。他有些口吃，但琴弹得非常好。所用琴名为"绿绮"，是传说中最优秀的古琴之一。他弹琴唱道："凤兮凤兮归故乡，遨游四海求其凰。有艳淑女在闺房，室迩人遐毒我肠。何缘交颈为鸳鸯，胡颉颃兮共翱翔。"这曲《凤求凰》令宾客大为赞叹，其中包括极其爱好琴乐的大美女：卓王孙之女卓文君。卓文君早就对司马相如有所耳闻，而这次宴会更使她对司马相如芳心萌动。司马相如对才貌双全的卓文君也非常仰慕，于是在宴席结束后，用钱收买了卓文君的贴身丫环，让其转达他对卓文君的爱慕。卓文君得知这个消息后，马上奔赴司马相如所住的驿站。

两人私定终身，担心遭受阻拦，司马相如便带着她连夜出了临邛南门，绕过平落，趁着夜色顺白沫江东下，由水路回成都。卓王孙对女儿卓文君不顾礼法，与人私奔的行为大怒，毅然断绝父女关系，不给她任何经济资助。司马相如夫妇为了生计，悄悄返回临邛当垆卖酒。后来卓王孙还是念及血缘亲情，态度有所转变，给了夫妇俩一大笔钱，司马相如和卓文君得以返回成都，过上衣食无忧的日子。

司马相如与卓文君的爱情故事伴随一曲《凤求凰》流传至今。平落古镇的江边仍保留

Wu, Prince of Liang[1] in the Han Dynasty（206 BC—AD 220）. After the death of the prince, Sima had to return to his hometown, Chengdu. During this time, a romance developed between him and Zhuo Wenjun who was a beautiful lady. Because of his talent in literature, Sima became the honoured guest of the magistrate of Linqiong County, which was a sensation there. One local merchant Zhuo Wangsun was very curious about the young man whom the magistrate had visited so frequently. One day, Mr. Zhuo invited Sima for a banquet at home. At the banquet, the elegant demeanour of Sima surprised all the guests. Although he spoke with a little stutter, he was good at playing the Chinese zither called Lv Qi[2]. While playing the zither, he also sang a song *Feng Qiu Huang*. In this song, he earnestly expressed his passion for courtship with straightforward words, which was highly praised by the guests, including Zhuo Wangsun's daughter Zhuo Wenjun, a very beautiful girl who loved music. She had heard about Sima before, and at the banquet, she admired him. After the banquet, Sima bribed Zhuo's maid with money and asked her to pass on his feelings of admiration to Zhuo. As soon as Zhuo learned of the information, she went at once to the inn where Sima was staying.

The two fell in love with each other. Worrying about the opposition from Zhuo's family, they decided to run away. They left Linqiong from its southern gate by night and returned to Chengdu by boat down Baimo River, in order to avoid passing by Pingluo Town. Knowing his daughter's elopement with Sima, Zhuo Wangsun burst into anger and disowned his daughter immediately. Later, the couple secretly came back to Linqiong and managed a small winehouse there, selling liquor to make a living. Gradually Zhuo Wangsun changed his attitude. He gave his daughter a large sum of money, which helped the young couple come back to Chengdu and live a happy life.

The love story of the couple as well as the song *Feng Qiu Huang* spread far and wide. The dock where they boarded the boat has been preserved at the riverside of Pingluo and retains the name of "Elopement Dock". The poet Zhang Hu of the Tang Dynasty（618—907）wrote a poem "Sima Xiangru's Zither Song" in memory of this romantic story.

Failure to Recognize the Master of Carpentry and Masonry: The Legend of Leshan Bridge

People in Pingluo are always benevolent and ready to do good deeds. In 1862, the first year of the reign of Emperor Tongzhi（1862—1874）in the Qing Dynasty（1616—1911）, a man named

---

[1] Prince of Liang was a noble title during the Han Dynasty.

[2] Lv Qi is the name of the Chinese zither of Sima Xiangru. In Chinese, "Lv" means deep green and "Qi" is used to describe something splendid. Sima's Lv Qi was said to be completely deep green and looked like an ancient tree twined by vines. Later it refers to the Chinese zither with superior quality.

着昔日他们乘船的码头，起名"私奔码头"。唐代诗人张祜则有《司马相如琴歌》一首纪念二人的爱情故事。

有眼不识祖师爷：乐善桥的传说

平落人乐善好施，清同治元年（1862），里人周善人等，打算建造乐善桥，于是推荐秋成武监造。秋成武认真研读了建镇造桥秘本，悟出了其中建桥的奥妙，就大胆施工建桥。在建桥过程中曾发生过一段鲜为人知的故事。动工修桥的工匠们都很勤劳，唯独有一位显得有点懒散。此人来历蹊跷，身高不足五尺，唇沾鼻涕，头发杂乱，走路一脚高一脚低，自号"跛鲁"，人称"跛师傅"。有一天，他来到工地，拜见了工头掌墨师和秋成武，自愿捐工。秋成武见他形貌古怪，不愿多说，就说了声师傅请自便吧。

跛鲁每天只顾埋头打石，也不与旁人交流。他边打石料边哼道："打困时和石醋睡，太阳下捉虱翻衣。红尘了愿留行影，有几高人识玄机。"大家听了都不明白，也就慢慢地冷落了他。光阴似箭，不知不觉到了年底。一天清晨，跛鲁对秋成武说："小老儿自知不甚济事，只打了几条毛石在那里，以后或许还用得上。"秋成武当时因为忙没怎么在意，跛师傅却转眼间不见了。几天后，桥拱顺利完成六洞，却发现有一个拱门需要塞尖。然而，查遍了所有备用的条石都不合用。正当大家着急之时，秋成武突然清醒过来说："跛老头不是说过

他留下条石吗？快去抬来试试。"于是大家七手八脚把条石都抬来试用，结果拿去一试，刚刚合适，而且是天衣无缝，连绣花针也别想插入。

周善人、秋成武等欢天喜地，掌墨师说："这几条石头如此神奇，莫非是鲁班爷下凡助我们不成？"这一提，众人都说："不说不像，越说越像。不是鲁班还有谁呢？他自号跛鲁，其实早就把名字都报了。"周善人说："这就是俗眼不识仙人。"乐善桥建成至今，巍然横跨江上。

—民俗文化—

建筑文化

古镇上共有33条老街，七弯八拐，曲径通幽。街道两旁保留着明清时期的古民居，街上木板房、小青瓦屋顶相连成片。建筑多为一楼一底的二层木结构建筑，一般为下层作铺面，上层作居室，体现出浓郁的川西风格。临江的一排排吊脚楼也给古镇增添了几分韵味。

Zhou Shanren, together with some other locals in Pingluo who often did good deeds planned to build a bridge and recommended Qiu Chengwu to be the engineer. Qiu studied books concerning how to build towns and bridges and began to build the bridge after comprehending the main points of bridge construction. There was one little-known legend during the construction. All the workers there were diligent and hard-working builders except for one unidentified man. This man was crippled and short, no more than five feet tall with a self-ascribed name of Lame Lu. He paid little attention to his appearance. One day, Lame Lu came to the construction site, and met the taskmaster and Qiu Chengwu, in the hope of joining the construction project as a volunteer. On account of Lame Lu's eccentric appearance and introvert disposition, Qiu Chengwu let him do whatever he wanted.

Every day, Lame Lu was absorbed in stone cutting and never communicated with others. Sometimes, he softly sang like this, "sleeping with stones when tired with work; catching the lice from cloth under the sun; leaving a trace in the world after fulfilling my promise; Any man could recognize the truth." However, nobody understood him and gradually gave him the cold shoulder. One year later, Lame Lu told Qiu Chengwu, "I clearly know I have not helped you so much, but I will leave a few lath stones for you. Maybe it will help you one day." Chengwu did not pay much attention to him because of some business in hand, and Lame Lu disappeared in a flash. A few days later, six arches had been built; however, the workers could not find any suitable stones to level the place of an arch. Everyone worried about it. Suddenly Chengwu thought of something and said, "Lame Lu left several lath stones before leaving. Why not have a try?" Workers immediately tried those stones, and to everyone's surprise, they were the perfect stones to level the arches. They were such a good fit that even a needle could not be inserted between the stones.

All the people were extremely delighted, and the taskmaster said, "Those stones were miraculous. Could it be that Master Luban[①] specially built them for us?" Everyone thought about it and agreed, "Could it be anyone else other than Luban? He had disguised himself as Lame Lu, so that people would not know his real identity." Zhou Shanren sighed, "This is a failure to recognize a great man." Since Leshan Bridge was built, it has stood majestically across the river.

—Folk Culture—

Architectural Culture

There are 33 ancient streets, winding their way through the town. On both sides of these

---

① Lu Ban (507 BC—444 BC) was a Chinese carpenter and engineer. He is respected as the Chinese god of builders and the master of carpentry and masonry.

饮食文化

平落古镇汇聚了众多美食，有奶汤面、碗碗羊肉、玉麦馍馍、河水豆花、烤笋子虫、竹笋烧鸡、汤白肉等。其中，奶汤面并非用牛奶煮的面，而是用新鲜猪骨、猪蹄、鸡等炖成香味浓郁的奶汤，将其盛入碗内，配以佐料，其汤雪白像牛奶一般，故得此名。河水豆花，采用本地生态黄豆加上取自白沫江的河水，经手工磨制而成。除此之外，名优白酒众多，文君酒、临邛酒最负盛名。

竹文化

平落是竹编之乡，尤以瓷胎竹编最具代表性。它以瓷器器皿为胎，用纤细如发的竹丝、柔软如绸的竹篾，依胎编织而成。其编织技艺要求高，难度大，整体比例匀称，给人以一气呵成之感。在图案设计方面，已从俗称"城墙垛垛"的简单花边发展到复杂多变的几何图案等自然图案。在编织技艺上，除了保持传统的细密编之外，又创造了特细编、疏编等10多种新工艺。瓷胎竹编工艺品，除了传统的花瓶、咖啡具等产品外，还有首饰盒、笔筒等。

茶文化

崃山产茶"十八堡"在历史上享有盛名，其中，花楸、天池、水口、盐井等堡，至今仍是

streets stand residences with the architectural styles of the Ming and Qing dynasties. Wooden houses and houses with tiles in a Chinese style stand one by one harmoniously. Most of these are two-storey wooden houses with storefronts on the ground floor and living rooms on the upper one, representing the typical architectural style of western Sichuan. Rows of stilted houses on the riverside also add charm to the town.

Food Culture

In Pingluo, there are a variety of delicious foods, including Naitang① Noodles, Stewed Mutton, Baked Cornmeal Mantou, Bean Curd Pudding, Roasted Bamboo Insects, Chicken with Bamboo Shoots, and Tang's Fatty Meat. Naitang Noodles gets its name from its milk-like stock. However, the stock is made with the fresh bones of pork meat or chicken rather than milk. Another recommended food is the Bean Curd Pudding which uses the finest local ingredients, for example the local soybean and the water from the Baimo River. In addition, there are many different types of liquor, such as Wenjun Liquor and Linqiong Liquor, both of which have high reputations.

Bamboo Culture

Pingluo is regarded as the home of bamboo weaving. One of the most representative bamboo products is Citaizhubian, a type of porcelain ware that is wrapped in bamboo knitting. Bamboo canes or sawali, as thin as a strand of hair and as soft as silk, are used to knit around porcelain ware such as a tea cup or a vase. The challenging process of knitting requires a high degree of technical knowledge to create a feeling of harmony throughout the well-proportioned structure. The design patterns vary from simple laces such as citywall battlements to complicated geometric shapes. In addition to the traditional dense knitting, more than ten new techniques are utilized, including fine-grained knitting and sparse knitting. In addition to the porcelain ware that is traditionally used such as vases or coffee sets, there are also some new choices like jewel cases or pen containers.

Tea Culture

Lai Mountain also called Qionglai Mountain has a long history of producing tea and is especially famous for its eighteen tea producing villages, including Huaqiu, Tianchi, Shuikou and Yanjing villages. These villages continue to produce tea even today. Huaqiu Villiage is the most famous tea producing area, boasting a type of tea that has a long-lasting aroma. Tea in Huaqiu used to be the drink for royals and in the time of Emperor Kangxi of the Qing Dynasty

---

① Naitang means the soup is like the milk in Chinese.

县内茶叶基地，尤以花楸第一堡最负盛名。所制成的茶，经久耐泡，具有独特的品质和香味。清朝时期，该堡主要制作皇家饮料，被康熙御封为"天下第一圃"，让花楸声名远扬。近年来，所生产的"花楸贡茶""花楸雪蕊"等茶叶，名扬海内外。

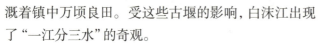
— 主要景点串游 —

乐善桥

七孔乐善石桥建于清同治元年（1862），有"邛南第一桥"之称。长120米，高16.6米，宽10米，属人行桥，后改建为公路桥。其桥洞一改普遍的半圆形，采用桃形，堪称川西一绝。

古堰

据《尚书·禹贡》记载，4000年前，大禹曾到邛崃治水，筑成古堰。汹涌的白沫江被分成了内、外两江，从此滋润平落千顷良田，水旱从人。该堰被称为"黄金堰"，后经改造由竹笼装卵石筑成，更加坚固。黄金堰附近还有一个堰叫安乐堰，建于清朝初年。分流的水穿吊角楼而过，也灌溉着镇中万顷良田。受这些古堰的影响，白沫江出现了"一江分三水"的奇观。

秦汉驿道

秦汉驿道遗址，又称"南方丝绸之路"，也被当地老人称为"剑南道"或"马道子"，位于平落镇骑龙山城隍岗，长约2千米，路面横宽4米，呈鱼脊形，是当时由成都经邛州、雅州通往吐蕃等少数民族地区的交通要道之一，也是韦皋出兵与吐蕃作战的主要路线之一。

（1616—1911）, it won high acclaim. Huaqiu is known as "The Finest Tea Garden under Heaven". Recently, Huaqiu Tribute Tea and Huaqiu Xuerui have become well known at home and abroad.

—Main Tourist Attractions—

Leshan Bridge

Built in 1862, Leshan Bridge which has seven archways is known as "The Finest Bridge in Qiongnan". With a length of 120 meters, a height of 16.6 meters and width of 10 meters, it used to be a bridge for pedestrians only, but today it allows the vehicles to drive across it. The regular arch which was built in the shape of a semicircle was replaced by a peach-shaped archway. This has been rated as the finest artwork in western Sichuan.

Ancient Weir

According to "The Tribute of Yu" in the *Book of Doucuments*, 4,000 years ago, King Yu[1] once came to Qionglai with a mission of curbing the flood. He built a weir here so that the turbulent Baimo River could be separated into inner and outer rivers to better the irrigation system for the fields in Pingluo. From then on, whether during a flood or drought, people were never worried about water for their crops. Thus, the weir is called Huangjin Weir or Gold Weir[2]. Later, it was rebuilt with cobblestone-stored bamboo baskets, which enabled it to be more firm and durable. Apart from the Gold Weir, there is also a weir called Anle Weir or Happy Weir built in the early period of the Qing Dynasty. It also irrigates the fields of the town, with the divided water flowing beneath stilted houses along the riverside. Because of the influence of these weirs, it is a marvelous spectacle to see one river with three divided waters in Baimo River.

Ancient Qin-Han Path

The Ancient Qin-Han Path is known as the Southern Silk Road or Jiannan Path. It is also called the Horses Path by the elderly living in this area. It lies in the Chenghuang Hillside of Qilong Mountain in the Ancient Town of Pingluo. With a length of two kilometers and width of four meters, the fishbone-shaped path is not only one of the most significant roads to minority areas like Tubo (Tibetan regime in ancient China) from Chengdu via Qiongzhou and Yazhou (now

---

① King Yu (2200 BC—2101 BC) is the leader of the Xia tribe. He is a legendary Chinese emperor who is famous for his great achievement in curbing the floods.

② In China, gold is very precious. It symbolizes wealth and good luck. The connotation of the name "Gold Weir" reflects people's best wishes on this weir which is regarded as precious as gold.

古造纸作坊

造纸作坊始于南宋，明末清初达到鼎盛。平落现存古造纸作坊74处，是古镇一大看点。宋代造纸的遗址位于距平落古镇3千米处的芦沟。芦沟也被称为"邛崃竹海"，此处生长的竹子是川西坝子常见的慈竹，是造纸的主要原料。因此，芦沟自古以来就是造纸重地之一。

Ya'an), but also one of the eleven major military routes to Tubo that General Wei Ao[①] often took.

Ancient Paper Making Workshop

Beginning in the Southern Song Dynasty (1127—1279), paper making technology reached its heyday in the late Ming Dynasty (1368—1644) and early Qing Dynasty. Now there are 74 existing ancient paper making workshops, which have become one of the main attractions of Pingluo. The paper making site of the Song Dynasty (960—1279) is located at Lugou, three kilometers away from Pingluo, which is referred to as the "Bamboo Sea of Qionglai". Sinocalamus affinis, one common type of bamboo of western Sichuan, flourish on the stony hill of Lugou. It is the main material for paper making. Thus, Lugou has become one of the important places of paper making since ancient times.

---

① Wei Ao (746—805) was a general in the Tang Dynasty. His greatest contribution lies in promoting the peaceful agreements with Nanzhao, a minority area in ancient China (an area in Yunnan Province now) and defeating Tubo.

5. 双流黄龙溪古镇

Huanglongxi Ancient Town, Shuangliu County

黄龙溪古镇简介

　　黄龙溪古镇位于成都平原南部，平坝与丘陵、府河与鹿溪河交汇处，是府河下游重要的风景旅游城填。距成都市区40千米，距双流县城35千米。东临本县籍田镇，西北面与新津接址，西南面紧临彭山县。黄龙溪镇古名"赤水"，据《仁寿县志》载："赤水与锦江汇流，溪水褐，江水清，古人谓之黄龙溪清江，真龙内中藏。"《隶读》著录《黄龙甘露碑》记云："黄龙见武阳事，铸一鼎，象龙形，沉水中……故名曰黄龙溪镇。"黄龙溪是国家4A级风景旅游胜地，是全国十大知名古镇之一，2007年被评为第三批中国历史文化名镇。

——传奇故事——

一江不容二龙：二龙相争传说

　　自古以来，黄龙溪一直有"二龙相争"的神话传说。"二龙"指的是中国古代神话中"烛龙"和"应龙"。据说，很久以前，烛龙最早居住在黄龙溪，它人面龙身，口中衔烛，在西北

A Brief Introduction to Huanglongxi Ancient Town

The Ancient Town of Huanglongxi is located in the south of the Chengdu plain, where the flat land, hilly land as well as the confluence of Fu River and Luxi River merge. It is an important scenic tourist town situated downstream of the Fuhe River. It is 40 kilometers from Chengdu, 35 kilometers from Shuangliu County, facing Jitian Town in the same county from the east. It adjoins Xinjin County in the northwest and Pengshan County in the southwest. The original name of Huanglongxi was "Chishui", meaning red water. According to *Renshou County Annals*, "When Chishui River and Jinjiang River converge here, water from Chishui is red while that from Jinjiang is clear. The ancient people attributed this phenomenon to the fact that a real dragon was hidden in the water". On the "Huanglong Ganlu Tablet", the record of *Lidu*, said that "after a dragon was reported to appear in Wuyang County, a tripod in the shape of a dragon was cast and sunk into the water to control the dragon. That is why it got the name Huanglongxi, which means Yellow-dragon River in Chinese. Huanglongxi has been recognized as a National AAAA-grade tourist attraction and is considered one of Ten Chinese Famous Ancient Towns. In 2007, it was rated as a Famous Historical and Cultural Town in China (the third batch).

—Legendary Stories—

Only One Dragon in a River: The Legend of "Fight Between Two Dragons"

The legend of "Fight Between Two Dragons" has been told in Huanglongxi for many centuries. The two dragons here refer to the Zhu Dragon[1] and the Ying Dragon[2] which appeared in Chinese ancient myths. It was said that long time ago the Zhu Dragon originally lived in Huanglongxi. It was a dragon with a human face, and it held a candle in its mouth. This candle could provide light in the darkness of the northwest where there was no sun. The Zhu

---

[1] Zhu Dragons are with human head and boa body. Zhu means candles in Chinese. In legends, the shift of the day and night is based on Zhu Dragon's blink of eyes and the shift of summer and winter is according to its breath.

[2] Ying Dragons are with wings and can fly. They are called Flying Dragons or Yellow Dragons.

无日之处照明于幽暗。它在河里游泳（指鹿溪河），把河水都染红了，因此，黄龙溪原名又叫赤水。另外，二郎神本来也是一条龙，是应龙，也是孽龙，后来经观世音菩萨点化，归到李冰手下治水。传说它能画地成河，导洪入海。

有一次，李冰派应龙二郎神治理鹿溪河，进入了烛龙的地盘，于是这两条龙就打斗起来。烛龙身披红甲，应龙二郎神身着青盔。一个能喷火吐焰，一个能翱翔九天。据称，当时这两条龙斗得难分难解，把小小的黄龙溪折腾得不成样子。后来烛龙看到当地老百姓为它们的打斗所害，流离失所，于是感到万分羞愧，一头扎进鹿溪河躲到北边钟山去了。应龙二郎神也觉得无颜面对乡民百姓，修好大佛堰（当地一水利设施）之后也远远地飞去了现在彭山的青龙场。后来，为了纪念这两条龙，人们每逢春节都要举行火龙灯舞，端午节要进行水龙舟赛。

龙形玄机：一街三庙

所谓"一街三庙"，指黄龙溪场镇弯曲的正街上排列得错落有致的三座寺庙。顺着江岸而下，依次是镇江寺、潮音寺（旧名乐善堂）和古龙寺。有传说称，古代黄龙溪人在镇江寺前的"王爷坎"和古龙寺内植下了四棵大榕树，现在仍然可见，意在镇住这条龙，不让其翻动。但是，当年刘备病故白帝城后，这条龙终于挣脱掉这四棵钉住它的古榕树，飞走了。从此，黄龙溪灾祸不断，黄龙溪先民仍供奉着这四棵树。后来的漫长年月中，黄龙溪又经历了许多社会动乱和灾祸。

到了明末清初，这里经常遭遇洪水，战乱不断，人民饱受其苦。为了能在这里长期生

Dragon usually swam in the Luxi River and dyed the water red. That is why the original name of Huanglongxi was Chishui, meaning red water. In contrast, Er-lang God was the original Ying Dragon. He was considered as an evil dragon who because of Merciful Buddha's teaching changed into being a good dragon and came to assist Li Bing[①] in curbing floods. The Ying Dragon was said to be very powerful. It could turn land into rivers and direct water into seas.

Once Li Bing sent Er-lang God to Luxi River where Zhu Dragon lived, Zhu Dragon mistook the reason as to why Er-lang God had invaded his territory. Er-lang God had to face a fight with Zhu Dragon. The Zhu Dragon got dressed in red armor while Er-lang God, the Ying Dragon in blue. Each dragon had particular traits, for example, the former could spray fire while the latter could soar high above in the sky. That day, the two dragons had such a fierce fight that there occurred a lot of damage to the properties of the local people. Realizing what they had done, both Zhu and Ying felt guilty. Zhu Dragon dived into Luxi River, swam to Zhong Mountain in the north while Ying Dragon flew far away to Qinglong Town in Pengshan County after the completion of Dafo Weir, a local water conservancy facility. Since then, the locals hold a Fiery Dragon Lantern Dance during the Spring Festival and a Water-dragon Boat Race during Dragon Boat Festival to commemorate the two dragons.

The Secret of Dragon-shape: "Three Temples in One Street"

The place called "Three Temples in One Street" is where three temples are situated on a winding main street of Huanglongxi Town. These temples are Zhenjiang Temple, Chaoyin Temple(old name: Leshan Hall) and Gulong Temple down the river. In this town, there are four ancient trees. According to a legend, the four banyan trees were planted by the locals in ancient times on the bank of the river, called Wangye Bank or Lord Bank which is in front of Zhenjiang Temple and inside Gulong Temple. These banyan trees are planted to prevent a dragon from rolling about. This dragon was said to be related to Liu Bei, the king of Shu Han Kingdom in the period of Three Kingdoms(220—280). However, when Liu Bei died in Baidi City, this dragon managed to free itself from these four old banyan trees and flew away. From then on, this town constantly suffered and it experienced great social turmoil and numerous disasters. Nevertheless, the forefathers here continued to worship the four banyan trees.

During the late Ming and early Qing periods, frequent floods and wars troubled this town and the locals suffered a lot. Three great families in this town, namely the He family, the Qiao Family and the Tang Family were the first migrants who settled in this town. These families

---

① Li Bing(c. 3rd century BC)was a Chinese irrigation engineer and politician of the Warring States Period(475 BC—221 BC).

活下去，并保世代平安，最先到这里的移民贺、乔、唐三家共同商议，请来一位风水老先生指点。老者看罢风水地脉，只留下一语："若要世代平安，只有请回黄龙天子！"为此，三家再三思虑后，一致决定将街道悄悄地修成龙的形状以保平安。据说，这条龙形街藏龙的妙计还暗指"卧龙"（诸葛亮）之意，因此，它同时暗指刘备和诸葛亮两条"龙"。由于两条龙力大难驭，于是又请来高人指点，在街上专门修建了三座寺庙用于镇龙。镇江寺抑龙头，由镇江王爷镇守；潮音寺卡龙颈，特奉观世音菩萨下手，也因捉龙捉七寸之理，所以潮音寺就建在紧挨着镇江寺不远的位置；古龙寺按龙尾，专请黄龙祖师亲为。这样一来，三寺结合，共同镇住这两条卧龙。再后来，三家又从青城山请来道教高师做法，使那四棵古榕树成为钉住龙头和龙尾的四根神针。其中暗藏的玄机奥秘，三家发誓永不泄露，否则就会失灵。于是，三家信守誓言，黄龙溪在后来的几百年里一直平安无事。

—民俗文化—

龙文化

黄龙溪因龙得名，因龙而灵，龙佛、龙寺、龙灯、龙舟构成丰富多彩的龙文化主题。黄龙溪"烧火龙"源于南宋。先人们根据"龙现武阳赤水"和民间流传中关于主宰光明与黑暗的"烛龙"与主管风雨的"应龙"神话及"龙生九子"的故事，在"舞龙"这个图腾文化的基础上，创造了独具特色的"火龙灯舞"，成为全国著名"火龙之乡"。黄龙溪火龙灯舞具有浓郁的乡土气息和川西文化风格，是成都地区保存较为完整的大型民俗群众文化活动之一。

invited an old Fengshui[1] master to give advice and bless the future generations. After the old man completed Fengshui here, he gave the families only one piece of advice, "If you want peace for generations, you have to invite the Huanglong (a yellow dragon) back!" For this reason, the three families unanimously decided to secretly build a street in the shape of a dragon to bless them with peace. It was said that the dragon-shaped street could call back the yellow dragon. Actually, the dragon-shaped street also implied Wolong, a sleeping dragon which was the pseudonym of Zhuge Liang, who was the military counsellor of Liu Bei. That was why it was effective to build a dragon-shaped street to attract the yellow dragon back again. However, people were afraid that the two dragons were too strong to be controlled. Thus, an expert was invited to give advice on how to solve this problem. Finally, three temples were built in the street to quell the two powerful dragons.

Zhenjiang Temple is located at the top of the street in such a way as if to control the heads of dragons with Lord Zhenjiang as the guard; Chaoyin Temple is situated in the middle of the street, appearing to be close to the necks of the dragons and Merciful Buddha has been especially invited to supervise the temple. Chaoyin Temple was built adjacent to Zhenjiang Temple in that the principle of catching a snake suggests hitting its heart; Gulong Temple holds the tails of the dragons, and the Founder of Huanglong Zen[2] was specially invited to be there. Thus, three temples were built to suppress these two dragons of the town. Later, a great master of Taoism from Qingcheng Mountain was invited to practice Taosit magic, enabling the four old banyan trees to become four magic needles that would nail both the heads and tails of the two dragons. The three families swore never to reveal this secret, otherwise the magic would not work any more. They kept their promise and Huanglongxi has been peaceful ever since.

—Folk Culture—

Dragon Culture

Huanglongxi was named after dragons and is famous for dragons. Thus, the dragon Buddha, the dragon temple, the dragon lantern, and the dragon boat formed colorful themes of the dragon culture. The unique Fiery Dragon Lantern Dance in this town originated in the Southern Song Dynasty (1127—1279). It was created based on the totem culture of the "dancing dragon" legends and stories. For example, the story of "the dragon appeared in Chishui Town, Wuyang County", stories about the Zhu Dragon in charge of brightness and darkness and the Ying Dragon in charge of wind and rain, and the story of "a dragon having nine sons".

---

① Fengshui means geomancy and geographical position.

② Huanglong Zen is a branch of Zen or Chinese Buddhism.

千年水码头

黄龙溪处于府河与鹿溪河的交汇口，河面宽阔，水势平稳，是天然码头。从成都来的下水船和从重庆、乐山来的上水船多在此停泊过夜，加上本地运送牧山特产的船只，使黄龙溪河面帆樯如林。黄龙溪历史上曾是蜀中，特别是成都对外交往的一条黄金水道，更是南方丝绸之路的物资集散地。"日有千人拱手，夜有万盏明灯"，实属锦江流域不可多得的天然码头，曾呈现过百货山积、帆樯如林的景象。

饮食文化

据县志记载，芝麻糕古时曾作为地方名点进献宫廷，而今也是黄龙溪现存唯一小有名气并批量生产的特色产品，有着丰富深远的历史背景和文化内涵。黄龙溪芝麻糕口感香甜，细腻绵软，老少皆宜，作为黄龙溪名牌产品曾荣获过多次奖项。

黄辣丁是取自锦江、鹿溪河中的野生河鲜，肉质细腻，无腥味。有两种吃法，一是以黄龙溪当地产的山椒、红辣椒提味，佐以香菜，汤色红亮，麻辣鲜香。二是用猪油、水、盐煮，不用太多佐料，保持原汁原味，一直煮到汤白为止，起锅时加入葱花，汤美鱼鲜，口味清淡。

猫猫鱼是用该地江河中野生的一种永远长不大的小鱼油酥而成，其中也包含俗称麻杆子、虾米的小虾，口味麻、辣、香、酥、脆，是佐酒的好料。

Therefore, Huanglongxi became the village of the fiery dragon, and became well known throughout the country. The Fiery Dragon Lantern Dance in Huanglongxi, a unique tradition with the style of western Sichuan culture, has become one of the best preserved folk cultural activities in the Chengdu area.

Water Wharf for One Thousand Years

Huanglongxi is a natural wharf with wide area and easy current, located at the confluence of the Fuhe River and Luxi River. In ancient times, downstream boats from Chengdu and upstream boats from Chongqing and Leshan mostly anchored here and stayed overnight, together with local boats shipping specialities of Mushan[1]. The view of Huanglongxi River was one of a nerver ending view of sails and masts. In history, Huanglongxi was once considered a golden waterway for central Sichuan, especially for Chengdu to communicate externally. Moreover, it functioned as a collecting and distributing center of materials on the Southern Silk Road. As the saying goes, "In the daytime thousands of people saluted, while in the evening ten thousand candles were lit", depicting the prosperity of the wharf. This was a rare natural wharf of the Jinjiang River, presenting a scene of merchandise and a forest of sails and masts.

Food Culture

According to the county annals, Sesame Cake, a famous local dessert, used to be presented to the royal court as a gift. This food has a profound historical and cultural significance, which today is the only local specialty that enjoys some fame and is being produced in quantity in Huanglongxi. Sesame cake tastes sweet and soft and is suitable for both the young and the elderly. It has won many awards as a famous dessert from the ancient town of Huanglongxi.

Yellow Catfish is a wild fish caught from both the Jinjiang River and the Luxi River. It has a fine flesh and has a very mild fish smell. There are two ways to cook it. One is to add flavor using wild pepper or red pepper that is grown in Huanglongxi and season it with coriander. With this method of preparation, the red soup tastes spicy and delicious. The second way is to boil it with lard, water and salt and nor to use too much seasoning. In this way, its original flavor is kept. When the soup turns white in color, it is ready. Chopped green onions are added for garnish. Both the fish broth and the flesh of fish taste fresh and light.

Maomao[2] Fish is a fried snack, made of small wild fish that would never grow up from the local river. There are also small shrimp that have a nickname of Maganzi or little shrimp. This dish tastes spicy, delicious and crisp. Eating it with wine makes it even more appetizing.

---

① Mushan is the short for Muma Hill in Shuangliu County, Sichuan Province.

② Maomao means small or little in Sichun dialect.

—主要景点串游—

古街坊

尽管经历了1700多年的历史变迁，古镇至今保留完整。现有明清时代街坊七条，街面全由石板铺成，两旁廊柱排列有序，街面平均宽度3.44米。

古寺庙

古镇内有三座完好的寺庙：古龙寺、镇江寺、潮音寺，位于黄龙溪正街，形成一街三寺庙，街中有庙、庙中有街的景观。镇外还有两座大寺庙，建筑宏伟，吸引了众多游人。

其中，潮音寺坐镇古街当中，古称乐善堂，是一座尼姑庵。临街五间，供奉观世音大士和弥勒佛。古时上元会、中元会、下元会都在此举行供天道场，祈祷风调雨顺。

镇江寺位于正街北首，与古龙寺遥遥相对，是千年码头王爷坎上的一座千年古刹，供奉镇江王爷杨泗以保平安，为旧时船帮祭祀集会的场所。寺前千年古榕寄生辣椒成为奇观。小小古镇成为佛教文化的集中展示点。

古建民居

唐家大院又称唐家烧房。唐家烧房已有300多年的历史，占地3亩，为传统的"前店后家"式格局，有两个天井，三开铺面经营自酿烧酒。从建筑角度来看，烧房又呈"日"字形

—Main Tourist Attractions—

Ancient Streets

The old town has been well preserved for over 1,700 years. Seven streets were built during the Ming and Qing dynasties. All the seven streets are paved with flagstones, lined with ordered pillars on both sides, and have an average width of 3.44 meters.

Ancient Temples

In the town there are three well-preserved temples: Gulong Temple, Zhenjiang Temple and Chaoyin Temple. They are all located on the main street of Huanglongxi, which forms a scene of three temples in one street enhancing each other's beauty. There are also two big temples outside of the town, with grand buildings, which attract many tourists.

Among them, Chaoyin Temple, known as a nunnery in the past, is located in the middle of the ancient street, with its original name Leshan Hall. The five rooms facing the street are used for the worship of Merciful Buddha and Maitreya Buddha. Since ancient times, at every Lantern Festival[1], Zhongyuan Festival[2] and Xiayuan Festival[3], the religious ceremonies of worshipping Heaven have been held at the temple to pray for favorable weather.

Located in the north of the main street and opposite to Gulong Temple across a great distance, Zhenjiang Temple is an ancient temple with a history of more than one thousand years. It is situated on an ancient wharf named Lord Bank, where Lord Zhenjiang whose name was Yang Si was both worshipped and was asked for blessings for peace. This temple also used to be a place for the sacrifice gathering of boat gangs in the past. In front of the temple, one can see an ancient banyan tree with parasitic peppers wrapped around, known to be a great wonder of this town. This small ancient town is famous for the intensified demonstration of Buddhist culture.

Ancient Civil Residences

Tang Compound was also called Tang's Wine Workshop. With a history of more than three hundred years, it covers an area of about a hacf acre. It has the traditional structure of a "front shop and rear home" [4], with two courtyards. Home-brewed spirit was sold in three front

---

[1] Lantern Festival, also called the Spring Lantern Festival, is a Chinese festival celebrated on the 15th day of the 1st lunar month in China.

[2] Zhongyuan Festival, also known as the Ghost Festival in China, is a traditional Buddhist and Taoist festival held on the 15th night of the 7th lunar month (the 14th night in southern China).

[3] Xiayuan Festival is held on the 15th of the 10th lunar month in China, for the worship of ancestors.

[4] Front shop and rear home is a traditional architecture home shop in China.

建造格局，分前后两厅，故而俗称"骑马庭"，现已十分少见。大院青瓦盖顶，为七柱穿斗木建筑结构，雕花门窗，具有典型的川西民居风格。

据记载，唐氏原是清初"湖广填川"的客家移民，唐家原为书香门第，以教书为业。后来，在开建场镇时，贺、乔、唐三家投了巨资，因而获得了场上米粮交易市场"打斗称粮"的管理经营权，人称"三把斗"。再后来唐家渐渐垄断了镇上的米粮交易，于是从第三代开始，便转而兼营酿酒。唐家烧房酿制的白酒，质好味醇。酒香不怕巷子深，一来二去唐家的酒名气越来越大，唐家烧房成为黄龙溪镇上名气最大的酒坊。随着家族酒坊的兴盛，唐家也成了黄龙溪最有实力和影响力的大家族之一。至今唐家酒坊遗址尚存，市场上还挂有"唐家酒厂"的牌匾。

古榕树

镇内现有树龄300年以上的古榕树六株，枝繁叶茂，盘根错节。雄浑厚重的枝干和浓荫蔽日的树盖，增添了古镇浓郁的古貌古趣。古镇在鹿溪河畔镇龙沟内还有一株外形酷似一条龙的千年古树乌柏树，外观非常奇特，有不少关于此树的美丽传说。

shops. The architectural structure of the wine-making workshop is represented in the shape of the Chinese character "日", that is, with both front and back halls. Therefore, this architectural style is called "Horse Riding Halls", which is rarely seen nowadays. The structure has a grey tile-roof, with carved doors and windows, adopting a wooden architectural structure of seven columns and tie construction, which demonstrates the typical style of western Sichuan civil residences.

According to historical records, the Tang family were originally Hakka migrants from Hunan, Hubei, Guangdong and Guangxi in the early Qing Dynasty (1616—1911). The Tang family was at first a literary family with teaching as the family profession. Later, the three families, Tang, He and Qiao, invested heavily in the construction of the town, and as a reward, they got the rights of managing and operating the weighing of the rice and grain in the town's market. They were called "Three Dous (a capacity measure for grain in China)". Eventually, the Tang family gradually monopolized the rice and grain trade in the town. During the third generation of their permanent residence in this area, the Tang family diversified into brewing spirits. The liquor brewed by Tang's Wine Workshop was of good quality and has mellow taste. As the saying goes, "Good wine needs no bush." That is to say, a good product sells itself. The Tang family's liquor gradually became increasingly famous and their workshop became the most well-known wine-making workshop in Huanglongxi. With the success of the family wine workshop, the Tang family became one of the most influential families in Huanglongxi. Till now, the site of the Tang's Wine Workshop remains, and in the market, there is still a plaque of Tang's Wine Workshop.

Ancient Banyan Trees

There are six banyan trees which are over 300 years old in the town, with luxuriant foliage, and knotted roots. The luxuriant branches and foliage add an antique beauty to this ancient town. In Zhenlong Gulley or Drangon-quelling Gulley near the riverside of Luxi River, stands a Chinese tallow tree of one thousand years old. It is aesthetically pleasing and resembles a dragon in shape and is thus used in many beautiful legends.

6. 蒲江西来古镇

Xilai Ancient Town, Pujiang County

西来古镇简介

　　西来古镇位于浦江县境内，距离成都市区84千米，东临寿安镇，南靠鹤山镇，西接复兴乡，北挨邛崃宝林镇。全镇面积78.87平方千米，约3.1万人。古镇森林覆盖率达到49.7%，空气质量甚优。气候温和怡人，水质优良，临溪河从中穿流而过，被誉为成都的"后花园"。西来古镇凭其古朴灵秀的自然美景与深厚的文化底蕴，于2005年被评为"成都市十大魅力城镇"。

—传奇故事—

神自西来：镇名传说

　　相传在康熙元年（1661），临溪河爆发了一场百年不遇、来势凶猛的洪水。洪水将上游张魁场关帝庙内供奉的木刻关帝神像冲到了临溪场（西来古名）一座叫西林寺的产田里。西林寺里住着一位德高望重的住持：静慈和尚。他认为关帝神像的到来是上天的安排，在与其他僧侣商量后，决定捐出寺庙的产田（寺庙里僧侣们衣食的主要收入来源），并在关帝

A Brief Introduction to Xilai Ancient Town

The Ancient Town of Xilai, 84 kilometers away from Chengdu, is located in Pujiang County. It is bordered by Shou'an to the east, Heshan to the south, Fuxing to the west and Baolai to the north. The town has an area of 78.87 square kilometers with approximately 31,000 inhabitants, with a coverage of lush forests that is close to 49.7% of the area. Located by the Linxi River with a mild climate, fine air quality and clean water, it has gained the name "back garden of Chengdu". In 2005, it was named one of The Top Ten Charming Cities/Towns in Chengdu for its natural scenery and fascinating culture.

——Legendary Stories——

God's Arrival from the West: Stories about the Name of the Town

It was said that there was a very heavy flood in the Linxi River in 1661, the first year of the reign of Emperor Kangxi (1661—1722). The flood took the statue of Guan Yu[1] in the Guandi Temple of Zhangkui, a town in the upper river of Linxi to the land possessed by Xilin Temple in Linxi Town original name of Xilai. In that temple, there lived a highly respected abbot called Jinci. He deeply believed that the arrival of the statue was not an occasional event but a plan by God. Thus, after discussing with his followers, he decided to repurpose the land around the temple which was a source of living for the whole temple. Thus, to publicize the loyalty of Guandi, a Guandi Temple was built in the very place where the statue was stranded. Generally, the gates of Guandi Temple face south however the gate at Xilai faces west, indicating that the statue of Guandi came from the west. Later, the weather there was favorable and people lived in peace and contentment.

In 1695, the 34th year of the reign of Kangxi, the magistrate in Pujiang inspected Linxi Town. He was confused by the name since there were so many places called Linxi. He proposed to rename the town. Considering that the statue of Guandi came from the west approximately 30 years ago and that it had brought prosperity and hope to this place, he suggested that the name be

---

[1] See foot ④ on page 55.

神像搁浅处新修一座关帝庙来供奉关公，以弘扬其忠义精神。通常，关帝庙的庙门都为南北朝向，只有西来的关帝庙门向西开，其含义有不忘关帝从西而来的意思。往后的临溪场风调雨顺，百姓安康。

到了康熙三十四年（1695），蒲江县令李绅文到临溪场来巡视，觉得取名为临溪场的地方很多，很容易混淆，便想重新为此地命名。考虑到30多年前关帝爷是从西而来，给这里带来了繁荣和希望，同时也借用佛教教义中"佛法西来"的典故，即唐玄奘把大藏三乘经从西取来之意，改临溪场为西来场。这就是"西来"名字的来历。

惜字积福：文峰塔传说

走进西来老街第一眼看到的便是耸立在正街东头的一座清朝时期建造的宝塔：文峰塔，又名"惜字宫"。文峰塔为三层六角形的建筑，塔身约10米高，四周刻有古典戏曲雕像和用九曲篆文写成的字。塔身下有个大的炉灶，用于烧写过字的纸，故名惜字宫。文峰塔反映了西来镇千百年来文化的积淀，也展现了西来人尊儒从文的思想。在塔内的报功堂上，正襟危坐着一位官神，目光如炬。相传凡是有人做了好事，有了功德，只需去给他报一声，这位官神便一丝不苟地将其记录在功德薄上。然后神灵们便根据功绩的大小来决定此人寿福的长短及其应享有的福祉。

关于惜字的传统有一段传说。相传，临溪河畔住着一位青年书生，他从小就喜欢书法，也写得一手好字。不过他有一个坏毛病，喜欢把写过的字片到处乱扔，并且不听别人劝说。后来有一天，他突然双目失明。当天夜里，他梦见一个白胡子老翁语重心长地说道："年轻人，这是你的报应啊！你想重见光明吗？就得爱惜文字。"第二天早上醒来，这位书生想起昨夜梦中老人的告诫，便拄着拐杖，去捡以前乱丢的字片。他每捡一箢，就倒进文峰塔烧掉，天黑时就去给报功堂的官神报个数。此后，无论是烈日炎炎的盛夏，还是寒风凛冽的严冬，他都从未间断过捡废纸片的行为，西来场的字片也被他捡得干干净净。他虔诚的举动感动了神灵，眼睛逐渐比以前好些，后来，这位书生的双眼竟完全复明了。

—民俗文化—

建筑文化

西来古镇保存了大量明清时期的川西民居。进入古镇，映入眼帘的是一条宽约3米的

changed to Xilai, meaning "from the west" in Chinese. In addition, this name also had another religious story that was taken into consideration, that of Monk Xuan Zang[1] who brought back the Mahayana scriptures from the west.

Cherishing Words Bringing Welfare: The Legend of Wenfeng Pagoda

Coming to the old street in Xilai, one will see a pagoda overlooking the street in the east. This pagoda was built in the Qing Dynasty (1616—1911) and is called Wenfeng Pagoda or Xizi Pagoda. It is a three-storey hexagonal structure with a height of 10 meters. It is engraved with ancient drama statues and seal characters, which not only embodies the cultural accumulation in Xilai but also reflects the local people's positive attitude towards Confucianism. As such, there was an emphasis on education. There is a big pot under the pagoda where waste papers with Chinese calligraphy were burned. That's why the pagoda is also called Xizi Pagoda, meaning treasuring the words. Inside, sat a solemn official whose eyes were sharp. It is believed that if someone performed good deeds, this official would be informed, and he would record them in a book with meticulosity. Furthermore, how long a man's life span was going to be or what welfare he enjoyed was decided by the Gods on the degree of good deeds he had performed.

As for cherishing words, there is an interesting story. A young scholar who lived near the Lixin River was interested in calligraphy since childhood. He was good at handwriting but also had a bad habit of throwing his paper around. What's worse, he refused to accept any advice. One day, he suddenly went blind. At night he dreamt of an old man who had a long gray beard. The old man said to him, "Young man, this is retribution. If you want to see the light again, you must cherish words." When he woke up the next morning, he recalled the old man's earnest warning and came to realize the truth. He went out with a stick to pick up all the pieces of paper he had thrown. When he had a full basket of waste paper, he dumped them near the pagoda and burned them. When it got dark, he reported to the official in the pagoda about what he had done during the day. He has kept doing this, no matter how bad the weather was. Finally, all the pieces of paper were picked up. It was his piety and perseverance that moved the God and he regained his eyesight eventually.

—Folk Culture—

Architecture Culture

A lot of ancient residential houses built in the Ming and Qing dynasties have been well preserved in Xilai. As one walks into the town, a three-meter-wide slabstone-paved street comes

---

[1] Xuan Zang is an eminent monk in the Tang Dynasty (618—907).

老街，由青石板铺设而成。老街两旁全是木质结构的瓦房，民居造型轻盈精巧，色彩朴素淡雅，是典型川西坝子建筑的缩影。古镇的建筑特色不仅在于这些保留的老房子，更在于古镇的整体布局。俯瞰全镇，会发现镇上的所有民宅呈"西"字形的建筑格局。

饮食文化

毛血旺，又称冒血旺，以鸭血为制作主料，火腿肠、鸭肚、猪心、豆芽等为辅料，口味麻辣。传统的毛血旺经过改良和创新，其汤汁红亮、麻辣鲜香、味道浓厚，是值得一尝为快的巴蜀名菜。

豆花是一道常见的四川乡村家常美味菜肴。制作时将锅内豆浆凝结分层，上层为清澈微黄的液体，下层为洁白的块状凝结物。此凝结物即为豆花。豆花内部多孔洞，较为松散，用筷子夹时易断裂。食时佐以农家自制的特色辣酱，开胃爽口，令人食欲大增。

禅茶文化

西来自古就有种茶的传统，其茶文化已有1700多年的历史。早在唐宋时期，临溪茶就曾作为一种专销茶，大量贩运至西藏地区，著名的茶马古道也由此而来。在这里，绿茶雀舌飘香，古镇环境幽静，节奏舒缓，加上西来本来的佛缘，形成了禅茶文化。

—主要景点串游—

古榕树

古镇临溪河边，排列着12棵树龄均在千年左右的古榕树，枝繁叶茂，遮天蔽日，奇特的树形极具观赏性。"夫妻树"是其中最奇特的，原本相邻的两棵榕树却在离地面约2米

into view. The street is lined with tile-roofed wooden houses which are light and ingeniously structured. These simple and elegant residential houses are representative of a type of western Sichuan architecture. In addition to the houses, the layout of the old town resembles the shape of the Chinese character "西" (means the west), which is also extraordinarily impressive.

Food Culture

Maoxuewang or Duck Blood in Chili Sauce, is a dish of Sichuan cuisine. This dish is a mixture of boiled blood curd that is garnished with sausage, duck gizzards, pig hearts and bean sprouts. It tastes spicy. After a series of trials to improve this dish, the new dish is thought to be more delicious and tasty. The broth is bright red in color, is spicy and has a fresh fragrance in taste. This dish is worth tasting.

Tofu pudding is a common family snack in the countryside of Sichuan. In the process of its production, the soybean milk stiffens with a clear, slight yellow liquid in the upper layer and a white block in the lower one. It is a tough job to pick the Tofu pudding with chopsticks because it is so soft and porous. Together with homemade chili paste, it usually increases one's appetite.

Tea-Zen Culture

The history of tea culture in Xilai is over 1,700 years old. Linxi tea has been well known since the Tang and Song dynasties. As a border-sale tea, it was authorized for traders to sell the tea to Tibet in massive quantity, which was how the ancient Tea-horse Road came into being. In this small town, fragrant green tea, the graceful environment, the slow pace of life and Buddhism, all together create the Tea-Zen[①] culture.

——Main Tourist Attractions——

Old Banyans

Along the Linxi River there stand 12 old banyan trees with an average age of one thousand years. These trees grow closely together and are so leafy that they even block the sunlight, forming a fascinating scenery. The "couple tree" is the most unique one among these because two old adjacent banyans have grown into one at one intersection, about two meters above the ground. Numerous roots grow at the place where they are entwined. Both the trunks of these trees extend two branches holding tightly ten centimeters below their joint as if a couple is embracing intimately. The left side of the thinner branch is thought to be the wife while the right is seen as the husband. According to a folk tale, a couple had once lived there during the reign of Emperor

---

① Zen is a dinstinct school of Chinese Buddhism, which has been strongly influenced by Taoism.

处合抱在一起。合抱处长出许多根须，交织缠绕，合抱处下方约10厘米，两棵树干又伸出两只长长的"手"紧紧相握，宛如夫妻合抱。左边较细的是"妻子"，右边较粗的是"丈夫"。传说南宋孝宗时，有夫妻二人草居于此，生前恩爱无比，死后紧紧拥抱而化为树。

文峰塔

在古镇中心院坝中，有一座清代建造的文峰塔。塔高约10米，分三层，外加宝顶，于清道光十三年（1833）建成。塔身成六棱状，每一层都是飞檐走角。塔身四周刻有古典戏曲雕塑，并配有用九曲篆文书写的诗文，此乃世间少有。

古戏台

在老街的上下段各有两座木结构大戏台，据说由钱姓和刘姓两家人各自修建而成，并且各竖起了一根灯杆。逢年过节戏台上唱大戏，灯杆上挂灯笼，老街上前来看戏的人摩肩擦踵，热闹非凡。

Xiaozong (1127—1194) of Southern Song Dynasty. They loved each other so much that they even died in a gesture of embracing, as if unwilling to depart. It is said that eventually, they turned into banyan trees.

Wenfeng Pagoda

There is a three-storey pagoda standing on the center square of the town with a height of ten meters. The six-sided pagoda has a roof crown on the top and each storey has cornice structures. It was built in 1833, during the 13th year of Emperor Daoguang (1821—1850) of the Qing Dynasty. The images of the main characters in traditional Chinese dramas were sculptured around the pagoda and the characters of the related prose for those images were written in seal calligraphy, which is quite rare.

Ancient Drama Stage

There are two wooden drama stages in the upper and lower sections of the old street. It is said that the stages were built by the Zhang and Liu families respectively with a lamp post on each stage. During one of the traditional festivals, lanterns are hung on the two posts representing the families. Local people flock to enjoy the drama.

7. 大邑安仁古镇

Anren Ancient Town, Dayi County

安仁古镇简介

　　安仁古镇，地处成都平原西部，距成都41千米。安仁镇在近代名噪一时，但其建镇历史可追溯至唐代。安仁县早在唐武德三年（620）就已建立（早于大邑建县50周年），隶属于剑南道邛州，其名取自"仁者安仁"之意。安仁镇以风格独特的古建筑群而闻名，现有全国重点文物保护单位及国家4A级旅游景区刘氏庄园、颇具明清建筑风格的刘湘公馆等古民居27座，还有风格中西合璧的公馆群。安仁古镇被誉为中国近代建筑的博物馆，有国家级重点镇、中国历史文化名镇（第二批）、成都市十大魅力城镇等美誉。

—传奇故事—

泥塑群雕：《收租院》的故事

　　刘文彩（1887—1949），安仁镇人，是当地的大地主。刘文彩庄园后面的收租院由一大一小两个四合院组成，各有一道东向大门。据说每到农历八月，刘文彩的"催租令"一下，

A Brief Introduction to Anren Ancient Town

The Ancient Town of Anren is located in the west of the Chengdu Plain, 41 kilometers away from Chengdu. Anren made its fame in modern times, but its history can be traced back as early as the Tang Dynasty (618—907). In 620, the 3rd year of the Wude Period (618—626) of the Tang Dynasty, Anren County was established, which was 50 years earlier than the establishment of Dayi County, under the administration of Qiong Prefecture of Jiannan Province. The name Anren is derived from the meaning of "the virtuous rest in virtue". Anren is known far and wide for its unique style of ancient buildings. The existing attractions include Liu's Manor which is a major national cultural heritage site and a national AAAA-grade tourist attraction, 27 ancient civil residences represented by the Mansion of Liu Xiang, with architectural styles from the Ming and Qing dynasties and the mansion complex, which combines both Chinese and Western elements. Anren, hailed as the museum of modern buildings in China, has earned many titles such as a Key National Town, one of Famous Historical and Cultural Towns in China (the second batch), and one of The Top Ten Charming Towns in Chengdu.

—Legendary Stories—

Clay Sculptures: The Story of Rent Collection Courtyard

Liu Wencai (1887—1949) was a local landlord in Anren Town who was portrayed as an archetype of the landlord class who was known to oppress the peasants in the old society (the old society generally refers to a period from 1928 to 1949). The rent collection courtyard at the rear of Liu's Manor consists of two shiheyuan, also called quadrangle courtyard, one of which is big and the other small, each with a gate facing east. It was said that in the 8th month of every lunar calendar year, as soon as the announcement of Liu Wencai's "rent collecting order" was given, the tenants would carry the grain they harvested after a year's toiling and come to the rent collection courtyard to pay rent. Each tenant had to pass the four steps of grain checking, grain screening, grain weighing and accounting. After paying their dues at each of the "four passes", quite a few tenants found that they could not afford to pay the fixed land rent. These tenants would be subject to torture, coercion, or even be displaced or separated from their families.

佃户们便带上终年辛苦劳作收获的粮食，前来收租院交租。一共有验谷、风谷、过斗、算账四道关。经过"四道关"层层盘剥后，不少佃户便因交不够"铁板租"，而会面临拷打、威逼，甚至是家破人亡、妻离子散的局面。

　　大型泥塑《收租院》陈列在大四合院里。真人大小的泥像，依次展现了送租、验租、风谷、过斗、算账、逼租、怒火等情景。人物面貌、体态栩栩如生，无一雷同。

　　送租：一条伸着长舌的恶狗旁站着一个汉子。他头戴草帽，身穿绸短衫，手执弹簧钢鞭，腰间挎着驳壳枪。他对面有一群衣衫褴褛的佃户，男的肩挑手推，女的背着竹篓，儿童替大人拉着鸡公车，向收租院源源不断地涌去。

　　验租：手拿念珠的刘文彩硬说面前的老大爷没交够租子，叫管账写了一张卖儿当壮丁的文书，强迫老大爷按手印。老大爷不答应，便被踢倒在地。儿子见了不顾一切地扑了上去，但寡不敌众，被袍哥打手一拥而上抓了起来。

　　逼租：一位双目失明的老大爷，儿子被抓了充壮丁，儿媳妇也被地主抢走给活活地折磨死了，只留下一个年幼的小孙女。老大爷倾其所有仍过不了验租关，刘文彩硬逼老大爷在一份卖身契上按了手印，上面写道："只因无力缴纳所欠刘家三斗租子，现将孙女儿抵押。"

　　怒火：一群拿着扁担的农民正要离开收租院。走在最后的一个壮年农民忽然转过身，放下箩筐扁担，双手握拳，瞪着刘文彩，似乎要冲过去和他算账。一个青年农民抓起一把

The large-scale clay sculpture group titled *Rent Collection Courtyard* is displayed in the big quadrangle courtyard. The life-size clay sculptures successively showcase the scenes of bringing in the grain for rent, checking the grain, screening the grain, weighing the grain, accounting, forcing payment of rent, and flaring in rage. Each of the characters is lifelike with unique appearances and postures.

Bringing in the rent: A man is standing beside a fierce dog with its tongue sticking out. He wears a straw hat and a silk shirt, holding a steel whip in his hand and carrying a mauser pistol in his waist. Opposite him are a group of ragged tenants streaming into the rent collection courtyard. The men are carrying loads of grain on their shoulders or are pushing carts; the women are carrying baskets of grain on their backs and the children are pulling handcarts for the adults.

Checking the rent: Liu Wencai who is fumbling with a string of prayer beads in his hand insists that the old man in front of him hasn't paid enough rent. He orders the accountant to write a contract selling the old man's son into forced labor and forces the old man to agree to give an imprint of his finger. The old man is kicked to the ground after he has refused to do so. Seeing this, his son rushes up desperately, but he is outnumbered and gets caught by a gang of Liu Wencai's thugs.

Forcing the rent: A blind old man is only left with his young granddaughter after his son was taken away for forced labor and his daughter-in-law was seized by the landlord and tortured to death. The old man still can't pass the rent checking yard even after he had given away everything in his possession. Liu Wencai forces him to put an imprint of his finger on an indenture which reads: "I hereby pledge my granddaughter for being unable to pay the grain of three dous[1] owed to the Liu Family."

Flaring in rage: A group of farmers with shoulder poles are about to leave the rent collection yard. A peasant in his prime walking at the end of the line suddenly turns around. He puts down the basket and shoulder pole, gripping his fists, staring at the landlord, in a posture that indicates that he is going to step forward to reason with Liu Wencai. A young peasant grabs an axe, takes a bow step and bends his body. His eyes are fixed on the windmill as if he can't wait to smash the man-eating machine. Another peasant wields his shoulder pole and looks as if he intends to confront Liu Wencai. An elder man next to him presses his shoulder with his left hand and gestures him not to act recklessly. There are five peasants in front of the two men. The one walking in the very front looks young. He is carrying his shoulder pole with his left hand and his right hand is clenched into a fist. His steps look firm and steady, as if he is determined to revolt.

---

① Dou ("斗") is a capacity measure of grains in China. One dou equals to 7.5 kilograms.

斧头，弓步俯身，双眼直视飞轮风谷机，恨不得砸碎这吃人的虎穴狼窝。一个农民抢起扁担正要冲向刘文彩，旁边一个年纪大一点的左手按住他的肩头，示意他不要蛮干。在这两人前面有5个农民，走在最前面的较年轻，他左手提着扁担，右手握着拳头，迈着坚定的步子，像是下定了决心，要抗争到底。

—民俗文化—

建筑文化：刘氏庄园

刘氏庄园由刘文彩及其兄弟陆续修建的5座公馆和刘氏家族的1处祖居构成，分布为南北相望的两大建筑群，占地总面积达7万余平方米，建筑面积2.1万余平方米，房屋共545间，是国内目前规模最大的近代地主庄园建筑群。整个庄园建筑群始建于清末，历经几次大规模的兴建和扩建，至民国末年形成现在的规模。

大邑刘氏庄园建筑规模宏大、气势非凡，颇具川西地方特色。整个庄园为一组中西合璧的建筑群，既有中国封建豪门府邸的遗风，反映了封建秩序及尊卑高下的等级关系，又吸收了西方城堡和教堂建筑的特色。主体风格体现了中国传统美学取向，细节上又融入了西方审美特征。

经过多年的调整、充实和发展，4个基本陈列已经形成：一是庄园老公馆刘文彩及其家人生活现场的复原陈列，并展出蜚声中外的大型泥塑《收租院》群雕；二是利用庄园新公馆

——Folk Culture——

Architectural Culture: Liu's Manor

Liu's Manor is composed of five mansions successively built by Liu Wencai and his brothers and an ancestral residence of the Liu Family, which are in two building groups in the south and north facing each other. The manor covers a total area of more than 70,000 square meters, with a construction area of more than 21,000 square meters, including a total of 545 rooms. So far, it is the largest modern landlord manor building complex in China. The construction of the whole manor began in the late Qing Dynasty (1616—1911) and it achieved its current scale at the end of the Republic of China (1912—1949) after several attempts of large-scale construction and expansion.

Liu's Manor in Dayi County is magnificent in scale and very imposing in outlook, embodying the local characteristics of western Sichuan. The manor as a whole is a group of buildings which combines Chinese and Western elements. It not only retains the legacy of a mansion of a wealthy feudal family in China, but it also reflects the feudal order and hierarchical relationship between superiors and inferiors. The manor also includes characteristics of castles and churches of European architecture. The main architectural style embodies the orientation of Chinese traditional aesthetics, yet the details are incorporated with European aesthetic characteristics.

After years of adjustment, enrichment and development, the manor has formed four basic displays: first, the life scene restoration display of Liu Wencai and his family members in the old mansion of the manor including the exhibition of an internationally famous large-scale clay sculpture group titled *Rent Collection Courtyard*; second, a western Sichuan folk customs display which vividly showcases the production and life of western Sichuan people in the former site of a new mansion of the manor; third, the exhibition of a rare collection of artefacts in the Manor Museum that holds sculptures of western Sichuan folk dwellings, contemporary and modern calligraphy, and paintings that were held in the former residences of Liu Wencheng and Liu Wenzhao; and fourth, a display of the restoration of the ancestral residence held in the former residence of the Liu Family.

Artcraft: Dough Figurine Huang

Dough Figurine, also known as Dough Modelling, is a type of popular traditional folk art carefully made by, among other processes, steaming, boiling, kneading, pinching wheat flour, and coloring with different pigments. "Dough Figurine Huang", known in Chengdu and the rest of the western Sichuan plain, refers to the artists who practice this art. These artists pass

旧址举办的川西民俗陈列，生动再现川西人民生产、生活方面的民俗风情；三是在刘文成公馆和刘文昭公馆旧址举办的庄园文物珍品馆馆藏精品陈列、川西民居雕刻及近现代书画陈列；四是在刘氏家族的老屋基原址举办的刘氏祖居复原陈列。

民间手艺：面人黄

"面人"也称为面塑，以小麦粉为主要原料，采用蒸、煮、揉、捏等工艺，辅以各色颜料精制而成，是深受广大群众喜爱的一项民间传统面塑艺术。"面人黄"世代相传，是成都乃至川西坝子著名的民间面塑艺人。其作品以三国、水浒、西游人物、雀鸟飞虫、家禽、农作物为主要对象。

—主要景点串游—

刘氏庄园

刘氏庄园以其独特的历史内涵以及其建筑本身对中国高超民间工匠艺术的充分体现而享誉海内外，是国际旅游组织认定的四川旅游发展"六朵金花"之一，在《四川省旅游发展总体规划》中被列为重点开发的旅游资源，现为国家4A级旅游区及全国青少年爱国主义教育基地。

民国风情街区

民国风情街区位于安仁镇中心，长760米，宽6～10米，民国时期兴建，包括树人街、裕

their knowledge of this art form to their future generations. The dough figurines are based on the characters from the *Romance of Three Kingdoms*, *Water Margin* and *Journey to the West* as well as birds and insects, poultry, and grain crops.

—Main Tourist Attractions—

Liu's Manor

Liu's Manor and its buildings are renowned both at home and abroad for their unique historic and cultural significance, which fully reflect the superb folk craftsmanship of China. It is one of the "six golden flowers" of Sichuan tourism recognized by the World Tourism Organization. It is listed as a key development tourism resource in "Overall Planning of Tourism Development in Sichuan Province", and recently Liu's Manor has been recognized as a National AAAA-grade tourist attraction, and as a national patriotism education base.

A Block with the Style of the Republic of China (1912—1949)

One street block with the style of the Republic of China is located in the downtown area of Anren. The street is 760 meters long and 6 to 10 meters wide. Built during the period of the Republic of China, this block consists of three old streets built in the style of that time that are named Shuren Street, Yumin Street, and Hongxing Street. These streets consist of many commercial and residential buildings including the original Anren Middle School, Anren Theatre, Paoge[①] Building, the Rice Market and ten mansions which combine Chinese and Western architecture (Anren has a total of 27 existing intact mansions which integrate Chinese and Western characteristics). Thus, this block is a charming complex that contains shops, accommodation, entertainment, leisure, restaurants and sightseeing. In recent years, the development in this area has included both the modern style of the Republic of China and the traditional style of western Sichuan culture, along with supporting facilities and activities such as Film Museum, Folk Gallery, Court Costumes of Qing Dynasty and National Costume Exhibition and Ethnographic Exhibitions and other thematic exhibitions open to the public.

Jianchuan Museum

Jianchuan Museum short for Jianchuan Museum Cluster, located in Anren, was built by a private entrepreneur named Fan Jianchuan. The museum covers an area of about 333,000 square meters and the building area of nearly 100,000 square meters is housed with more than 8 million artefacts in its collection, of which 404 are national first-class cultural relics. The museum's

---

① Paoge is a folk gang in Sichuan and Chongqing.

民街、红星街三条民国老街，及原安仁中学、安仁剧院、袍哥楼、米市和中西合璧的10座公馆（安仁现有保存完好的中西合璧的公馆共27座），是一个集购物、住宿、娱乐、休闲、餐饮、观光等于一体的综合体验街区。近年还推出了展现民国时期摩登风情和川西文化的民国风情街，配套开放了电影博物馆、素人画廊等设施，以及清代宫廷服饰暨民族服饰展、民族志展等主题展览。

建川博物馆

位于安仁古镇的建川博物馆，全称建川博物馆聚落，由民营企业家樊建川创建。博物馆占地33.3万多平方米，建筑面积近10万平方米，拥有藏品800余万件，其中国家一级文物404件。博物馆以"为了和平，收藏战争；为了未来，收藏教训；为了安宁，收藏灾难；为了传承，收藏民俗"为主题，分为抗战、民俗、红色年代、抗震救灾四大系列30余座分馆，已建成、开放25座场馆。该馆是目前国内民间资本投入最多、建设规模和展览面积最大、收藏内容最丰富的民间博物馆。

artifacts are themed with "Collecting Wars for Peace; Collecting Lessons for the Future; Collecting Disasters for Safety; and Collecting Folk Customs for Heritage". It has planned to construct more than 30 exhibit halls, based on four main series of the War of Resistance against Japan, Folk Customs, Revolutionary Period, and Earthquake Relief. 25 halls have been completed and are open to the public. This museum is a non-governmental museum with most private funding, the biggest building and exhibition area and the richest collection in China to date.

8. 雅安上里古镇

Shangli Ancient Town, Ya'an City

上里古镇简介

上里古镇地处雅安市雨城区北部，位于雅安、邛崃、荥经、名山四地交界处，距离雅安27千米。上里初名"罗绳"，是我国历史上南方丝绸之路上的重要驿站之一。上里镇东、北、西三面为丘陵山地，中南部为山丘围着的平坝，城镇边缘东、南、西三面都有河流和小溪围绕。古镇东北的一条沟谷里有一湾名为白马泉的清泉。

古镇最高峰名叫黑岩坪，海拔1725米。河谷平坝是农田，最低处海拔905米。山丘岭上林木植被茂密，生态环境质量佳。古镇属于亚热带湿润季风气候，夏无酷暑，冬无严寒，气候温和，四季分明，雨量充沛。

——传奇故事——

天降甘露：白马泉传说

上里名泉"白马泉"，原名"龙渊"。关于此泉得名有多种传说。一说与唐僧的白龙马相关。相传唐僧西去取经分走南、北两条路，曾在南路经过白马泉。唐僧师徒到了上里，便进庙膜拜。白龙马在寺庙外等待师傅时，因为口渴饮用了泉水，泉水立即涨潮朝拜。其原因在于这一泉水与东海相连，因而知晓白龙马的真实身份为龙王之子，故行涨潮朝拜之礼。当地僧人见到这一情景，感到非常奇怪。等唐僧师徒离开上里后，他们立即围了泉水，建造水池，以解决当地居民的生活用水问题。后来，寺庙住持高僧得到观音菩萨的点化，得知整个事件的原委，便将其奉为圣泉，引得乡亲们竞相朝拜。后来，"龙渊"改名为"白马泉"。为了纪念这一传说，如今白马寺内的香炉上仍有以唐僧取经为主题的浮雕装饰。

又有传说称，宋乾道年间（1165—1173），四川西南地区连续三年大旱，附近州县的官民都来到白马泉求雨，而这个时候正巧遇到泉池涨潮，随后便是风雨交加，天降甘露。好雨给老百姓带来希望，让田里的禾苗重生。官员们将这一情况呈奏给皇上，皇帝封白马泉

A Brief Introduction to Shangli Ancient Town

The Ancient Town of Shangli is situated 27 kilometers north of Yucheng District, Ya'an City. Lying where Ya'an, Qionglai, Yingjing and Mingshan adjoin and called Luosheng in the past, Shangli was one of the important post stations on the Southern Silk Road. Surrounded by hills on the east, north and west, the town has hill-girted flatland in the middle and south, with rivers and brooks on its east, south and west fringes. The Baima Spring winds across a gulley in the northeast. Mount Heiyanping, towering 1,725 meters above sea level, is the highest place, whereas the flatbed in the river valley, 905 meters above sea level, is the lowest part. Thick vegetation on the hills make the town a recommendable tourist attraction. With a temperate subtropical humid monsoon climate, this town has a temperate climate. There are four distinct seasons and with rains that occur frequently.

—Legendary Stories—

Timely Rain: The Legend of Baima Spring

Baima Spring was originally hailed as "Longyuan" (Dragon Pool). There are many popular legends about this spring. One legend associates the spring with the white horse of a Buddhist monk of Tang Dynasty named Xuanzang. Xuanzang and his disciples were said to take the south and north routes on their pilgrimage to the west. One day when heading south, they rode past the spring in Shangli, dismounted and offered sacrifices at a local Buddhist temple. The horse was left outside to wait for them. It felt thirsty and drank the water from the spring. To everyone's surprise, the spring welled up profusely in honor. Actually, the spring was connected to the East Sea, and it recognized the real identity of the horse which was a son of the East Sea Dragon King. Surprised at the miracle, the local monks dammed up the spring immediately after Xuanzang and his disciples had left. They aimed to make a drinking water pool for the local communities. Later the eminent monk and abbot of the temple found out about the whole story through their communication with Guanyin (Merciful Buddha). Thereafter, Longyuan was renamed as Baima Spring (White Horse Spring) and worshipped by the local people as a holy site. The Xuanzang-themed relief sculpture in memory of the event is still visible on the incense

池为"渊泽侯"。

另有一民间传闻说，观音菩萨路过上里古镇，见到百姓们遭受旱灾之苦，便大发慈悲，倾尽瓶中之水，于是天降甘露三日，解除了旱情。其中的一滴甘露洒落于白马泉，泉水自此长年不竭。后人得知是菩萨相助，于宋代永乐年间依托这一泉水靠山修建了观音殿，并把山岩雕刻成观音像长年供奉，同时把该泉命名为"观音泉"以表达对观音的谢意。现在的白马寺观音大殿里供奉的"十八罗汉拜观音"雕像塑于唐代，殿里的泉水就是"观音泉"，这也是中国佛教唯一在大殿内有泉水的建筑物。

筑桥遇仙：二仙桥得名

二仙桥位于上里古镇西边约200米处的陇西河上。二仙桥为高卷拱单孔石桥，桥面两侧筑有石栏，上面雕刻着龙头、龙尾，桥头有正面浮雕神像和"二仙桥"三个大字，和周围的景致相映成趣，自成一景。相传清乾隆年初，该桥建了两次都被洪水冲毁。乾隆四十一年（1776）该桥第三次建成。走近二仙桥，可以清晰地看见桥旁刻字记述的先后三次建桥的过程。

关于这三次建桥，民间还流传着这样的传说：清乾隆年初，为了方便两岸居民的生活交通，当地衙门打算在陇西河上修建拱桥。前两次修建，桥均在建成之际因遭遇洪灾而被冲毁。后来当地人经过高人指点，得知洪灾是河里居住的龙族肆意游走而造成的。清乾隆四十一年居民再次修建该桥。修建之时，他们在桥身的两侧分别刻了龙头、龙尾，目的是"镇龙"，避免洪灾再次发生。神奇的是，这座桥第三次建成后历经一个半世纪，都未再发生洪水毁桥的事件。

burner in the Baima Temple.

The second legend associates the spring with a three-year drought in southwest Sichuan, during the reign of Emperor Qiandao (1165—1173) of the Song Dynasty. The imperial officials and civilians swarmed to the Baima Spring to pray for the rain. The pool welled up gushingly and was followed by a rain storm, promising a new hope for people as the dying crops revived. Officials reported this miracle to the emperor, and the emperor conferred the title of Yuanzehou (The Lord of Pool) on the pool.

The third legend associates the spring with Guanyin or Avalokitesvara[①] Bodhisattva, who passed by during a local drought. Shocked by the intense suffering, Guanyin showed mercy by draining out a water bottle to create three days of rain and put the drought to an end. However, one of drips fell beside Baima Spring and turned the dry spring into a limpid perennial spring. Later on, a hall was built adjacent to a mountain to house the spring, and a figure of Avalokitesvara Bodhisattva was carved on the massif. The spring was named Guanyin Spring or Avalokitesvara Spring, expressing people's gratitude for the deity. *Eighteen Arhats Worshipping Avalokitesvara Bodhisattva*, a statue worshipped in the hall, was built in the Tang Dynasty (618—907). With the Avalokitesvara Spring right in the center of it, the hall is the only one of its kind in China.

The Meeting with Gods in Bridge Construction: The Naming of Er-xian Bridge

The Er-xian Bridge spans over the Longxi River, around 200 meters west of the town. The stone bridge has a high arch and railings on the deck with dragon heads and tails in relief. The bridgehead is featured with gods in relief and calligraphic work that depicts the Chinese characters "二仙桥"(means Er-xian Bridge). These form a delightful contrast with the surroundings. Twice ruined by floods after completion in the early Qianlong period (1736—1795) of the Qing Dynasty, it was rebuilt in 1776, the 41st year of the same period. An epigraph work adjacent to the bridge gives an account of the three construction projects.

Another legend associates the construction of the bridge with the local government's plan to improve the local transportation infrastructure in the Qianlong period of the Qing Dynasty. The bridge was twice ruined by flood shortly after completion. Later, a well-known prophet attributed the damage to the dragons inhabiting the river. When the bridge was rebuilt in 1776, the 41st year of the Qianlong period, the builders embossed dragon heads and tails on the railings to quell the dragons and to preclude further disasters. To the amazement of everyone, the bridge has not been damaged by flood for more than one and a half centuries since the third reconstruction.

---

① Avalokitesvara is a bodhisattva who embodies the compassion of all Buddha.

"二仙桥"名字的由来,有民间传说称在第三次建桥竣工当日,附近州县名士前来祝贺,人们来到桥头准备踩桥定名时,发现有两位乞丐坐在桥头拦住踩桥的人们。众人正想上前理论,这两个乞丐便跳进河里,河水立刻显出两个石包,大家才大悟,原来这二位并非乞丐,而是两位神仙,于是便将此桥定名为"二仙桥"。

—民俗文化—

建筑文化

古镇民居保存较为完好,体现了明清时期风格,大多为青瓦民居,木结构建筑。清道光四年（1824）所建的韩家大院是古镇的代表性建筑之一,原是清代官吏韩廷藩的私人府邸。大院由七个院落组成,正所谓"七星抱月"。整个建筑物的门、窗、枋、檐都用浮雕、

镂空雕和镶嵌雕刻作装饰,同时用楠木、银杏等为木料,使得雕刻之物栩栩如生,神态逼真。该大院独具地方建筑特色,为穿斗式木结构和青瓦屋面组成的四合天井古建筑群,接近地表处采用石墩做柱基,石板铺地和嵌镶地角坊。这种形式的建筑有较高的抗震和防潮性能,同时以变化无穷的民间雕刻艺术展现了淳朴的造型和浓郁的生活气息。

小镇的街道相对狭窄,两边为老式铺面,街道呈"井"字布局,取"井中有水,水火不容"之意,用水来牵制火,希望小镇和平安定。街中心有较宽阔的戏坝子,前面有二重檐歇山顶戏楼,是川中场镇罕见的建筑设计。

饮食文化

挞挞面是全手工面条,和拉面较相似。将新鲜面块放在案板上甩挞（不同于拉面）,最终成厚薄均匀、宽窄适宜的面条,再放入大锅宽水煮熟。面条熟后,选配数十种不同的调料,有令人食欲大增的大块牛肉,也有红亮油闪的墩墩肉等。入碗大

Folklore also associates the name "Er-xian", meaning two gods, with a miracle on the completion date of the third reconstruction. At the time many high-society people arrived to attend the inauguration ceremony. They were about to name and cross the bridge in celebration when two beggars seated at the approach came up to forbid their passage. People were about to contest this when the beggars jumped into the river and transformed into two monoliths. People came to realize that the two beggars were two gods, so the bridge was named Er-xian out of respect for them.

—Folk Culture—

Architectural Cultrue

Houses in Shangli are mostly well-preserved, demonstrating the styles of Ming and Qing dynasties. Most of them are wooden houses with grey tiles. A representative one of this style of housing is Han's Grand Courtyard built in 1824, the 4th year of the reign of Emperor Daoguang (1821—1850). It served as the mansion of Han Tingfan, a notable Qing government official. The grand courtyard has seven smaller courtyards, reflecting the concept of "Seven Stars Surrounding the Moon". All the doors, windows, tie beams and eaves, made of Chinese phoebe nees or gingko timber, are embossed, hollowed or inlaid as a vivid embellishment. Characterized by the local style, the grand courtyard is an atrium-featured compound with a dark grey-tiled roof and a wooden tie-beam structure. Stone plinths serve as posts at the floor end and flagstone flooring and inlaid stone thresholds are also provided. The structure of the house is highly resistant to earthquakes and humidity. The various folk-style carvings on this structure exhibit plain but strong domestic features.

The streets in the town are relatively narrow, lined with conventional-style storefronts. The streets form the shape of a large net like the Chinese character "井", meaning water well. This design was inspired by the concept of "suppressing fire with water", expressing the best wishes of peace and tranquility. In the center of the neighborhood is a large outdoor theater, with a hip roof that has a double-layer eave design. This is rarely seen in central Sichuan towns.

Food Culture

Tata noodles are handmade noodles akin to Lamian[①] noodles. Fresh dough is hurled onto the chopping board and it is then shaped into noodles that are equal in thickness and width. The noodles are then cooked thoroughly and served with many ingredients, such as beef and red oily pork cubes and seasonings to taste. Tata noodles look pearly white and smooth and it has a unique

---

① Lamian is a kind of Chinese hand-pulled noodles.

方，口味独特，有质感洁白、入口滑爽、不黏牙、弹力好、筋度高的特色。

乌骨鸡炖山药是"野"山药和"土"鸡的结合，是上里具有浓郁地方特色的美食。野山药优在口感细嫩略脆，入口化渣，土鸡肉则醇香油亮。炖好后，汤色油黄，香飘宜人，闻则欲食，食则无忘。这道菜不仅味道鲜美，而且为滋补身体之佳品。

—主要景点串游—

文峰塔

文峰塔又称"字库塔"，建于清同治五年（1866）。塔下有字纸炉，为上里古代官宦人家和文人燃烧字纸之用。

高桥

高桥建于清乾隆十四年（1749），为三卷拱桥。桥上、桥下东西两端各有一人行道。桥上、桥下皆可通行，享有"清代立交桥"之美誉。

九世石牌坊

九世同居石牌坊建于清嘉庆六年（1801），记载了陈氏家庭九代同居、人口逾千、共聚一堂的历史。陈氏家族被誉为汉族第一大家庭，两次受到朝廷嘉奖，因而建立家谱石坊。

taste. It's elastic-like and chewy.

Stewed Silkie with Yam is a combination of wild yam and free-range silkie, which is a delicacy with strong local characteristics in Shangli. The cooked yams taste tender, slightly crisp and are melting soft. The silkie meat tastes great. The broth smells fragrant, looks oily and tastes appetizing and unforgettable. This dish prepared with local ingredients is not only delicious but also tonic.

——Main Tourist Attractions——

Wenfeng Pagoda

Wenfeng Pagoda, also known as Ziku Pagoda, was built in 1866, the 5th year of the reign of Emperor Tongzhi (1862—1874) in the Qing Dynasty. At the foot of the pagoda stands a burner in which ancient rich men and literati burned used calligraphy paper.

Gaoqiao Brigde

Gaoqiao Bridge is a bridge with three arches. It was built in 1749, the 14th year of the Qianlong period of the Qing Dynasty. The bridge has an upper deck and a lower deck at the eastern and western ends respectively, permitting passage at both levels. Therefore, it enjoyed a high reputation as a flyover in the Qing Dynasty.

Jiushi Stone Paifang

Jiushi Stone Paifang[①] or Nine-generation Stone Paifang was built in 1801, the 6th year of the reign of Emperor Jiaqing (1796—1820) in the Qing Dynasty in memory of the Chen family. This is a big family with nine generations living under one roof. Totaling a family tree of more than 1,000 people, the household was then famed as the largest Han family and twice authorized by the imperial court to establish their own genealogical records and paifang.

---

① Paifang is a traditional style of Chinese architectural arch or gateway structure.

9. 理县桃坪羌寨

Taoping Qiang Village, Li County

理县桃坪羌寨简介

　　桃坪羌寨位于阿坝州理县境内，距县城40千米，距成都139千米，是国家级重点文物保护单位。桃坪羌寨距今已有2000多年历史，所有建筑均由石头垒砌而成，是目前世界上保存最为完整且尚有人居住的碉楼与民居融为一体的建筑群，享有"自然空调"之盛名。羌寨完善的地下水网、迷宫似的巷道和雄伟古朴的碉楼，被人们誉为羌族建筑文化艺术"活化石"，桃坪羌寨也被称为"神迷壮丽的东方古堡"。

——传奇故事——

桃花圣地：桃坪得名

　　桃坪羌寨依山而建，一条杂谷脑河经寨子缓缓流过。其历史可追溯到公元前111年，寨子至今仍保存着原始羌寨的风貌。如今寨里住着约100户"格尔麦阿嘎"人，在羌语里是

A Brief Introduction to Taoping Qiang Village

Taoping Qiang Village is subordinate to Li County of Aba Tibetan and Qiang Autonomous Prefecture. Geographically, it has a distance of 40 kilometers from Li County and 139 kilometers from Chengdu. With a long history of more than 2,000 years, the village is an important national cultural heritage site. In the village, all the buildings are constructed with stones. Currently, Taoping Qiang Village owns most of the preserved architecturally designed compounds in the world which are still in use. They combine the architectural style of the Qiang ethnic Minority's Diaolou, a kind of watchtower, with that of the local residential houses. Owing to the special architectural structure of Qiang Diaolou, the village is not only well known for its magnificence and beauty, but also for its fame of "natural air-conditioning" (Qiang Diaolou is warm in winters and cool in summers). The village is honored by both Chinese and foreign scholars as the "representation of architecture of the Qiang Minority" and "a mysterious and magnificent oriental maze", owing to its complete and fine underground water networks, accessible pathways, and maze-like architectural art.

—Legendary Stories—

The Wonderland of Peach Blossom: The Naming of Taoping

Taoping Qiang Village is built on the mountain, with a river named Zagunao flowing through. Its history can be dated back to 111 BC. Currently, the buildings and structures in Taoping still remain in the original style of Qiang architectural compounds. In this village, there are around 100 families called "Ge'er Mai Agha", which means families of the ancient alleys in the Qiang language.

The original name of Taoping was "Chixi Village", which meant a red creek. It was said that in the creek flowing through the village, the pebbles were red. Hence, it got the name. Later, it was renamed to Taoziping, also called "Qiezi" in the Qiang language, meaning that immortals had visited the place.

According to a legend, Taoping was once a barren and desolate place. People worked very hard but could barely survive. However, the simple folk custom here and the industrious

"古巷人家"的意思。

桃坪羌寨最早名为"赤溪寨"，据说当时流经桃坪的一条小河中石头呈红色，因此而得名。后来又改名为桃子坪，羌语为"切子北"，意思是神仙来过的地方。传说很早以前桃坪是一个土地贫瘠、四周荒凉的地方，人们辛劳耕作，却只能勉强度日。但这里淳朴的民风、寨民们的勤劳最终感动了神灵，天神木比塔洒下树种，顿时漫山遍野长满了桃树。春天，桃花芬芬，香气袭人，整个寨子沉浸在花的海洋里。花果成熟的季节，这里硕果累累，果香四溢。据寨中老人说，以前桃坪除了早熟桃以外，还有六月桃、七月桃和八月桃，一年之中这里有半年的时间都满是花果。人们幸福地生活在这世外桃源中，因此，这个盛产桃子的地方就被称为桃子坪，后来简称"桃坪"。

火娃盗火：白石神传说

走进桃坪羌寨，会发现寨子中所有的庄房和碉楼上都放有一块或多块洁白的石英石，这是历年来羌族人民信奉和崇拜的图腾：白石神。传说，很久以前寨子中没有火，羌民们生活得非常艰苦，人们吃不到熟食，不能取暖，不能抵御野兽的攻击。到了夜晚整个寨子被黑暗笼罩，黑夜带给人们无尽的恐惧。为了给这个地方带来光明，寨里一位名叫"火娃"的英雄决定上天取火。他不畏艰险，排除万难，最终得到了白石。他击石生火，造福这里的人们，为寨子带来了文明。所以人们将这位英雄奉为白石神，白石也成了纪念这位英雄的图腾。

在羌文化中，白石崇拜又与生殖崇拜紧密结合，因为白色象征着纯洁和亘古不变，这使

villagers moved their gods. The God Mubita shed seeds from trees and these seeds immediately grew into peach trees, covering the mountains. In the spring time, these trees blossom with a beautiful fragrance and the whole village is immersed in a sea of flowers. During harvest time, one can smell the fruit everywhere. The elderly men in the village recall that in past years, besides the harvest of the early maturing peach, there were a series of peach harvests that took place in June, July and August. These village people spent almost half of the year harvesting peaches. Therefore, this place which is abundant in peaches is called Taoziping.[①] Later the name changed into Taoping in short.

Fire Boy Stealing the Fire: The Legend of White Stone God

Walking into the Taoping Qiang Village, visitors will find one or more white quartz stones placed on the roofs of the villagers' houses or Diaolou. These white stones serve as the Qiang people's totem for the White Stone God. It is said that a long time ago, people in the village led a hard life, as there was no fire in the village. Hence, the villagers had no cooked food, no warmth in winters and in their defense against monsters, they did not have a fire to light the dark night, all of which brought endless fear to them. In order to bring light to the village, a young man called "Fire Boy" decided to steal fire from heaven. On the way to heaven, the fearless hero overcame all the difficulties and obstacles that he confronted and ended up with a harvest of white stones (the quarts) which could be used to make fire. With the fire brought by the young man, villagers led a better life and their civilization started. Thereafter, Fire Boy was enshrined as the White Stone God, with white quartz stones serving as his totem.

In the culture of the Qiang ethnic group, the worship of white quartz stones is closely related to their reproduction worship, for the color white, in their eyes symbolizes unchanging purity, which provides them with an approximate impression of "life", and further expounds the value of "human reproduction". Meanwhile, white stones in Qiang people's heart are also symbols of their God of heaven, God of earth, God of fire and the divinity of ancestors, which reflects their traditional values of hierarchy, namely "Gods are above humans, and humans are above animals". The white stones, apart from serving as a symbol of worship for the Qiang people, are also used in building as part of the classical architecture as including the glaring white quartz gives the stone-piled houses a sense of spirituality and aliveness.

---

① Taozi means peach in Chinese. Ping in Chinese refers to a flat ground in a mountain. Taoziping refers to a place famous for peaches.

古羌族人产生了物体可以逐渐转化为"生命"的朦胧意识，进而又将其引申到"人种繁衍"的生殖观念上。同时，白石也是羌族人民心中群体神灵的图腾，它是天神、地神、火神以及祖先神灵的象征，充分体现了羌族人民"人在畜上，神在人上"这一传统价值观。白石不仅是羌寨人民信奉的对象，也是对这些雄伟古朴建筑的点缀和装饰。洁白耀眼的白石与羌族建筑完美结合，使这些石块垒砌而成的建筑更加灵动，富有生气。

—民俗文化—

建筑文化：碉楼

碉楼是整个羌寨的标志性建筑，主要以土、石和木料为原材料。建筑格局多为四角梯形，一些碉楼也呈六角或八角形，高九层，约30米，各层四面开有射击窗口。在羌民聚集地区，每隔一段距离就会有一座碉楼与其他村寨相连，碉楼内部楼层之间狭窄陡峭，具有"一夫当关，万夫莫开"之势。一座座坚挺有力、苍凉雄劲的碉楼是羌寨人民集体智慧的结晶，更是灿烂文明的标志，成为羌族文化传承的主要实物载体。

饮食文化：羌餐

颇具草原游牧民族特色的羌餐是羌寨的主要特色之一，讲究原生态属性，以肉食为主，

—Folk Culture—

Architectural Culture: Diaolou

Diaolou, a kind of watchtower, is the representative architecture of the Qiang Village. These Dialou are basically constructed with earth, stones, and wood. The Diaolou is mainly shaped in the form of a four-angle trapezoid. Some are also shaped as six-angled trapezoids or eight-angled trapezoids. They often have nine storeys and are about 30 meters in height. In the four directions of each storey, there are windows for shooting at the enemy, that is, for safety. In the inhabitation of the Qiang people, these towers were built at particular distance intervals to connect one village with another. As they are generally built with steep and narrow stairs inside, these towers are regarded as fortresses where one man guards the pass. Even ten thousand enemies are unable to get through. In all, the strong and powerful Diaolou is believed to be the part of the collective wisdom of the Qiang people, as well as a symbol of their glorious civilization, serving as the main cultural carrier of the people of Qiang ethnic minority group.

Food Culture: Qiang Food

One of the main specialties of Taoping Qiang Village is their Qiang food which is characterized by nomadic style flavors. Meat takes priority in a meal, and various local herbs serve as a garnish. Their snacks, such as, those made of potatoes or corn, Tuotuo Meat (lump pork) and home-made grape wine are very good. Besides these snacks, one may also taste delicious Qiang preserved pork, field mushrooms and walnut flowers. With a combination of traditional ethnic cooking methods and pollution-free ingredients, one may not only taste the unique flavor of the special Qiang cuisine but also have a glimpse of the Qiang culture.

Embroidery Culture: Qiang Embroidery

Qiang embroidery is the concentrated embodiment of the Qiang people's arts and aesthetics. It also serves as gorgeous treasure of the cultural inheritance of China for more than one thousand years. Qiang girls, from an early age, are trained in the traditional art of embroidery, and generally become experts of this art as they grow up. They value the art of embroidery, because each girl needs to make her own wedding clothes and "Yunyun Shoes" for their wedding ceremony, otherwise, their bridegrooms may feel disgraced. Today, Qiang embroidery has become one of many popular souvenirs and collections for tourists and collectors from around the world.

兼搭多种当地野菜。洋芋坨坨、玉米苞苞、坨坨肉、自酿葡萄酒等小吃回味悠长。除小吃外，羌家腊肉、野山菌、核桃花等特色菜也值得品尝。原生态的食材与民族传统厨艺相结合，人们不仅可以品尝到独特的羌菜风味，还可从中窥见羌族文化。

刺绣文化：羌绣

羌绣是羌族艺术审美价值的集中体现，也是中华民族千年文化的珍宝。羌族姑娘自小学习刺绣，待到成年时皆练就了驾轻就熟的刺绣工艺手法。按照羌族的传统婚嫁礼俗，姑娘出嫁时必须穿着自己绣成的嫁衣，还有上好的"云云鞋"方能出阁，否则男方会觉得很失体面。如今，羌家绣品已经成为中外游客和收藏家青睐有加的纪念品和收藏品。

歌舞文化

羌族歌舞奔放豪迈，是羌族具有代表性的传统文化项目之一。按表现形式可分为独唱、对唱和集体对歌等，著名代表作有《花儿纳吉》《改盘歌》等。羌族人民以丰富多样的歌舞形式来表现该民族的劳动生活、婚嫁习俗和祭祀信仰，其歌舞节奏明快，热情奔放，耐人寻味。

—主要景点串游—

羌绣馆

羌绣馆位于新寨，这里集中展示、出售各种羌绣，同时也是绣娘培训、材料存放的地方。羌绣馆于2010年开设，也是里县最早开设的多功能馆厅。他们将传统的羌绣技能与现代时尚完美结合，赋予羌绣新的文化内涵。

杨家大院

杨家大院是羌寨保存得比较完好的古老羌寨建筑，距今已有上千年历史，用传统的材料和古朴的垒砌方式修建而成。这座古宅四通八达，户户相通，虽经千年风雨的洗礼，但在"5·12"汶川大地震中丝毫未损。

陈家羌碉

陈家羌碉是目前历史最为悠久的住宅碉楼，也是桃坪羌寨最古老的建筑，见证了长达

Singing and Dancing Culture

Qiang singing and dancing, which is bold and passionate, is one part of the local traditional cultural programs. In their expressive forms, Qiang singing and dancing programs are presented in solo, antiphonal singing and collective singing in antiphonal styles. The most prominent masterpiece includes *Huaernaji*, *Gaipan Song* and others. In their leisure time after work, Qiang people indulge in a variety of rhythmic, enthusiastic and enchanting singing and dancing to visualize the scenarios of their work, marriage, sacrifice and worship.

——Main Tourist Attractions——

Qiang Embroidery House

The Qiang Embroidery House is situated in the new village. The House is used for embroidery demonstrations, sales, embroidery workshops for women and for storage of materials. The Embroidery House was established in 2010. It is one of the earliest multi-functional embroidery houses for the Qiang ethnic minority. Staff in the House combine perfectly traditional Qiang embroidery skills with modern fashionable subjects, giving Qiang embroidery new cultural dimensions.

Yang's Grand Courtyard

Preserved as a relatively complete ancient Qiang house, Yang's Grand Courtyard, built with traditional materials in traditional ways of construction, has witnessed a history of a thousand years. Though so many years have passed, the courtyard that extends in all directions and connects all doors remained intact during the massive earthquake on May 12th, 2008.

Chen's Diaolou

Chen's Diaolou is the oldest residential tower in history as well as the oldest building in Taoping Qiang Village. It has witnessed the history of Taoping for more than 2,000 years. A bell is installed at the top for sending messages, for military defense purposes. However, unlike other Diaolou, Chen's Diaolou is also a residence for the head of the village. Thus, its internal structure is more complex because it is a combination of both a house and a watchtower. There are underground channels on the ground floor for military defense in case they need to escape during a war. The second floor is a living area with kitchens and living rooms. On the third floor, there is a terrace (balcony), where female members of the family do needlework or chat. The fourth floor is a warehouse for storing food. The remaining storeys are mainly used for military purposes, and include lookouts and a signals transmission station. Thanks to the special design

2000多年的羌寨历史。楼顶的钟口用来传递消息，为军事防御之用。然而，与其他羌碉不同的是，陈家羌碉还供土司头人居住，其内部结构更为复杂，为罕见的"房碉结合"的形式。碉楼底层设暗道，供战时防御或逃生之用。二层为生活区，有厨房、居室等。三层设碉楼平台（阳台），是羌族妇女们做针线、聊天的地方。四层为仓，储存粮草。其余各层主要用于瞭望、释放信号等军事目的。这座羌碉虽年代久远，但依然牢固如初，得益于其特殊的设计及精湛的工艺，凝结了羌族先人的智慧。

地下水网

羌寨有一个迷宫般的地下水网，引自雪山的水，由暗渠进入寨区，再由主干渠分流到各家各户。地下水网不仅给寨子提供源源不断的水流，而且具有防御功能，如遇战事，寨民们可通过暗渠藏身或逃生。

and superb craftsmanship of their clever ancestors, Chen's Diaolou remains as solid as ever after even thousands of years.

The Underground Water Network

What underlies the entire Taoping Qiang Village is a maze-like underground water network, through which melting water from snow mountain flows into the village area and is redirected to all households. The underground water network does not only ensure a steady water supply for the village, but also serves as a shelter for villagers in case of wars.

10. 甘孜丹巴古镇

Danba Ancient Town, Ganzi Autonomous Perfecture

丹巴简介

　　丹巴，位于四川省甘孜藏族自治州，距州府康定137千米，距省会成都368千米。丹巴旧称"诺米章谷"，藏语指"山崖上的城"。它位于长江上游，典型的高山峡谷地貌，最高海拔5820米，最低处1700米，呈垂直分布。境内峰峦重叠，河流纵横，峡谷深邃。其独特的地形地貌，造就了丹巴融雪山、森林、海子、温泉、草甸、大河为一炉的神奇美丽的自然风光。丹巴还拥有旖旎的民族风情和古老的历史文化。丹巴是嘉绒文化的发祥地之一，素有"千碉之国"之称。梭坡古碉群、甲居藏寨、土司官寨、莫斯卡格萨尔石刻、中路石棺墓群等独特的人文景观与丹巴壮美的自然风光交相辉映，为丹巴赢得了"童话世界""中国最美乡村""中国景观村落"等美誉。

—传奇故事—

克歌降妖：碉楼

　　丹巴自古有"千碉之国"之称，在梭坡、中路、蒲角顶等碉楼集中的地方，高耸的古碉连绵起伏，气势非凡。碉楼，羌语称"邓笼"，早在汉代就开始在羌族地区发展盛行。丹巴的碉楼是由世代生活于此的嘉绒藏族所建，历史已愈千年。关于碉楼的修建，当地流传着这样的传说：很久以前，大渡河河谷中有妖魔专门摄取男童灵魂，于是谁家生了男孩，为了

A Brief Introduction to Danba Ancient Town

Danba, located in Ganzi Tibetan Autonomous Prefecture in Sichuan Province, is 137 kilometers away from Kangding, the seat of the prefecture, and 368 kilometers away from Chengdu, the capital of Sichuan Province. Danba was formerly known as Nuo Mi Zhang Gu, meaning "the town above the cliff" in Tibetan. Located in the upper reaches of the Yangtze River, it has a landscape ranging from rolling ridges and peaks to deep canyons and rivers, and an undulating elevation with the highest altitude reaching 5,820 meters, the lowest 1,700 meters. Its unique terrain has created a beautiful blend of natural scenery with snow-capped mountains, verdant forestry, alpine lakes, hot springs, marshy grassland and raging rivers. Danba also boasts distinct folk customs and a long history with a rich culture. Known as the Kingdom of Thousands Watchtowers, Danba is one of the cradles of ancient Jiarong culture[1]. The Suopo ancient watchtower clusters, the distinctive Jiaju Tibetan Village and the Headman's Village, the Gesar Stone Carvings in Moska, and the ancient sarcophagi in ZhongluVillage are a testament to Danba's unique cultural identity and heritage. The juxtaposition of Danba's rich cultural and historical relics and splendid natural scenery has garnered it a reputation of a "fairy tale world" and "one of the most beautiful villages in China".

—Legendary Stories—

Defending Evils: Diaolou

Since ancient times, Danba has long been known as "the Kingdom of Thousands Watchtowers". The ancient *dialu*, or fortified watchtowers, dominate the majestic skyline of the villages of Suopo, Zhonglu and Pujiaoding. Diaolou, also known as Denglong among the ethnic Qiang, began to develop and prevail as early as the Han Dynasty (206 BC—AD 220). The Diaolou were built over a thousand years by Jiarong Tibetans, who have lived in this region for generations. The legend has it that a demon in the Dadu River valley was fond of swallowing

---

[1] Jiarong or Gyalrong refers to the culture of the Jiarong Tibetan group, a branch of China's Tibetan ethnic minority. The Jiarong culture is a characteristic sub-culture of the Tibetan culture.

保佑男孩生长，便要修筑碉楼，以御妖魔。男孩长一岁，就加修一层碉楼，打炼一坨毛铁。等到男孩18岁长大成人，碉楼修到18层，毛铁打炼成钢刀，钢刀于是就被送给男孩作为成人礼，鼓励他克敌降妖。丹巴的建筑故而以"碉楼"为特色。

众山之首：墨尔多神山

墨尔多山起于阿坝州鹧鸪山，山脉在马尔康、丹巴、大小金川境内伸展，绵延上千里。其主峰位于大渡河源头、大小金川交汇处，海拔5000米，山势险峻，风光奇绝，古往今来为人顶礼传颂，为藏地圣山。关于墨尔多神山，在嘉绒地区也流传着一个古老传说：很久以前，神山之首空悬已久，喜马拉雅山神发起了一个集会，召集青藏高原的各路山神，通过讲经和比武来选出众神之首。

集会开始后，各山神齐聚一堂，纷纷按旨就坐，只剩下一把龙头扶手玉石雕花椅。这时，一位山神自东而来，环顾四周，未见空位，便坐在龙头椅上。这一举动直接惹怒了其他山神，

这位从东方来的山神不慌不忙说道："讲经说法排座次，擂台比武分高低，佛言佛语为依据，何方获胜归何方。场中既然无我坐席，想必是大家要推我登首席了。"群神不服，欲与他辩经说法。谁料到东方来的山神佛法造诣精深，经历七七四十九

boys' souls. Therefore, when a boy was born, his family would build a tower to protect him from the evil spirit. Following his birth, the family would smell and forge iron and add one storey to the watchtower every year. By the time thc adolescent was 18 years old, the watchtowers would have risen to 18 storeys. In addition, the iron would be forged into a sword. The sword would be presented to the boy at his coming-of-age ceremony to encourage him to defeat this demon.

The Head of the Mountains: Moerduo Holy Mountain

Moerduo Mountain range starts from Zhegu Mountain in the Aba Tibetan and Qiang Autonomous Prefecture and stretches thousands of li[①] across Maerkang, Danba and Greater and Lesser Jinchuan. Located at the source of thc Dadu River and the intersection of the Greater and Lesser Jinchuan, the rugged main peak, 5,000 meters above sea level, offers sublime scenery and is worshipped as one of the holy mountains of the Tibetan area since ancient times. There is an ancient legend about the mountain. Once upon a time, the position of the ruler of the holy mountain had been vacant for a long time. A Himalayan God convened a meeting of various mountain gods in the Qinghai-Tibet Plateau to select a supreme ruler through scripture debating and a tournament.

When the rally started, all the mountain gods gathered together and were seated upon the decree, leaving only a jade carved dragon throne chair unoccupied. A mountain god from the east having just arrived from the east, looked around and found no vacant seat. Therefore, he seated himself on the dragon throne's chair. It immediately provoked other deities. The god from the east said calmly, "The throne chair is left for the one who wins the debate and the joust. Since there is no seat left in the field, presumably you all permit me to ascend to the throne." The rest of the immortals were unconvinced and vied to debate the scripture with him. Why did he think that he had achieved profound attainment in Dharma? During the seven days of seven sets of debates, he defeated all his opponents one after another. During the nine days of nine sets of debates that followed, he made a clean sweep at the tournament. All gods were willing to submit to defeat and thus elected him as chief. When he took off his hat to the deities, they found that he had a bald head that glimmered brightly. Thereupon, the gods chanted in unison, "Moerduo! Moerduo!" A long time ago when Buddha inspected the world, he found a beautiful and fertile land in the East where people were valiant and industrious. Buddha predicted that Dharma would be widely spread and practiced in this place one day. The land is known as Moerduo, meaning "glittering bald head" in Sanskrit. That day when the gods saw Moerduo with their own eyes, they were all awed. After this tournament, all the gods in the surrounding mountains submitted themselves to him and were conferred with titles of nobility.

---

① Li（"里"）is a traditional unit of length and is equal to 0.5 kilometer or 0.311 mile.

天辩经后，把群神一一击败。随后又经历九九八十一天比武，大获全胜。群神不得不服，推举他为首领。当他摘帽向众神致意时，大家发现他是秃顶，而且熠熠生辉，于是众神齐声高呼："墨尔多！墨尔多！"原来佛祖在视察天下时，曾发现东方有一地方山川秀美丰饶，人民勤劳勇敢，预言佛法将在此地弘扬。这个地方就是墨尔多，梵文中又作"秃顶闪光"之义。今日众神亲见墨尔多即生敬仰之情。这次比武之后，四周群山皆臣服于墨尔多，随后，他将周围神山都册封排位。

就在墨尔多准备离去之时，错过讲经比试的山神"多尔基"（金刚神）不服墨尔多，决意与他分高低。墨尔多爽快地答应了他，表示愿让多尔基先动手。说时迟那时快，多尔基举刀直指墨尔多，墨尔多腾空一跃，大刀直接砍在了墨尔多脚下的岩壁上。就这样，多尔基共挥刀108次，墨尔多也向山头跳了108次，山脚到山顶共留下108道砍痕。如今，山脚至墨尔多山顶共有108层阶梯。

—民俗文化—

建筑文化：千碉之国

丹巴以其丰富的古碉建筑而闻名于世，享有"千碉之国"的美誉。丹巴现有数量最多、分布最广、功能及外型最为齐全的古碉遗存。据载，丹巴自汉代起建造古碉，在明清达到鼎盛，其数量曾达到3000余座。而目前，据统计丹巴境内仍存古碉562座。丹巴高碉皆为石砌碉，现存四角、五角、八角、十三角四种类型，其功能主要为家碉和寨碉两类。家碉由单个家庭修建，一般与家宅相连，用于家庭物资储藏和防卫。寨碉由部落、土司或村寨修建，用途各异，如作为界标使用的界碉，还有建筑在山梁上或山谷中的风水碉和烽火碉，战时承担攻防任务。

服饰文化：三片

丹巴妇女的传统便装俗称"三片"。一片为头帕，当地人称"巴惹"。中老年人一般戴素色，已婚少妇的"巴惹"绣有彩线花边和花卉图案，未婚少女的"巴惹"前面两角还系扎彩线束。其余两片为前后围腰。在节庆日，当地妇女通常会穿百褶裙和齐膝外套，有的还会佩戴披肩，头戴发箍，项系珠串等，格外典雅华贵。

When Moerduo was about to leave, Duoerji, or Vajradhara, who missed the debate and tournament, decided to have a sword competition with him. He readily agreed and let Duoerji strike first. Duoerji went at him with a sword as fast as he could. He leapt up and sliced off the rock at his feet. Duoerji attacked at Moerduo 108 times and each time Moerduo sprang over and successfully dodged, leaving 108 cut marks from the foot to the top of the mountain, and naturally those 108 cuts became today's 108 stairs.

──Folk Culture──

Architectural Culture: The Kingdom of Thousands Watchtowers

Danba is famous for its fortified Diaolou and enjoys the reputation of the "Kingdom of Thousands Watchtowers". It has the most widely distributed and the largest number of existing towers with various functions and of different configurations. According to historical records, Danba Diaolou was started during the Han Dynasty and reached its peak in the Ming and Qing dynasties with the number of towers surpassing more than 3,000. Presently, there are still 562 towers in existence in the region, all of which are made of stones. The Diaolou features four major types of watchtowers, including those that are in the shape of a quadrangle, a pentagon, an octagon and in a tridecagon style. They used to function as residential and communal towers. The residential towers were built by a single family, usually connected with a homestead to store household goods and for defense. The communal towers were built by tribes, chieftains or villages for various uses, such as boundary markers, or fengshui or beacon towers. These towers were built on a ridge or in a valley for wartime defense.

Costume Culture: Sanpian

Danba women's traditional dress is commonly known as Sanpian, also called "three pieces". One of these three pieces is used as a headscarf, or Ba-re known by locals. The elderly generally wear them in plain colors, while young married women wear ones with colored lace and floral patterns. Unmarried girls wear theirs with colored threads tied to the front. The other two pieces are two waistcloths worn over in the front and in the back. During festivals, local women will wear pleated skirts and knee-length garments, and some will wear shawls, hair bands or bead necklaces, exuding an air of refinement and elegance.

──Main Tourist Attractions──

Jiaju Tibetan Village: A Fairy Tale World in Tibetan Region

Danba Tibetan Village has been named as the most beautiful village among five others in

—主要景点串游—

藏区童话世界：甲居藏寨

丹巴藏寨被《中国国家地理》杂志评为"中国最美六大乡村古镇之首"，而丹巴藏寨又以甲居藏寨最为有名。"甲居"在藏语中意为百户人家。数百户藏寨错落有致地依偎在山谷中，在皑皑雪峰、碧水青山的映衬下，仿若一个美妙的藏区童话世界。甲居藏寨由古石碉式藏房组成，完整地保存了嘉绒民居的样貌，富有传统藏式风韵。

天堂之谷：党岭

党岭以温泉、红叶和高山湖泊而闻名。景区内有30多个高山湖泊，镶嵌在山谷中，宛如明镜。葫芦海是党岭最具观赏价值的湖泊。湖水清澈见底，雪山环绕，植被繁茂，宛若仙境。党岭的秋色尤为绚烂，层林浸染，色彩斑斓，美不胜收。

天然盆景：牦牛谷

牦牛谷又叫东谷河谷，沿岸高山耸峙，河水清冽，丛林丰茂，奇峰异石遍布，海子散落于河谷，被誉为"天然盆景"。牦牛谷最为著名的是温泉。附近很多人视该温泉为吉祥之地，纷纷来此沐浴。

China by *China National Geography* while Jiaju Village tops the list for its scenery in Danba. Jiaju means 100 households in Tibetan. Dozens of traditional Tibetan residential houses which are nestled in the valley against the backdrop of snow-capped mountains present a picturesque view. The Jiaju Tibetan village features traditional Tibetan fortress-like houses, offering a rare glimpse into the Tibetan style residences that are perfectly preserved.

Dangling: The Valley of Heaven

Dangling is reputed for its hot springs, red leaves and alpine lakes. There are more than 30 alpine lakes studded in the valley. The highlight is called Hulu Lake. The crystal clear water against the snow-capped mountains and virgin forests presents a picturesque, fairy-tale like vista. Dangling is at its best in autumn, when the valley is ablaze with fall hues.

Yak Valley: The Natural Bonsai

Yak Valley is also known as East Riverdale. It is lauded as a "natural bonsai", with its towering mountains, limpid rivers, lush vegetation, towering peaks, grotesque rocks and lakes scattered around. Yak Valley is most noted for its hot springs. Believers nearby regard this spring as an auspicious place and visit it constantly.

11. 泸定磨西古镇

Moxi Ancient Town, Luding County

磨西古镇简介

　　磨西古镇位于四川省甘孜州泸定县以南，贡嘎山东麓，毗邻国家5A级风景区海螺沟冰川森林公园。磨西古镇与泸定县城距离约52千米，距成都约304千米。"磨西"为古羌语，原意为"宝地"，指贡嘎山东麓水土丰美、适宜人居的难得的地理环境。磨西古镇旧称"磨西面"，为院系氏后裔磨西人所居，其建镇历史最早可追溯到汉代。磨岗岭古道是茶马古道的重要节点，这一交通要道使磨西成为川藏通道上物资供应和人口集散重镇。从当地的民族组成来看，磨西镇汇聚了汉、彝、藏等多民族人口，是川西多民族文化的汇聚地之一。磨西镇建筑多是具有清代建筑格调的农舍，全镇建筑沿一条古老的自流灌溉渠自然延伸分布。

——传奇故事——

语言误解：磨西得名

　　磨西镇名的来历，除古羌语的释义"宝地"外，还有一个有趣的传说。"磨西"一词本是

A Brief Introduction to Moxi Ancient Town

The Ancient Town of Moxi is situated to the south of Luding County, Ganzi Tibetan Autonomous Prefecture, Sichuan Province and at the eastern foot of Gongga Mountain. The town sits adjacent to Hailuogou Glacier National Forest Park which is a national AAAAA-grade tourist attraction. It is about 52 kilometers away from Luding County, and about 304 kilometers from Chengdu. The name of the town "Moxi" derives from the transliteration of the ancient Qiang minority language, originally meaning "the place of treasure", which is a complimentary comment of its abundant, livable geography and its environment which is situated on the eastern foot of Gongga Mountain. The original name of the town was Moximian or Moxi Facet, as it was once populated by the descendants of the Yuanxishi[①] Moxi people. The initial construction of the town can be dated back to the Mogang Ridge during the Han Dynasty (206 BC—AD 220), which served as an important traffic node of "The Tea-horse Ancient Road". This enabled the town to become a vital place for the transportation of goods and the movement of people on the Sichuan-Tibetan Route. Moxi's population distribution consists of ethnic populations from the Han, Yi and Tibetan tribes, making the town itself a habitation of multi-ethnic cultures in western Sichuan. The architecture of the building in Moxi is mostly in the style of farmers' residences during the Qing Dynasty (1616—1911), all of which naturally stretch alongside an ancient gravity irrigation channel.

—Legendary Stories—

Language Misunderstanding: The Naming of Moxi

Other than the derivation of the name "Moxi" which is mentioned above, another version regarding the name is well known and quite interesting: The pronunciation of "moxi" derives from the Tibetan language, signifying "do not know". It is said a long time ago, a team of Han businessmen once traveled there and inquired about the name of the place to a Tibetan Lama (a Tibetan monk) who was sitting beside the temple. The Lama replied with "moxi" in the Tibetan

---

① Ancient Chinese were given two surnames before Qin Dynasty (221 BC—206 BC), as one surname "Xing" was inherited from the patriarchal line, and the other surname "Shi" was inherited from the maternal line.

藏语，是"不懂"之意。据说在很久以前，早期的茶马古道上，有一队汉商途经此处，由于不熟地理，不知何处，正好遇见一喇嘛在寺边打坐，便问其此地何名。喇嘛当然不通汉话，只是用藏话回答了"磨西"，表示不懂所问的是什么，而汉商也不通藏语，以为喇嘛回答此地地名，于是把"磨西"当成了地名，从而一传十，十传百，经年流传至今，磨西便也由此得名。

—民俗文化—

建筑文化

磨西古镇修筑在一个东、西、北三面绕水环山的倾斜平台上，南高北低。一条从北山峡谷蜿蜒而上的石道，在古镇的入口岔成两条并行的马路，一条往东通向贡嘎雪山，一条往南通向100千米外的康定。丁字形小街以外，村落和楼房紧凑地聚拢在一起，低头相向，亲密攀谈。磨西镇的建筑风格大多保留了清末民初民居建筑特色。置身其中，走在青石板铺就的老路上，仿佛回到了近百年前的时光。镇中核心位置是一座由法国传教士修建的哥特式天主教堂，从中传出的礼拜祷告钟声已回响百年，中西文化的交融给古镇增添了另外一番情趣。

婚嫁习俗

磨西保存着彝族各种传统的习俗，尤其是婚嫁习俗，代代相传。结婚当日，无论路途

language, meaning he did not know what the question was as he was unable to understand the Han language. The Han businessmen took the reply "moxi" as the name of the place as they did not know the Tibetan language, either. Therefore, the initial misunderstanding spread a great distance and has lasted to this day.

——Folk Culture——

Architectural Culture

Moxi is built on a tilted platform surrounded by water and mountains from the east, west and north. The platform itself rises higher to the south and lower to the north. A winding stone road from the northern valley winds through the town and branches off into two parallel roads, one that heads for Gongga Snow Mountain, and the other that heads toward Kangding County which is 100 kilometers away. Somewhere beyond the T-shaped street, villages are closely inter-connected with buildings, as if they are facing and murmuring to each other. The style of architecture in Moxi has been largely preserved since the time of the late Qing Dynasty and up to the early period of the Republic of China (1912—1949), making one feel as if he is visiting the past when walking through the town. At the center of the town is a gothic style Catholic church which was built by French missionaries. The church bell has rung for a century, giving the ancient town a special flavor of a mixture of Eastern and Western cultures.

Marriage Customs

The people of Moxi have preserved a variety of traditional customs from generation to generation, and in particular, marriage customs. On the day of the wedding, a bride must be carried on the back of strong young men till she reaches her bridegroom's house no matter how long the distance is, because the people of the Yi ethnic minority group have a saying: "A bride off the back is not valuable." However, a bridegroom has to be particular about the way he carries his bride on his back. Different from the way that it is done today, a bride's legs must not be separated. She needs to cross her legs and lean on the man's back. On the wedding day, the bride must be dressed in a pleated skirt and embroided clothes, with "Chalva", a traditional cloak, on her shoulders. Her head has to be wrapped with layers of veils, and another big red veil is used to cover her whole body. The bride is supposed to accept gifts from her younger bridesmaids after she is carried to the bridegroom's house. In the evening, the guests join in a singing contest and partake in a feast.

远近，新娘都得由年轻壮小伙一路轮流背着到婆家，因为彝族有句俗话是："不背的新娘不珍贵。"背新娘的方法极为讲究，和我们现在所知道的背法不一样，非常忌讳双腿叉开。新娘必须双腿交叠，侧卧在小伙身上。婚礼当天，新娘身穿崭新的百褶裙和贴身的绣花衣，身披擦瓦尔（一种彝族披风）。新娘头上裹着好几层帕子，最后全身再用一个大红帕子遮住。就这样新娘历经迢迢路途被小伙子背到了新郎家里，接受小伴娘们的礼物。入夜后，除了把酒言欢，大家还会进行唱歌比赛，比一比谁更深情。

—主要景点串游—

金花寺

磨西镇位于甘孜藏族自治州，邻近西藏自治区，按理说这里应该是藏传佛教之地。古镇的尽头却坐落着一座"奇妙"的寺院：金花寺。这座寺庙是宗教融合的象征。寺庙左上方的屋顶悬挂着太极图，乃为道教；右上方的屋顶悬挂万字图，是汉传佛教；而正中间却是达喇图，典型的藏传佛教。信步在这里，听着僧人的低声喃喃，心中即便有再多杂念也跟着烟消云散。

天主教堂

磨西古镇的地理和文化中心是一座建于百年前的天主教堂。百年来，它给这座位于茶马古道上的西陲小镇增添了令人意想不到的异域风情。天主教堂始建于1918年。当时的

──Main Tourist Attractions──

Jinhua Temple

It is generally presumed that Moxi would adopt the religion of Tibetan Buddhism, as it is located in Ganzi Tibetan Autonomous Prefecture which is adjacent to the Tibetan Autonomous Region. Surprisingly, at the end of the town lies a "miraculous" temple: Jinhua[①] Temple. This temple is a symbol of the combination of religions. On the upper left side of the temple's roof hangs the diagram of the universe (an emblem of Taoism), representing the existence of Taoism; whereas on the upper right side of the roof hangs the painting of thousands of subgraphs which is a typical representation of Chinese Buddhism. A painting of Lama (Tibetan monk) is hung in the middle of the roof. Walking around the temple and listening to the monks' murmuring, one feels refreshed and calm.

Catholic Church

At the center of Moxi lies a Catholic church that was built a hundred years ago. For a century, the church added an unexpected exotic flavor to this town in western China on the Tea-horse Ancient Road. The church started to be built in 1918 and was sponsored by the Kangding Catholic parish. For religious purposes the parish decided to build a religious facility on the important traffic route connecting Sichuan and Tibet. Both the church and residences were completed in 1925. However, what remains now is the church only. The church was designed by French missionaries who later followed suggestions from locals and infused the church with traditional elements of temples in southwest China. Typical of that traditional form is the upturned eaves on top of the church, which signifies an integration of Chinese and Western cultures. This Catholic church later became the soul of Moxi architecture.

Luding Bridge

Luding Bridge is an important national cultural heritage site. It was initially built in 1705, the 44th year of the reign of the Kangxi Emperor (1662—1722) in the Qing Dynasty, thus it has a history of more than three hundred years. The calligraphy on the bridge plaque is said to be written by the Kangxi Emperor himself. The body of the bridge is three meters wide and 101 meters long; and is fastened by thirteen iron links. Originally, the bridge was constructed by wood which was connected by iron links. After repeated repairs and reconstructions, Luding Bridge today is basically made of stones and cement. Historically, the bridge served as an

---

① Jinhua means golden flowers in Chinese.

天主教康定教区出于宗教目的，决定在磨西这一川藏交通要道修建宗教场所，并于1925年建成了教堂和住房，而今只有这座教堂保存完整。该教堂的整体设计由法国传教士主持，听取当地人建议后，教堂又融入了中国西南地区传统庙宇的样式。最典型的莫属教堂顶部的飞檐样式，让其颇具中西合璧之象，从而成为磨西镇建筑的灵魂。

泸定桥

泸定桥为全国重点文物保护单位。它始建于清朝康熙四十四年（1705），迄今已有300多年历史了，屹立桥头的"泸定桥"三字据说由康熙皇帝御笔所题。桥宽3米，长101米，本为由铁链铰接的木质桥，桥身主要由13根铁链固定，经近现代多次整修加固后，现主要结构已由木质改为石料或混凝土。泸定桥是当地重要的交通设施，也一直是川藏交界地区的咽喉要道。1935年5月29日"飞夺泸定桥"的胜利让泸定桥逐渐为人所知，而今这座历经沧桑的铁索桥不仅继续发挥着交通要道的作用，同时也成了人们缅怀先烈、追忆历史的圣地。

important traffic infrastructure in the local area and an opening of the Sichuan-Tibetan boarder. On May 29th, 1935, a decisive battle of the seizure of Luding Bridge gave this bridge a world-renown reputaion. The Luding Bridge has undergone vicissitudes and serves not only as a traffic facility, but also is known to be a memorial structure of the revolutionary martyrs and their glorious history.

12. 洪雅柳江古镇

Liujiang Ancient Town, Hongya County

柳江古镇简介

柳江古镇坐落于眉山市洪雅县西南的花溪河边，距离县城30多千米，距离成都市区150千米，是四川十大著名古镇之一。古镇始建于南宋绍兴十年（1140），距今已有800多年历史，古名"明月镇"。后因镇上的柳姓家族和姜姓家族出资修建了一条石板长街而更名为柳江场，即今天的柳江古镇。古镇四面环山，花溪河与杨村河穿镇而过，风景优美，一年四季雨雾朦胧，享有"烟雨柳江"的美称。柳江古镇声名远播，素有"云南丽江，四川柳江"之说，曾荣获"全国特色景观旅游名镇""国家级优美乡镇""全省十大最美村落"等称号。

—传奇故事—

柳江四大家族

清末民初的柳江有"曾、张、杨、何"四大家族，势力庞大，对柳江镇的政治、经济和文化产生了极大的影响。民间有一种说法："曾家的房子，张家的丫头子，杨家的顶子，何家的谷子。"意为曾家楼阁华丽，张家丫头漂亮，杨家官位显赫，何家稻谷盈仓。

曾家的房子

"曾家园"的主人和设计者名叫曾艺澄，曾就读于重庆大学建筑系。其父名叫曾益寿，

A Brief Introduction to Liujiang Ancient Town

The Ancient Town of Liujiang is located 30 kilometers southwest of Hongya County, Meishan City and 150 kilometers from Chengdu. It lies on the bank of Huaxi River. With its splendid landscape, Liujiang is considered as one of the most fomous ancient towns in Sichuan Province. The town, with a history of more than 800 years, was built in 1140, the 10th year of Shaoxing during the Southern Song Dynasty (1127—1279). Originally named "Mingyue Town", Liujiang was named for two big families in town, i.e., the Liu family and Jiang family. These two families financed the construction of a flagstone street in town, after which Liujiang became famous as a local market. Surrounded by mountains on all sides, Liujiang has the Huaxi and Yangcun rivers running through the town. Liujiang is widely known for its picturesque scenery and is often compared to Lijiang, a world-famous ancient city in Yunnan Province. Enveloped in rain and mist throughout the year, this town resembles a beautiful watercolor painting, and is therefore often referred to as "misty Liujiang". Liujiang is recognized on several award lists, such as "National Featured Tourist Towns" "National Beautiful Towns" and "Top Ten Beautiful Villages in Sichuan Province".

—Legendary Stories—

Four Big Families of Liujiang

During the late Qing Dynasty (1616—1911) and the early period of the Republic of China (1912—1949), Liujiang was dominated by a few wealthy families, named Zeng, Zhang, Yang and He. The four families were so powerful that they had great political, economic and cultural influence over Liujiang. An old folk saying goes, "Zeng's house, Zhang's maids, Yang's power, and He's grains", meaning that the Zeng family owned a beautiful courtyard, the Zhang family had beautiful maids, the Yang family held high positions and the He family possessed a full granary.

Zeng's Courtyard

The owner and designer of Zeng's Courtyard or Zengjia Yuan was Zeng Yicheng, who

清朝咸丰年间在柳江街上开了家药铺，后来做青山生意发了财，成为了柳江一代名绅。曾艺澄为纪念其父，花了10多年的时间，按照繁体"寿"字布局，精心修建了"曾家园"，享有"半潭秋水一房山"的美誉。

张家的丫头

张家世代书香门第，是柳江有名的文墨世家。张带江是清代著名书法家，以秀丽、遒劲的"带江体"独树一帜。张家对选用丫头的要求非常高，传说其鼎盛时期家中丫头近50人，个个窈窕标致、温婉动人，不仅聪明能干，且略通书琴，遂远近闻名，成为一方美谈。

杨家的顶子

杨家官场势力大，其代表人物为民国时期的杨宇楼。他先后担任过北洋军政府云南省中英禁烟会秘书、国民政府贵州省湄潭县知事、国民政府重庆江北县知事等要职。后来，他加入了"新民主主义建国社"，并利用自己的影响力多次营救被捕的中共地下党员，为四川省的解放事业做出了重大贡献。

何家的谷子

何家的代表人物何肇南曾中过晚清的秀才，20世纪20年代初在军阀陈洪范手下任辎重营长兼峨眉知县。1924年他转投军阀刘成勋，任骑兵团长。1927年他回到洪雅，和其兄弟将搜刮的民脂民膏运回柳江扩充家财，贩卖鸦片，盘剥农民，到1937年时已占有良田6000多亩[①]、山林50000亩，年收租谷万担以上。后来又做了木材生意，且在工、商、金融业都有投资，成为一方富豪。

忠贞爱情：夫妻树

古镇向来多古树，柳江古镇上主要生长着许多古老的榕树、桢楠、麻柳、梧桐，甚至还有全川最大，据说已有200年历史的黄桷兰树。这些古树和寄居在上面的藤蔓植物又形成了"树中树""夫妻树"等奇观。夫妻树由相邻的一棵梧桐树和一棵榕树融生而成，树干相偎相依，树冠枝叶伸展，树叶不分

---

① 1亩≈666.7平方米。

studied architecture in Chongqing University. Dating back to the Xianfeng years (1851—1861) of the Qing Dynasty, Zeng Yicheng's father, Zeng Yishou operated a herbal medicine shop in Liujiang. He later made a fortune in the lumber industry, and therefore became a well-known figure in Liujiang. In honor of his father, Zeng Yicheng spent ten years designing this courtyard, shaping its layout based on the traditional Chinese character "壽" which appeared in his father's given name. This character is pronounced "shou", which means longevity in Chinese. The exquisite design of Zeng's Courtyard has received tremendous praise, putting it on par with the esteemed Suzhou Gardens.

Zhang's Maids

For generations, the Zhang family attached great importance to education and nurtured a few scholars. One of them, Zhang Daijiang, was a famous calligrapher in the Qing Dynasty who developed a calligraphic style of his own which was characterized by its striking beauty and vigor. The Zhang's were highly selective with their maids. At the best of times, the Zhang family had around 50 female servants, who later became known far and wide for their legendary beauty, elegance, wisdom and competence.

Yang's Power

Many members of the Yang family held high positions of power. The most prominent among them was Yang Yulou. Yang held a series of key positions, from Secretary of Opium-prohibiting Council of Yunnan Province under Beiyang Military Government to Magistrate of Meitan County of Guizhou Province and Magistrate of Jiangbei County in Chongqing during the Republic years. He later joined the "Society of New Democratic Country" and rescued arrested underground Communists on numerous occasions, thus contributing greatly to the liberation of Sichuan Province.

He's Grains

He Zhaonan, once a Xiucai, meaning a scholar who passed the imperial exam at the county level, was a representative figure of the He family. In the 1920s, he worked for a warlord named Chen Hongfan as Head of Army Supplies and Magistrate of Emei County. In 1924, he was employed by another warlord named Liu Chengxun and served as the Colonel of the Cavalry. In 1927, he returned to Hongya and greatly expanded his family wealth with money exploited from local peasants. He and his brothers further enslaved local peasants by selling opium to them. In 1937, the family of He owned over 6,000 mu[1] of farmland and 50,000 mu of forests, collecting

---

① One mu ("亩") is equal to 666.7 square meters.

彼此，你中有我，我中有你。

"夫妻树"名称源于一个美丽的传说：从前，天庭里有位美丽的仙女私下凡间，游历山水。当仙女经过柳江古镇时，被这秀丽的山水和淳朴的民风深深吸引，便决定留在柳江生活。仙女每晚都会去清澈的杨村河沐浴，享受同大自然的亲密接触。一天，当地一位少年上山砍柴时迷了路，无意间目睹正在沐浴的仙女。少年傻了眼，仙女此时也看到了他，四目相对的瞬间互生情愫。此次尴尬的邂逅便开启了一段美丽的情缘，少年和仙女很快坠入爱河，不久结为夫妻。他们在婚礼时互相许下了"在天愿作比翼鸟，在地愿为连理枝"的誓言。

他们美丽动人的爱情传到了村中一个恶霸的耳中，当他看到如花似玉的仙女时，顿时起了强占的念头。夫妻俩得知了恶霸的计划，为躲避他的骚扰，便逃到两棵大树下搭茅棚居住。一天深夜，恶霸带了几名打手来抢仙女，少年奋起反抗，可惜人单力薄，被打手打昏后用绳子吊死在其中一颗榕树上。仙女见丈夫已死，也不愿独活，遂在旁边的梧桐树上自缢身亡。夫妻俩死后，原本分开的两颗树竟然越长越近，最后融生在一起，根连着根，枝并着枝，好像是同心携手的夫妻俩，似乎实现了其"在天愿作比翼鸟，在地愿为连理枝"的誓言。古镇居民为了纪念仙女与少年的爱情，从此便把这两棵树称为"夫妻树"。

—民俗文化—

雅女文化

柳江素有雅女之乡的美称。西蜀洪雅，人杰地灵。瓦屋青衣，雅女动人。烟雨柳江，大美之地。古镇湿润的气候、宁静的山水、深厚的文化底蕴养育了古镇的一代代儿女，特别是古镇的女孩子，出落得玲珑娇艳，五官精致，肌肤白皙，气质清新，聪慧典雅。俗话说："来到柳江，忘了家乡；来到花溪，忘了家妻。"雅女以花为貌，以鸟为声，以柳为态，以冰雪为肤，素有"贞、烈、孝"的美誉。

饮食文化

钵钵鸡是柳江民间的特色菜肴，选用当地跑山鸡，将鸡肉及鸡杂煮熟后串成串浸泡在鸡汤、鸡油以及辣椒、花椒、芝麻等多种香料调成的汁液里，有红油和藤椒两种口味，鸡肉滑嫩弹牙，麻辣鲜香，深受食客喜爱。

蛋裹圆又名香碗或镶碗，是柳江古镇地方菜的代名词。制作方法是将上好的猪肉剁成末，与淀粉、鸡蛋、芹菜、盐、香油等调和，然后再将其捏成圆条状，外表裹上鸡蛋皮，用蒸的方式烹饪，熟透后取出切成片，趁着热劲吃味道最好，老少皆宜，一直是柳江民间"九大碗"的重头菜。

over 10,000 dan[①] of grain per year in rent. Later running a successful lumber business and investing widely in industry, commerce and finance, He Zhaonan became a local tycoon of his time.

Loyalty of Love: Fuqi Tree

A variety of aged trees grow in Liujiang, including the Banyan, Nanmu, Ash, and the Sycamore. It is also said to be the home to the biggest ficus tree in Sichuan, which has a history of 200 years. These old trees, along with other plants and vines that live on them, form spectacular views such as the "Fuqi Tree" (Couple Tree) and "Tree of Trees". "Fuqi" means "husband and wife" in Chinese. The "Fuqi Tree" is in fact the coupling of a sycamore tree and its adjacent banyan tree. Leaning against each other, with shared crowns and branches, the two interdependent trees have literally joined together.

The name "Fuqi Tree" comes from a beautiful legend. Once upon a time, there was a beautiful fairy living in heaven. One day, without permission, she secretly descended to earth and started to travel around the world. Upon her arrival at Liujiang, the fairy at once fell in love with the spectacular landscape and friendly people, and thus she decided to stay for a while. Every night, she went to bathe in the clear waters of the Yangcun River, enjoying nature's bounty. Once, a young man lost his way while collecting firewood. He was struck senseless when he accidentally caught sight of the bathing fairy. As soon as their eyes met, they developed strong feelings for one another. This awkward encounter led to a romance. The fairy and the young man fell in love and decided to get married soon afterwards. At the wedding, they made a beautiful vow to each other, "Let us be lovebirds in the sky, and to entwine our roots on earth."

However, it wasn't long before their touching love story spread to a local villain. As soon as he discovered how striking the fairy was, the villain wanted to make her his own. When the couple learned of the villain's plan, they immediately fled and found a hiding place under two big trees, where they built a thatched cottage. Unfortunately, the villain was able to track them down, and one night, the villain and his henchmen came to take the fairy away by force. The young man resisted to the last, only to be knocked out and then hanged from the big banyan tree. When she learned of the death of her husband, the fairy lost her will to live. She hung herself from the sycamore tree, close to the banyan tree where her husband had been hung. After the couple's deaths, the two separate trees began to grow towards one another, and finally grew into one. As an embodiment of the couple's beautiful vow, the consort trees with linking roots and interlocking branches resemble the fairy and the young man holding hands. In order to commemorate this beautiful love story, people in Liujiang named the two trees "Fuqi Tree".

---

① Dan（"担"）is a capacity measure of grains in China. One dan equals to 10 dou, around 70.5 kilograms.

酥油千层饼又名酥锅盔。制作时先要起面，再将撕去表膜的猪生板油、八角、茴香、三萘、花椒、生姜、精盐、味精等食材剁成的馅抹在拉长的面皮上，经卷压成形，上煎锅煎烤，最后放进炉膛烘脆。做好的锅盔外表金黄，酥脆适口，香醇美味。

—主要景点串游—

曾家园

曾家园由地主曾艺澄花费长达10年的时间精心修建而成。宅园占地11621平方米，总建筑面积5402平方米。该建筑融合了川南民居和西洋建筑元素，是四川省少见的晚清、民国时期民居庭院建筑范例。2013年3月被国务院列为第七批全国重点文物保护单位。

吊脚楼

吊脚楼是古镇标志性的景点之一。

吊脚楼取材于当地山区的树木，屋基由卵石垒砌而成。它临江而建，掩映在一棵遮天蔽日的大榕树里。吊脚楼、大榕树，再加上一汪柳江水，形成了此处独特的美景。

─Folk Culture─

Yanv Culture

Liujiang is known as the home to "Yanv", or "girls from Hongya County". Located in western Sichuan, Hongya County is a land of picturesque scenery and distinguished people. Liujiang, the "Land of Great Beauty", has nurtured generations of people with its humid climate, tranquil ambiance and deeply-rooted culture. Girls in Liujiang are especially charming. They are widely known for their beauty, elegance and wisdom. An old saying goes, "If you come to Liujiang, you will forget your hometown; if you come to the Huaxi River, you will forget your wife at home." This is due to the Yanv's refined faces, sweet voices, slim figures and fair skin, as well as their reputation for being faithful, tough and caring.

Food Culture

Benben Chicken or Bobo Chicken is a local specialty. Free-range local chicken and giblets are boiled, sliced, and strung together on bamboo skewers. These skewers are then soaked in a pot of spicy sauce made of chicken soup, chicken fat, peppers, peppercorns, and sesame seeds. The dish comes in two flavors: chili-oil and local peppercorn. The flavor of the tender chicken and Sichuan spices is well received among customers.

Danguoyan, an omelet stuffed with minced pork, also named "Xiang Wan" (flavorful bowl), is a signature dish of Liujiang. Quality pork is minced and mixed with starch, eggs, celery, salt and sesame oil. Shaped into round bars, the mixture is then covered with egg and steamed. When it is well-cooked, the bars are sliced and ready to serve. The dish tastes better when it is hot. Popular with both old and young, Danguoyuan has always been a must-eat at local "Jiu Da Wan", which is a kind of local banquets.

Also known as Crispy Pancake, these multi-layered pancakes start with leavened dough, which is then stretched into long strips and covered by filling made of lard, anise, ginger and other condiments. Rolled in small pies, pan-fried and then baked in an oven, the delicious pancakes come out with a crispy golden layer on the outside.

─Main Tourist Attractions─

Zeng's Courtyard

Zeng's Courtyard was built by the landlord Zeng Yiceng, who devoted 10 years to its meticulous construction. The yard occupies an area of 11,621 square meters, of which 5,402 square meters is occupied by buildings and structures. Blending architectural features of

古镇老街

古镇老街全长约500米，保留着从民国初期到改革开放不同时期不同风格的建筑，有"百年建筑博物馆"之称。

老街格局与四川众多的场镇相似，水渠穿街而过，厚重的石板路承载着历史的沧桑。老街人头攒动，游人们赏古树、品小吃、玩纸牌，为古镇增添了不少生气与活力。

southern Sichuan civil residences with features from European buildings, Zeng's Courtyard is an architectural model of the rarely-seen civilian residences between the late Qing Dynasty and the early period of the Republic of China in Sichuan. In March of 2013, Zeng's Courtyard was listed as one of the national key cultural protection sites by the State Council of China (the seventh batch).

Stilted Houses

Houses that are built on stilts are one of the most iconic sights in the ancient town. Built with local timber, these buildings are based on a foundation of pebbles and stones. Hidden behind the dense shade of old banyan trees along the Liujiang River, they produce a distinctive beauty of their own.

The Old Street

About 500 meters in length, the Old Street has been called a "Museum of Century-old Buildings", because it is lined by buildings of various styles ranging from the early period of the Republic of China to the period of the Reform and Opening-up. The layout of the street is like many other ancient towns in Sichuan. Water channels run along the street, covered by heavy stone slabs that carry the weight of history. The Old Street is always crowded. Tourists can enjoy the beauty of the old trees and the tasty street snacks while watching the locals play cards, which add life and vitality to the street.

13. 宜宾李庄古镇
Lizhuang Ancient Town, Yibin City

李庄古镇简介

李庄古镇位于宜宾市翠屏区东部，素有"万里长江第一古镇"之称。全镇面积71.52平方千米，场镇面积2平方千米。古镇建制历史悠久，自梁代大同六年（540）起设六同郡。李庄自然景色秀丽，人文景观荟萃，文物古迹众多，其建筑文化及民俗文化使李庄声名远播。2005年被评为第二批中国历史文化名镇，2008年被授予国家4A级旅游景区之称。

—传奇故事—

潜心学术：建筑学伉俪

20世纪30年代，由于战争，多家文化学术机构辗转迁移至四川南溪县李庄，一大批知名

A Brief Introduction to Lizhuang Ancient Town

The Ancient Town of Lizhuang is located in the eastern part of Cuiping District, Yibin City, known as "the first ancient town along the Yangtze River". The town covers an area of 71.52 square kilometers, and the main part of the town is two square kilometers. Its history can be dated back to the Liang Dynasty (502—557). As early as 540, the 6th year of the Datong period, Liutong County was established here. Lizhuang boasts beautiful natural scenery, varied cultural landscapes and numerous cultural relics, in particular its architecture and folklore culture. In 2005, these gave the town the reputation of a Famous Historical and Cultural Town in China (the second batch), and it was named as a national AAAA-grade tourist attraction in 2008.

—Legendary Stories—

Perseverence in Academic Research: The Couple in Architeture

In 1930s, due to a number of wars, many cultural institutions moved to Lizhuang, in Nanxi County, Sichuan Province where a large number of well-known scholars gathered. In 1940, the Research Institute of History and Language in Academia Sinica moved here, too. The Society for the Study of Chinese Architeture, an academic community which specializes in the study of ancient architecture, also moved to the small town with all their documents and reference books. Despite extremely difficult conditions, the members of this community continued their research on ancient architecture and published many professional works. The couple Liang Sicheng[1] and Lin Huiyin[2], together with their colleagues, completed a number of classic works of architecture, such as the *History of Chinese Architecture*, and *Image of the History of Chinese Architecture* (English version), etc.

When they were writing the book *History of Chinese Architecture*, Liang Sicheng and Lin Huiyin lived a very difficult life. Soon after her arrival in Lizhuang, Lin Huiyin started suffering from lung disease, and during the same period, the long-lasting war, the soaring cost

---

① Liang Sicheng was a Chinese architect and scholar.

② Lin Huiyin was a Chinese architect and writer.

学者云集于此。中央研究院历史语言研究所也于1940年迁往此地。营造学社，是专门从事古代建筑研究的学术团体，其成员携带着图书资料租住在李庄上坝月亮田。营造学社在极其艰苦的条件下，坚持古建筑调查与研究，期间出版了大量专业著作。梁思成、林徽因夫妇与同仁在此克服困难，完成了《中国建筑史》《图像中国建筑史》（英文稿）等一批建筑领域经典著作。

在写作《中国建筑史》的日子里，梁思成、林徽因的生活相当困难。一方面，林徽因饱受身体病痛的困扰，到李庄不久，就换上肺病，卧床不起。另一方面，夫妻俩不得不面对战事不断、物价猛涨、经费拮据的问题。他们的朋友纷纷伸出援手。傅斯年瞒着俩人向中央研究院代院长朱家骅写信求助。费正清和费慰梅也多次来信劝他们去美国治疗。然而，都被梁思成和林徽因二人婉拒。

后来，梁思成的大妹梁思庄从北平辗转越过日军防线到李庄探望兄嫂。随后，费正清也来到李庄。在亲人和朋友的陪伴下，这对伉俪在李庄度过了漫漫长夜，迎来了期盼已久的胜利。李庄的艰苦生活磨练了他们的意志，同时也给予了他们思想的火花，最终，在这个小镇，梁思成完成了中国首部建筑经典之作《中国建筑史》。

科学报国：李庄克隆之父

生物学家、教育家童第周是中国当之无愧的"克隆之父"。他用鱼作材料，进行了一系列的实验胚胎学研究，开创了我国克隆技术之先河。他所取得的成就离不开在李庄开展的一系列先驱实验。1941年抗日战争期间，童第周受聘为同济大学生物系教授，来到李庄。尽管条件十分艰苦，但他始终坚持做实验，甚至不惜以花光所有积蓄为代价，举债6万元买下一台德国造的旧显微镜。他利用干电池、煤油灯，甚至窗台上的阳光，开始了中国最早的克隆技术研究，并取得了领先世界的生物胚胎研究成果。

1943年初，童第周教授邀请了英国著名学者李约瑟博士来校讲学。李约瑟博士在李庄

on commodities and financial scarcity also gave rise to hardship in life. Their plight made their friends sad. Fu Sinian, one of their friends wrote to Zhu Jiahua, acting president of Academia Sinica for help, without letting the poor couple know. Other friends like Fei Zhengqing (John King Fairbank) and Fei Weimei (Wilma Canon Fairbank) also wrote letters to the couple, persuading them to go to the United States for a better medical treatment and a good life. Lin Wheiyin and Liang Sicheng were very grateful to their friends but declined all their help.

In October of 1942, Liang Sizhuang, the eldest younger sister of Liang Sicheng went to Lizhuang from Peking, by crossing the Japanese occupied areas and visited the couple. She was followed by Fei Zhengqing. In the company of relatives and friends, they lived through the hardship in Lizhuang, and ushered in a long-awaited victory. In this town, Liang Sicheng completed writing the *History of Chinese Architecture*, which is known to be the first classic work of Chinese architecture.

Patriotism in Scientific Researches: The Father of Cloning from Lizhuang

Tong Dizhou, the biologist and educationist, deserves the honor of "the father of cloning" in China. He carried out a series of experimental embryology studies on fish and started "cloning" technology in China. His achievements cannot be separated from the pioneering experiments carried out in Lizhuang. During the War of Resistance against Japan in 1941, Tong Dizhou came to Lizhuang, and was employed as a professor of biology at Tongji University. Although the conditions were very poor, he insisted on conducting his experiments. He used all his savings and even borrowed money to buy an old German microscope in order to continue with his work. He made use of dry batteries, kerosene lamps, and even rays of sunlight coming through his window to conduct the experiment. He was the first to begin the study of China's cloning technology and was considered as the world's leading researcher for working with biological embryos.

In early 1943, Professor Tong Dizhou invited Dr. Joseph Needham, a famous British scholar to lecture at Tongji University. During his time at Lizhuang, Dr. Joseph Needham visited Dr. Tong Dizhou's biology laboratory with great curiosity. When he saw that in his so-called "biology laboratory", there was only one microscope and a few goldfish for trial, he could not believe that Professor Tong had attained such great achievements which had attracted worldwide attention in the biological field in such poor conditions. Dr. Needham repeatedly praised Professor Tong's achievements in this field as a miracle. In Lizhuang, there were many experts and scholars like Tong Dizhou. They served the motherland in such a way that they carried forward the tradition of the Chinese nation through persistence, diligence and academic spirit. These scholars shouldered the heavy responsibility of scientific research.

期间，十分好奇地参观了童第周的"生物实验室"。当看到仅有一架显微镜和几条养着供做试验的金鱼时，他简直不敢相信童第周能在如此艰苦的条件下取得令生物学界瞩目的研究成果。这位洋博士连连称赞这简直是奇迹。实际上在李庄，有许多如童第周一样的专家学者，他们秉承执着、勤勉的学术精神，肩负科学研究的重任，以这种特殊的方式报效祖国。

—民俗文化—

民俗活动

李庄是个古风古韵浓郁的小镇。这里的民俗活动也别有一番情趣，如舞草龙、放龙灯、划花船、表演"牛儿灯"、川剧清唱等，都是年节里乡亲们喜爱的文娱活动。其中，舞草龙尤为特别，参与舞龙的全是女子。逢年过节或有重大庆祝活动时，她们都要进行舞龙表演，一招一式，丝毫不逊须眉，成为李庄最具独创性的民俗活动之一。

建筑文化

李庄的建筑非常有特色，比如席子巷就很好地体现了川南古镇民居建筑的风格。这是一条青石板路面的窄巷，两旁的民居多为木榫穿斗结构的二层小青瓦房屋，冬暖夏凉，错落有致。每间房屋门面外还有两扇齐腰矮门，称为"腰门"，别具独特韵味。上面的屋檐把仅有几米宽的街道遮盖住。站在街市上观天，仅见一丝天空，故席子巷又称"一线天"。

饮食文化

李庄的特色美食，最具代表性的当属"一花二黄三白"，即花生，黄辣丁和竹荪组成的"二黄汤"，白肉、白酒及白糕。其中，李庄白肉尤为出名。白肉指选料、火候、刀工、佐料颇为独特的蒜泥白肉。这种白肉长、薄、透亮。起初因其长，曾

—Folk Culture—

Folklore Activities

Lizhuang boasts rich traditions and distinctive folk activities. There are many popular recreational activities held here during the Spring Festival, including the straw-dragon dance, the dragon lantern play, the flower boat race and Sichuan Opera performance without makeup. The straw-dragon dance is a special folk activity because the dragon dancers are all women. At every Spring Festival or on other major holidays, these women perform the dragon dance. This has become one of the most original folk activities in Lizhuang.

Architectural Culture

Buildings in Lizhuang are very distinctive. Mats Lane boasts examples of the architectural style of residence in southern Sichuan. This is a narrow slabstone-paved lane lined with residences. Most of these residences are two-storey houses built with Chinese-style grey tile. They are well-proportioned, warm in winter and cool in summer. Each facade has two waist-low doors, known as a wicket, which adds the architecture a unique style. The extended eaves overhang most of the street which is only a few meters wide. Standing on the street and looking upward, one can only catch a glimpse of the skyline. Therefore, Mats Lane is also called Yixiantian, meaning a thread of sky or a thin strip of sky.

Food Culture

The most representative delicacies in Lizhuang are summarized as "one hua, two huang, three bai[1]". They refer to the following dishes: peanut (pronounced as huasheng), yellow catfish (pronounced as huanglading), two-yellow-soup which is cooked with yellow catfish and bamboo fungus, sliced boiled pork (pronounced as bairou), alcohol (pronounced as baijiu) and rice cake (pronounced as baigao). Among these, sliced boiled pork is the most well-known dish of Lizhuang, which is also called "Sliced Boiled Pork with Garlic Sauce". This dish is special because of the choice of fresh food ingredients, the intensity of the heat, and the unique skills needed for slicing the pork which are long, thin and bright. Originally, this dish was called "the wrap of the feet" and later was renamed because people thought that the name was unsuitable. During war time, many teachers and students who moved here with their institutions of higher education liked to eat the sliced pork dish. Even some foreign teachers came to taste the famous

---

① Hua, huang and bai are three colors in Chinese, which are respectively the initial sound of six representative dishes in Lizhuang.

被称为"裹脚肉"，因此名不雅，后来改为李庄白肉。关于这道菜还有一个趣闻。当时，许多随高等学府和研究机构搬迁至李庄的专家、师生都喜欢吃，外籍教师也常来，但因语言不甚流利，常常拍屁股表示要品尝用上好猪腿肉做成的这道名菜。在当地，素有"到李庄不吃蒜泥白肉，等于没到李庄"之说。

—主要景点串游—

张家祠

李庄镇西的张家祠堂，占地近4000平方米，因堂内有两广总督张之洞题写的"宏我汉京"匾额而闻名天下。清道光十九年（1840），由张师德为首的张氏族人集资660两银子，从族人手中购得大宅。为表达张氏子孙爱敬祖先之心，专辟为追远根本的宗祠之用。

这座宗祠的主体为四合院式木结构建筑，上为正祠，下为厅房。其厅房的50扇窗门别具特色。每扇均用上等楠木精工雕刻了两只仙鹤，50扇窗共100只仙鹤，形态各异，栩栩如生，四周配以飞彩流云，谓"百鹤祥云窗"。梁思成先生在考察时也为这样精湛的建筑艺术而惊叹。张家祠百鹤窗、文昌宫、奎星阁、禹王庙九龙碑被并称为"李庄四绝"。

旋螺殿

旋螺殿位于李庄镇北2.5千米外的石牛山上，建于明万历二十四年（1596），初名文昌宫，后更名为旋螺殿。殿呈八角形，通高25米，进深、面阔均为8米。外为三重檐，内实二层。青色筒瓦，塑八条垂脊，垂脊上各置垂兽和走兽。屋面坡度平缓，宝顶及八个翼角的起翘均不甚高，比例匀称，线条柔和，风格独特，造型奇丽。整个建筑不用一颗钉子却极为牢固。1956年螺旋殿被评为四川省重点文物保护单位，2006年被列为全国重点文物保护单位。

pork dish. As their Chinese was not very fluent, they often slapped their thighs to give the waiter a hint, showing that they want to order this dish. There is a saying, you have not really visited Lizhuang unless you have tasted "Sliced Boiled Pork with Garlic Sauce".

—Main Tourist Attractions—

Zhang's Ancestral Temple

Zhang's Ancestral Temple is located in the west of Lizhuang, covering an area of nearly 4,000 square meters. The temple is famous for a horizontal inscribed board written by Zhang Zhidong, Viceroy of Guangdong and Guangxi. A man called Zhang Shide raised some silver to purchase the big house from his clansmen in 1840, the 19th year of Daoguang (1821—1850) during the Qing Dynasty and considered it to a temple where Zhang Shide and his clansmen expressed their respect and love for their ancestors.

The main part of this ancestral temple is a wooden building which is built in the quadrangle-courtyard style and consists of a main hall in the north and sitting rooms in the south. The sitting rooms have 50 unique windows, each of which is made of fine Nanmu (a kind of Chinese phoebe nees timber) planks carved with two cranes. So altogether there are 100 vivid cranes in different shapes, with moving clouds surrongding them. Hence, this type of window has the name as "windows with auspicious clouds and 100-white-cranes". The exquisite architectural art of the windows was highly praised by Mr. Liang Sicheng, a great architect in China when he visited Lizhuang. The windows of Zhang's Ancestral Temple, together with Wenchang Hall, Kuixing Pavilion and the Nine-dragon Stele (stone tablet) in King Yu's Temple, are reputed to be the "four wonders" in Lizhuang Ancient Town.

Gyraulus Temple

Gyraulus Temple is located on Shiniu Mountain, 2.5 kilometers away from the north of Lizhuang Town. It was built in 1596, the 24th year of Wanli (1573—1620) in the Ming Dynasty with the name Wenchang Temple. Later it was renamed Gyraulus Temple. The temple is built in the shape of an octagon, and it is twenty-five meters high and eight meters long and wide. Although the temple appears to have three tiers of eaves there are in fact two. Roofed with grey semicircle-shaped tiles, the temple has eight roof ridges decorated with various animal heads and squatting animals. With a slightly sloped roof, the whole temple is known for its good proportion between the top and the eight slightly upward eaves. The temple has soft lines, a unique style and marvelous shapes. The whole building is quite strong even though it was built without any nails. In 1956, it was listed as An Important Provincial Cultural Heritage Site. Gyraulus Temple was awared the title of An Important National Cultural Heritage Site in 2006.

东岳庙

东岳庙为李庄古镇内又一著名古建筑，曾是同济大学工学部所在地。东岳庙始建于明正德年间（1506—1521），供奉东岳大帝。现东岳庙重建于清道光七年（1827）。由大山门、丙灵殿、玉皇楼、岱宗殿、十二殿等建筑组成。

Dongyue Temple

Dongyue Temple is another famous ancient building in Lizhuang, which was once the seat of the Engineering Department of Tongji University. It was built in the reign of Zhengde(1506—1521) in Ming Dynasty, and dedicated to the God of Mount Tai. The Dongyue Temple was rebuilt in 1827, the 7th year of Daoguang(1821—1850) during the Qing Dynasty. Among them, Dongyue Temple consists of many buildings and structures including the Mountain Gate, Bing Ling[1] Hall, Yuhuang[2] Pavilion, Daizong[3] Hall and Twelve Hall.

---

[1] The Lord of Bing Ling is said to be the third son of God Dong Yue, who is a mountain god.

[2] Yuhuang refers to the Jade Emperor who is in charge of all the gods.

[3] Daizong is another name for Mount Tai in present-day Shandong Province.

14. 合江福宝古镇

Fubao Ancient Town, Hejiang County

福宝古镇简介

福宝古镇位于川南泸州市合江县，距县城42千米，是国家级福宝森林公园的门户。古镇始建于元末明初，其选址较为独特，场是一座山，山是一座场。场镇空间大起大落，层次丰富。古镇原名为"佛保场"，因当时交通不便，生活艰难，于是人们在精神上寻求寄托，修建了大量庙宇，期盼得到佛祖庇佑。1949年后更名为"福宝场"。古镇是自贡到贵州古盐道的必经之处，一度为大漕河（又名蒲江）流域政治、经济、文化交流中心。迄今，场镇仍较为完好地保留着明清时期山地建筑的原貌，被中外专家誉为"中国山地建筑精华"。2008年被评为第四批中国历史文化名镇。

—传奇故事—

行善得福：秀娥传说

相传很久以前，当地有个名叫秀娥的女子。她美丽贤惠，心地善良，常常帮助遇有急难的乡邻和路客，深受人们敬慕。

有一年，纵贯此地的大漕河流域遭遇天灾，水涝成灾，疫病流行。唯独秀娥所居住的群山环抱之地没有受到洪水侵扰，过往行人无不惊奇，称这是一片"福天"。然而，"福兮

A Brief Introduction to Fubao Ancient Town

The Ancient Town of Fubao is located in the south of Sichuan, 42 kilometers away from Hejiang County, Luzhou City. It is viewed as the portal to Fubao Forest Park, a national tourist attraction. Built in the late Yuan Dynasty (1206—1368) and early Ming Dynasty (1368—1644) in a mountain site that is considered relatively unique, this town enjoys a large area of different and rich landscapes. It was originally called Fobao, which means a place blessed by Sakyamuni. People in this region lived a hard life and had very poor transportation facilities, so a lot of temples were built to seek both spiritual guidance and Buddha's blessing. After 1949, it was renamed Fubao, meaning a place with good luck and treasures. As this was the only transportation passage from Zigong City to the ancient salt path of Guizhou Province, the town became known as the political, economic and cultural communication center in the Dacao River basin, also known as the Pujiang River basin. Today Fubao is preserved relatively well, with the original mountain buildings of Ming-Qing[①] styles still standing. Fubao has been highly praised by both Chinese and foreign experts as "one of the outstanding representatives of Chinese mountain architecture". In 2008, it was listed as one of the Famous Historical and Culturual Towns in China (the fourth batch).

——Legendary Stories——

Good Deeds Deserve Blessing: The Legend of Xiu-e

Many years ago, there was a woman named Xiu-e who was beautiful and kind hearted. She often helped people out with their problems, and thus had gained the respect among the villagers. One year, a flood in Dacao River basin gave rise to the spread of epidemic diseases. However, the hill-surrouding village where Xiu-e lived was the exception. It was therefore regarded as a lucky place, but it was not long before calamities befell this place. Bandits invaded and plundered the village and Xiu-e's house was no exception. The family endured many misfortunes. Her son starved to death and her husband fell ill. Her mother-in-law was so worried that she cried herself blind. Xiu-e went to the river bank sadly, hoping to prepare a grave for her son. Unexpectedly,

---

① Ming-Qing refers to the period of the Ming (1368—1644) and Qing (1616—1911) dynasties.

祸所伏"，这里虽未受天灾，却横遭人祸。盗贼轮番到此抢劫，秀娥家中被盗贼洗劫一空，儿子饿死，丈夫病倒，婆婆急得哭瞎了眼。秀娥伤心欲绝地到河畔为儿子挖墓坑，竟挖出了一块卵石，那卵石色泽美丽、光滑透明、金光闪闪，她将石头捧回了家，奇迹突然发生了：儿子复活了，丈夫病好了，婆婆眼明了，囤里有了粮食，全家人欢欢喜喜。秀娥忽然意识到这块卵石是宝物，能为人消灾避难，带来福泽。于是，她拿起卵石，走村串户，所经之处，雨住天晴，田禾转青，病人痊愈。

秀娥不辞辛劳地行走于各个村庄。忽然，一阵大风袭来，卷走了她手中的卵石，还将她吹落在屋后的山腰上。秀娥疲累不堪，便坐下来歇息，谁料她就此沉睡过去，化成了一磴巨大的石头。从此，人们认为这里是块福地，便纷纷迁徙来此定居，将此地取名为"福宝"。后山腰那磴巨石被称为"飞娥石"，石侧建造了一座神庙，供奉秀娥。神奇卵石的故事越传越远，小镇也因此兴盛了起来。

逐疫驱邪：合江傩戏

傩戏是一种古老的民间艺术。傩，是古代民间逐疫驱邪的一种巫术仪式。合江傩戏又名"赵侯坛"或"端公戏"。赵侯坛是庆坛类傩戏，据传以隋朝嘉州刺史赵昱为坛神，因赵昱曾被封侯，故尊称赵侯。相传赵昱与兄赵冕曾师从于李珏，在四川道教圣地青城山修道。隋末，应朝廷之邀，赵昱出任嘉州刺史。在任期间，遇到犍为蟆蛟作怪，水患淹没了庄稼、农舍。赵昱率领全县军民与蟆蛟奋战，并亲自执剑入水。在沿岸军民呐喊助威下，他挥剑力斩蟆蛟，平息了水患。为纪念赵昱治水德政，人们在灌口立祠以祭，以"灌口神"水神祀之。每到腊月，人们就举行仪式，戴着面具，跳傩舞，在坛场正中立"正一玄皇上赵侯圣主"字牌，以庆坛酬神。

she dug out a smooth and transparent pebble that had a shining golden shimmer. When she took it home, a miracle occurred. Her son revived, her husband fully recovered and her mother-in-law regained her sight. What's more, the grain bin was full again. Xiu-e realized that the pebble that she had found was a rare treasure which could eliminate disaster and bring good luck to people, so she took it to other places which were in distress. To everyone's surprise, wherever she went, if there were heavy rains, the rain would stop, and the sun would shine again. The field would become green and people recovered from illness.

Xiu-e took great trouble to walk to villages far and wide. One day, suddenly there was a strong wind which not only blew both the pebble away from her hand, but also blew herself away, and she finally landed on the mountain side behind a house. Xiu-e was so tired that she sat down to rest. She sunk into a deep sleep and never woke up again but instead she changed into a stone statue. Since then, this place has been regarded as a lucky place and many people settle down here, hence the name "Fubao". The large stone was called the "Flying Stone of Xiu-e", and there was a temple built beside the stone so as to enshrine and worship Xiu-e. With the story of the magical pebble spreading far and wide, the town thrived from then on.

Diseases and Devils Expel: The Legends of Hejiang Nuo Opera

In ancient times, Nuo was a witchcraft ceremony that was practiced to eradicate diseases and devils. Based on Nuo, Nuo Opera is an ancient folk art. Hejiang Nuo Opera also called "Zhao Hou Altar" or "Duangong Opera", is a very popular local opera that is performed in Hejiang County. Zhao Hou Altar, was an altar Nuo Opera named after Zhao Yu, the governor of Jiazhou[1] in the Sui Dynasty (581—618). Zhao Yu was respected and given the title of Lord Zhao. It was said that Zhao Yu and his brother Zhao Mian had learned Nuo Opera from Li Yu, who grew up in the holy land of Taoism, that is, Mount Qingcheng of Sichuan Province. During the late Sui Dynasty, when Zhao Yu was assigned as the governor of Jiazhou, an evil dragon often troubled the people. Floods ruined crops and farmhouses. Zhao Yu led both the military and civilians to fight against this evil dragon, and even fought with the dragon in the river himself. People who were watching the fight encouraged him to swing his sword and chop up the dragon. As soon as he did that, the flood was curbed. To commemorate his contributions to taming the flood, people built an ancestral temple for worship at Guankou, enshrining Zhao Yu as the river God which they called "Guankou God". Every lunar December, the local people hold a ceremony, where they wear masks and perform the Nuo dance. A tablet with the words "Zheng Yi Xuan[2] Emperor Zhao Hou" is usually set in the center of the temple for worship.

---

① Jiazhou refers to today's Leshan City of Sichuan Province.
② Zheng Yi Xuan is a branch of Taoism.

一民俗文化一

建筑文化

福宝古镇高低错落、鳞次栉比的屋宇千姿百态，排排吊脚木楼错落有致，随山势起伏。小街宽处七八米，窄处仅1.5米左右。建筑多为明清风格。雕梁画栋，见证岁月峥嵘；飞檐翘角，沐浴风雨沧桑"。青石街道，环境幽雅，建筑古朴，具有深厚的历史文化底蕴和珍贵的建筑美学价值。

回龙街是全镇现保存最完整的一条古街。沿回龙桥而上，在大青石铺成的街道两旁，民房一间靠一间，大小不一，形成九龙巷、刘家巷、包青巷、柴市巷、鸡市巷等五条巷道，街道全长450米，是当时最热闹繁华的地段，回龙桥、三宫八庙、惜字亭等古建筑也掩映其中。

唢呐文化

福宝文化源远流长，民间艺术种类繁多，如演灯戏、对山歌、打连枪、耍花灯、舞狮子等。其中，福宝贯打唢呐尤为出名，2007年被列入"四川省首批非物质文化遗产名录"。

福宝贯打唢呐是以唢呐为主奏，鼓、锣、钵、梆等打击乐器为伴奏的鼓吹乐。"贯打"指吹打结合，浑然一体。福宝唢呐为师徒传承，曲调和曲牌名众多，内涵丰富，主要分为人物情绪、山野风光、动物情态三类。福宝贯打唢呐发端于唐代，发展于宋元，完善于明清，成为人们喜庆欢乐、排解忧伤、振奋精神、鼓舞士气的重要文化形式。

—Folk Culture—

Architectural Culture

Fubao boasts houses that are in rows upon rows in a picturesque disorder along the mountainside. There are many houses, which are built on stilt which are over the surface of water or soil. Streets are seven or eight meters at the widest part and one meter and a half at the narrowest part. Most of the recidences are of the Ming-Qing architectural style. Carved beams and painted rafters have witnessed the changing years while cornices and upswept eaves have embraced the wind and rain. Bluestone-paved streets as well as quiet and elegant environments are examples of the simple and unsophisticated architecture that embodies both deep historical and cultural significance and precious aesthetic values of architecture of this period.

Huilong Street is the best-preserved street in the whole town. Walking along Huilong Bridge, one may find houses of different sizes on both sides of the bluestone-paved street, which consist of five alleys, namely Jiulong, Liujia, Baoqing, Chaishi, and Jishi Alley. One may also enjoy other scenic spots here, such as the Huilong Bridge, Three Halls and Eight Temples, and the Xizi Pavilion which are tucked away among the houses on the street. The whole street is 450 meters long and it used to be the busiest street in that area.

Suona Horn Culture

Fubao culture has a long history. There are various types of cultural dances and plays, including the Lantern Play, the Dueling of Folk Songs, and Lion Dances. The most famous music in this area is played on the Fubao Guanda Suona Horn which was rated as The First Batch of Intangible Cultural Heritage of Sichuan in 2007.

Fubao Guanda Suona Horn refers to a piece of music that uses the suona horn as the main instrument and percussion instruments such as a drum, gong, pa[①] and pang-tzu for accompaniment. "Guanda" means the harmonious combination of wind and percussion instruments. This art is handed down from master to apprentice. There are many melodies and musical scores, where people's emotions, natural scenery and animals' expressions and postures are demonstrated. The Guanda Suona Horn was created during the Tang Dynasty, developed in the Song and Yuan dynasties, and perfected in the Ming and Qing dynasties, becoming an important cultural form for people to express joy and happiness, eliminate grief, boost spirits and enhance troop morale.

---

① Pa is a Chinese musical instrument, and its shape is like an earthen bowl.

饮食文化

福宝原始森林盛产竹笋，故以清水笋尖、玉兰片、竹笋、竹荪等绿色食品为主的竹系列"熊猫宴"颇为出名。

福宝风味小吃早在清末就享誉川南黔北，有传统的酥饼、豆腐干、油炸糍粑块儿，还有地道的岩蜂糖、山区老腊肉、泉水豆花、梅子酒、山花蜜等特色美食，风味独特。

—— 主要景点串游 ——

三宫八庙

福宝古镇"三宫"指清源宫、万寿宫、天后宫。"八庙"即五祖庙、土地庙、张爷庙、禹王庙、火神庙、灯棚、王爷庙、观音庙。这些庙宇布局合理，格局基本完好，大都设有戏楼、厢楼、天井、板壁，框架穿隼，雕梁画栋，但现皆已成为民居。除王爷庙、灯棚、观音庙不在回龙街，其余的庙宇占了回龙街的五分之二。

回龙桥

回龙桥建于清道光二十年（1840），全长25米，桥面宽4米，拱高6米。桥的中央部位镂雕有一条龙，桥中挂有剑，雄跨于白色溪上，又名回龙河。桥街全用大青石铺就，栏杆是大青石雕刻成的歇山式房顶式样，是当时福宝大漕河谷地区唯一的一座石拱桥。

每当赶集的时候，回龙桥就成为最热闹的地方。现在桥栏大部分已经拆除，两旁建起了门面，开出了店铺，桥面宛然已成街面。故穿行回龙街，不免见街不见桥。进入街房，从窗户看出去，才发现漕河在下面穿街而过。

Food Culture

Fubao forest abounds with bamboo shoots. In the town, there is a grand banquet named Panda Feast which serves mainly dishes cooked with such bamboo ingredients as tender tips of bamboo shoots, dried slices of tender shoots and edible fungus found in bamboo groves. Just because it serves these green dishes, the feast becomes quite popular among the locals.

Since the late Qing Dynasty, Fubao snacks have enjoyed great fame in the south of Sichuan and the north of Guizhou. There are various traditional snacks that have a unique flavor, including flaky pastries, dried bean curd, fried glutinous rice cakes, authentic local preserved meat, bean curd pudding, plum wine, and mountain flower honey.

—Main Tourist Attractions—

Three Halls and Eight Temples

Three Halls refer to Qingyuan Hall, Wanshou Hall and Thean Hou Hall. The Eight Temples include Temple of Five Ancestors, the Earth God Temple, Zhangye Temple, Yuwang Temple, Fire God Temple, Lantern Show Temple, Wangye Temple and Guanyin Temple. All the temples are arranged among other rooms systematically and have relatively intact arrangements. Most of the temples here consist of a theatrical stage, wing-room, courtyard, wooden partition and so on. These are carved with beautiful paintings or ornaments and have become dwellings now. Except for the Wangye Temple, the Temple of Lantern Show and Guanyin Temple, the other temples are built on Huilong Street, occupying two fifths of all.

Huilong Street

Huilong Street was built in 1840, the 20th year of Daoguang (1821—1850) during the Qing Dynasty with a length of twenty-five meters, width of four meters and height of six meters. There is a dragon pattern carved on the center of the bridge, and a hanging sword in the middle of the bridge. Stretching across the Huilong River, this bridge is paved with bluestones, and has a gable and hip-roofed handrails. All these features make Huilong Bridge the only stone arch bridge in Dacao River basin of Fubao.

Every time people went to a fair, the road on the bridge served as a busy market. The bridge has now become a street. Most of the handrails have been torn down, and shops line both sides of the bridge. When you walk along the bridge, a street rather than a bridge comes into view. Only when you step into a shop on the side of the bridge and look out of the window, can you catch the sight of Dacao River that flows below the street.

惜字亭

惜字亭位于一棵大黄楝树下，建成于清乾隆五十五年（1790），仿八卦图造型，共六层八方，高约8米，每层每方都刻有图案各异的浮雕。它是"天后宫"烧钱化纸的地方，所以又叫"字库"，俗称"化钱炉"。该亭虽不宏大壮观，但于浓荫下也颇显古朴。据说，从前镇里的文人很爱惜字画，即使有不如意之作，也不乱扔，需选一良辰吉日，放到"字库"中予以焚化。后来，镇上的人把这里视为圣寺，建亭保护，惜字亭也由此名闻天下。

Xizi Pagoda

In 1790, the 55th year of Qianlong (1736—1793) during the Qing Dynasty, Xizi Pagoda was built next to a big live oak. The pagoda is eight meters high and imitates the structure of Bagua, an eight-pattern diagram, with six tiers and eight eaves. There are reliefs with different patterns on each tier. Xizi Pagoda belongs to Thean Hou Palace and it is used for burning imitation paper money for use of the dead. Therefore, it is also called "word stock", commonly known as "money-burning furnace". Xizi Pagoda is not grand but instead is simple and unsophisticated and is situated against dense foliage. It is said that poets and literary men would never throw away their used drafts of works away, because they cherished calligraphy and paintings very much. Instead they would choose a lucky day and burn these drafts of their work in the "word stock". Later in time, people regarded this place as a holy place and built a pagoda here. From then on, Xizi Pagoda has become well known far and wide.

15. 乐山罗城古镇

Luocheng Ancient Town,
Leshan City

罗城古镇简介

　　素有"中国诺亚方舟"之称的罗城古镇，位于乐山市犍为县东北部，占地95平方千米。古镇始建于明末崇祯元年（1628），以其独树一帜的建筑风格享誉中外，时至今日仍保留着部分明清时代老四川文化的人文风貌。镇中心的主街凉厅街形如一艘巨大的船，俗称"船形街"。1982年，一位澳大利亚人受其奇特造型的启发，以其为模板在墨尔本建造了一座"中国城"，罗城古镇从此蜚声海外。1992年，罗城古镇被四川省政府批准为"省级历史文化名镇"。2007，古镇"凉厅街"被列为省级文物保护单位。

—传奇故事—

筑舟求雨：船形街的由来

　　罗城古镇坐落在一个椭圆形的山丘顶上，古镇的主街为"凉厅街"，也被当地人称为"船形街"。关于船形街的由来，当地流传着这样的传说：罗城古镇地处铁山北麓，无大江河流，

A Brief Introduction to Luocheng Ancient Town

Known as "China's Noah's Ark", the Ancient Town of Luocheng lies in the northeastern part of Qianwei County, Leshan City, covering an area of 95 square kilometers. Built in the first year of the reign of Emperor Chongzhen (1628—1644) during the Ming Dynasty, this ancient town is famous for its unique architectural style, and the preservation of traditional Sichuan culture from the Ming and Qing dynasties. "Liangting Street," meaning "Cool Hall Street" in English, is the main street running through the center of the town. It resembles a big boat, and hence got its popular name Boat-shaped Street. Luocheng started to gain international acclaim in 1982, for an Australian built a "Chinatown" in Melbourne using the old town's unique configuration as a model. In 1992, Luocheng Ancient Town was listed as a Provincial Heritage Town by the Sichuan Provincial Government. In 2007, "Liangting Street" was listed as a provincial cultural heritage site.

——Legendary Stories——

Building a Boat for Rain Pray: Origin of the Boat-shaped Street

Luocheng is located at the top of an oval-shaped hill. The town's main street "Liangting Street" is commonly called "Boat-shaped Street" by the locals. There is a legend recounting how the street was constructed. Situated at the foot of the northern Tieshan Hill, without direct access to water, Luocheng suffered from constant water shortages since ancient times. Farm land became arid due to prolonged droughts, leading to crop failures and poor harvests. The old town therefore became well-known as a "dry wharf". The local town's people had to walk quite a few miles away to fetch drinking water.

During the Chongzhen years in the late Ming Dynasty, an outsider Xiucai[1] Zhang came to Luocheng. While enjoying a cup of tea at a tea house, he saw the locals there sighing and moaning, and noticed that they would drink every drop of tea that was in their tea cups before leaving. Out of curiosity, Xiucai Zhang asked the old man sitting next to him what was going

---

[1] See foot note [2] on page 37.

自古缺水，常常久旱不雨，农田龟裂歉收，历史上是远近闻名的"旱码头"。当时，百姓要到十几里以外的地方挑水喝。

明末崇祯年间，有个外地人张秀才来到此地，坐在茶馆里喝茶，看到茶客们一个个唉声叹气，临行时还把茶杯里的水喝得一干二净，便向邻座的一位老人打听缘由。老人叹息道："这镇上缺水。罗城旱码头，滴水贵如油呀。"张秀才沉默良久，念出四句口诀："罗城旱码头，客商难久留。若要不缺水，罗城修成舟。"众人听后齐声赞叹，于是一致推举张秀才做造"船"的领头人。张秀才带领数百名能工巧匠，大兴土木，撤旧屋建新房，不到三年时间，大"船"便修成了。修"船"是为了求雨，所谓"舟在水中行，有舟必有水"。

菩萨"断案"：灵官庙传说

为了求水，镇上又于朝乾隆十九年（1754）在船形街的尾部修建了灵官庙，庙内供奉灵官菩萨，祈求天降甘霖。灵官庙属于道教，因为犍为没有道教，只好把铁山的佛教僧人请来暂时管理。灵官庙香火通常很旺，据说灵官菩萨很灵验。

传说清末罗城发现一无头尸体，按清朝法典要限期破案，大案办不穿，县太爷要丢乌纱帽。当时的李县太爷坐阵"丰泰栈"小楼，让下属明查暗访，毫无下落。眼看快到期，县太爷以酒解愁。喝闷酒时，听到灵官庙钟声，心一动去向"灵官"求助。县太爷命手下人买来香蜡钱纸求"灵官"显灵，祷告：小官今人命案办不穿，望"灵官"保佑我三天内捕获凶手，定重塑金身。

on. Sighing, the old man replied, "This town is in desperate need of water. Luocheng is a dry wharf where a drop of water is more expensive than a barrel of oil." After a long silence, Xiucai Zhang blurted out, "Luocheng, the dry wharf can not make merchants stay. A boat has to be built in the town to keep water flowing." The saying drew immediate praise from the locals, who unanimously nominated Xiucai Zhang to be the leader of "boat-building". With Zhang's leadership and hundreds of skilled craftsmen's hard work, in less than 3 years' time, this grand construction project transformed Liangting Street with a completely new look, i.e., a big boat. People believed that the street shaped as a boat would bring rain, because of the saying, "A boat rides in water, and where there is a boat, there is water."

Settling Lawsuits: Legend of Lingguan Temple

In order to pray for rain, a temple was built at the "tail" of the Boat-shaped Street in 1754, the 19th year under Emperor Qianlong's reign (1736—1795) during the Qing Dynasty. In this temple, a Taoist god "Lingguan" was worshipped. However, this temple was managed by some Buddhist monks who were from the Tieshan Mountain, which were nearby, because Taoism was not practiced in Qianwei County. It was said that many prayers had been answered by Lingguan, and therefore the temple was always crowded with an endless stream of pilgrims.

Legend has it that a headless corpse was found in Luocheng during the late Qing Dynasty. According to the law of that time, the case needed to be solved within a limited period, otherwise, the county magistrate would lose his position. At that time, Magistrate Li ordered his men to conduct a thorough investigation, but they found no clues. Magistrate Li was drowning his sorrow in a restaurant when the bell toll from Lingguan Temple gave him a flash of inspiration to ask Lingguan for help. Magistrate Li ordered his men to buy offerings for a tribute and went to Lingguan in person to pray. Earnestly, he pleaded, "Lord Lingguan, please help me capture the murderer as soon as possible. I will definitely repay you by refurbishing the golden statue of your holiness."

Magistrate Li was very fond of eating cooked fresh pig's front feet which a butcher gave to him everyday. The next day after he had prayed to the God Lingguan, Magistrate Li found that the cooked pig feet had tasted different. After an immediate investigation, the chef confessed that the butcher had delivered the pig's hind feet instead of the front feet that day. That was why the taste was different. Feeling deceived and furious, Magistrate Li ordered that the butcher be arrested. As his agents made their way to the butcher's shop, they found a grease-covered butcher who was scared and suspicious. They immediately seized him. However, he was not the one who delivered the pig's hind feet. This butcher was mistaken for the one the agents were looking for. The butcher was escorted back to the courtroom. Magistrate Li, serving as the judge and banging his gavel, condemned the butcher loudly, "You butcher—you are not only good

　　这位县太爷最爱吃猪前蹄，每天由屠夫送货到官厨。在求拜"灵官"的第二天，县太爷发现蹄味不对。原来，县太爷喜欢吃前蹄，而这次屠夫忘了留前蹄，以后蹄代替。官厨把详情告诉了县太爷，听后他对屠夫的欺骗行为非常生气，于是立即发令将屠夫抓来。差人快到屠宰店时，大声叫道："抓住他。"此刻，从店里另跑出一个屠夫，差人一见此人如此古怪，又满身油腻，误以为是将猪后蹄充前蹄的屠夫，赶紧抓住，押送到公堂上。李县太爷将惊堂木一拍，大声斥道："你会砍，还瞒本县太爷，你知罪吗？从实招来。"屠夫听到"你会砍"，吓得周身打抖，乞求说："大老爷饶命，我罪该万死，人虽然是我砍的，但是某人叫我砍的。"县太爷心想，嘿！全明白了，想不到踏破铁鞋无处找，得来全不费工夫，急忙追问："那人头呢？"屠夫说："交与主谋了。"很快主犯也被抓到。李县太爷为感激灵官菩萨之灵验，亲自买回金粉为菩萨重塑金身。还送一大匾，匾上刻有"感灵显应"四个金光闪闪的大字，送匾那天是农历六月十五日，从此罗城群众就将这一天定为"灵官会"日期（通常灵官会为农历四月二十六日）。继后又整修庙宇，并在庙前建一戏台，修一拱门，既为庙门，又如衙门，因而构成一巧妙的船形。从此以后此地成为集市贸易中心，船形象征风调雨顺后的五谷丰登。

——民俗文化——

麒麟灯

　　罗城镇的"麒麟灯"是当地特有的一种民间歌舞，又称送子舞，被列入四川省非物质文

at chopping, but also good at deceiving! How dare you! Confess immediately!" The moment he heard the word "chopping," the butcher became very scared. Trembling with fear, he cried, "Master, please forgive me. Even though I know I am guilty for a crime for which ten thousand deaths cannot atone, you should know I did not kill out of my own will. Somebody else asked me to do it." Shocked, Magistrate Li realized that the butcher was involved in the case of the headless corpse, "Now I understand! We discovered the clues." He then hurriedly interrogated the butcher, "Where is the missing head?" he asked. The butcher answered, "I have already given it to the mastermind." With clues provided by the butcher, the principal culprit was soon caught. With tremendous gratitude for God Lingguan's help, Magistrate Li decided to fulfill his promise by gilding Lingguan's statue. He also adorned the temple with a big plaque inscribed with shining characters to commemorate the magical apparition of Lingguan. That day henceforth became known as the day of the Lingguan Fair. That day henceforth became known as the day of Lingguan Fair (traditionally, the day of Linguan Fair falls on the 26th day of the 4th lunar month). The temple was later refurbished with a drama stage and an arch built in front of it. The arch, shaped like a boat, served as the gate to the temple and served as a symbol of good harvests. Lingguan Temple has since become the marketing and trading center of Luocheng.

——Folk Culture——

Kylin Lantern Dance

The Kylin[①] Lantern Dance, also known as the "Son-delivering Dance", is a local performance that includes both singing and dancing. It has been recognized on the list of Intangible Cultural Heritage of Sichuan. The performance, given during Chinese New Year celebrations, is believed to herald a year of luck and happiness. A Taoist legend says that a young scholar named Dong Yong fell in love with the seventh daughter of the Jade Emperor. She was called the Seventh Fairy. However, the Queen Mother did not approve of their romantic relationship. She forced the Seventh Fairy to leave Dong Yong and took her back to the Sky Palace, where the Seventh Fairy later gave birth to a son. After the Seventh Fairy had been taken away, Dong Yong buried his immeasurable sorrow and resentment by focusing his undivided attention on his studies. Ultimately, he won first place in the highest imperial examination. When the good news traveled to the Jade Emperor, he decided to send his grandson back to his father, Dong Yong. Escorted by a celestial general, Dong Yong's child rode a Kylin to reunite with his father at Huixian Bridge in Chang'an. This is the story of "The Son Delivered by a Kylin" in Chinese folklore, which was the origin of the Kylin Lantern Dance. What is unique about the

---

① Kylin is a kind of unicorn in China.

化遗产保护名录。每逢春节，罗城古镇都要耍麒麟灯，庆贺新年佳节，寓意吉祥幸福。相传，七仙女与董永相爱，被王母娘娘强行带回天宫后生下一子，董永强压悲愤，一心苦读，高中状元。玉帝闻讯后，派一名天将护送董永的儿子乘坐麒麟下凡，在长安会仙桥将其子归还董永，这就是民间传说"麒麟送子"的由来。整个灯舞围绕麒麟送子到人间的故事情节展开。其独特之处不仅在于它有较完整的故事情节，同时还在于从服饰、音乐到表演动作，都借鉴了传统川剧的表现形式，具有显著的地域文化特色。

商贸娱乐

罗城"船形街"的两侧是木结构的长排旧瓦屋，临街一面屋檐异常宽大，形成了叫作"凉厅子"的罕见长廊，其支撑点是100多根立在六边体长条石柱上的旧圆木。两边凉厅房屋中有杂货铺、丝绸店、饭馆等。每逢赶集、庙会或年节的时候，方圆数十里的乡民成群结队前来镇上，出售农副产品或竹木家具，换回生活用品和生产工具。到了晚上，各色各样的灯笼高悬，如龙形灯、狮形灯、象形灯、牛形灯、麒麟灯、守护灯等，使夜色更为美丽迷人。人们在这里品茶、划拳、喝酒、吃夜宵、听川剧、看灯影戏、观木偶戏或地方民歌演唱、玩龙灯、耍狮子舞、玩纸牌、下棋等，尽情享受古镇的风味，沉浸在古朴浓厚的乡土情调里，度过祥和安宁、悠然自乐的时光。

铁山武术

从古至今，古镇习武之风盛行，明、清时开有数家武馆，著名的武师不乏其人，至今仍有许多弟子。罗城镇背靠铁山，地势险要，历来为兵家必争之地。自元、明以来，习武之风甚浓。从清康熙年间起，罗城人代代以练武为能事，武馆林立，逐步形成了以回族海氏为代表的北派武术和以汉族朱氏为代表的南派武术，涌现了一大批清代科举武生。有两个代表人物，一个是清光绪年间名震川西南的罗城红灯教起义首领、南派武侠、汉族人黎天东，一个是20世纪30年代享誉海内外的北派武术大师、回族人蔡静斋。随着时间的推移，铁山武术的影响力已不及当年深远，但罗城人尚武之心却并未消失，古镇武风已经渗入当地人的骨髓。如今的罗城出现了新一批的铁山武术继承者，他们继承先祖留下的宝贵财富，诠释着中华武术的博大精深，托起了铁山武术的希望。

—主要景点串游—

船形街

船形街始建于明末崇祯年间，是古镇的中心，整条街坐东向西呈船形结构，东西长，南北短，全长209米，最宽处9.5米，最窄处1.8米，像一把织布的梭子，所以有"云中一把梭"的美称。从高处俯视，又像是一艘搁置在山顶上的大船正劈波斩浪，扬帆起航，所以又有"山

Kylin Lantern Dance is not just its story, but also its clothing, music and performance, all of which draw on traditional Sichuan Opera and therefore reflect the distinct local and regional culture.

Commerce and Entertainment

On both sides of the Boat-shaped Street lie long rows of historical tile-roofed houses. Eaves facing the street hang over it, supported by over 100 logs on hexagonal stone pillars. This forms a shady corridor called a "Liang Tingzi" or "Cool Hall". Grocery stores, silk shops and restaurants abound along this street. The street is always crowded during town fairs and holidays, when villagers from dozens of miles away come to sell their agricultural products or bamboo-made furniture and buy their daily necessities and farm tools. In the evenings, various lanterns are hung along the street, adding charm to the beautiful night sky. The latterns come in different shapes such as dragon, lion, elephant, ox and unicorn. Immersed in tranquility, harmony and happiness, the local people lead a simple and leisurely life in the old town, enjoying an array of activities such as drinking tea and beer, eating local snacks, listening to Sichuan Opera and local folk songs, watching lantern and puppet shows, watching and performing dragon or lion dances, and playing cards and chess.

Tieshan Martial Arts

Throughout history, the study of martial arts has prevailed in this ancient town. Several schools of martial arts were manned by kung fu masters in the Ming and Qing dynasties, and their followers can still be found today. Abutting Tieshan Mountain, Luocheng has always been a town of great military importance due to its difficult-to-attack geographic location. The practice of martial arts has been popular ever since the Yuan and Ming dynasties. Generations of people in Luocheng have taken great pride in practicing kung fu, which can be dated back to the Kangxi years (1662—1722) in the Qing Dynasty. During this time frame, kung fu schools proliferated, martial talents abounded, and two sects of martial arts gradually formed: the North School represented by the Hai Family of Hui ethnicity, and the South School represented by the Zhu Family of the Han people. Two prominent figures stood out as kung fu masters. One was Li Tiandong, a Han from the South School, who led the well-known "Uprising of the Red Lantern[①]" during the Guangxu years (1875—1908) in the Qing Dynasty. Another was Cai Jingzhai, a Hui from the North school, who was well known both at home and abroad in the 1930s. During this time there was a waning interest in the martial arts, however, the spirit of Tieshan Martial Arts was so deeply entrenched in the locals, they never lost their love and respect

① The Red Lantern was a secret civil gang in Sichuan Province.

顶一条船"的美称。船形街建筑风格为川南民居的穿斗木构架式，梭形的街面是船底，两边的建筑是船舷，古戏楼是船舱，灵官庙是船尾。船形街的修建代表着罗城文化精英和能工巧匠对水文化的殷切愿景。

古戏楼

别具特色的古戏楼位于船形街中心的"船舱"位置，于1984年古镇维修时重建。古戏楼在明清时又称"万年台"，是人们比武、演唱川剧的文化娱乐场所。戏楼四角宝顶雕梁画栋，戏台正中横匾上书"神听和平"，寓意川剧娱人酬神、人

神共庆的功能和特色。两边有对联："昆高胡弹灯曲绕黄粱，生旦净末丑功出梨园"，分别描述了川剧的五个戏种和五个角色，包括《海登法师》《中国变脸王》《四川茶馆》在内的多部电视剧曾在古戏楼取景拍摄。

灵官庙

灵官庙位于古镇东端，建于清乾隆十九年（1754），分别在清咸丰九年（1859）、民国八年（1919）进行了重新修葺。主建筑为两重式结构，前有正殿，后有观音，基本上保持了原貌。

for kung fu. Today, a new generation of martial successors has begun to emerge in Luocheng. Endowed with the legacy of their ancestors, they are now exploring the profound nature of Chinese kung fu, ushering in a bright future for Tieshan Martial Arts.

——Main Tourist Attractions——

The Boat-shaped Street

The Boat-shaped Street, located at the center of the town, was built during the Chongzhen years in the time of the late Ming Dynasty. The street is long from east to west, and short from north to south, creating a unique boat-like shape. The street spans 209 meters in length, with a maximum of 9.5 meters and minimum of 1.8 meters in width. Due to its resemblance to a weaving spindle, the street has been called the "spindle in the mist". From a bird's eye view, the street looks like a big boat landing on top of the mountain, ready to sail off and catch waves. Hence it is also called the "boat on the peak". The street is of the vertical truss style popular in the civil residences of southen Sichuan. At street level, it resembles the bottom of a boat, the buildings along the street are the sides of the boat, the Old Opera House is the cabin and Lingguan Temple the stern. As a symbol of the water culture in Luocheng, the Boat-shaped Street is a symbol of collective wisdom and excellent craftsmanship.

The Old Opera House

Located at the heart of the Boat-shaped Street, the distinctive Old Opera House was rebuilt in 1984 when Luocheng was under restoration. Commonly known as "Wannian Tai" or "Stage of Ten Thousand Years" in the Ming and Qing dynasties, the Old Opera House was an entertainment and cultural center for Sichuan Opera. Painted beams form the pyramid roof, and a plaque hanging in the middle of the stage says "May God hear harmony", signifying that Sichuan Opera serves as a bond between humans and God. There are Chinese couplets hanging on both sides of the stage, "Beautiful singing of Kun, Gao, Hu, Tan and Deng occurs in dreams; Masterly performance of Sheng, Dan, Jing, Mo, Chou follows hard work in troupes." Kun, Gao, Hu, Tan and Deng refer to the five tunes of Sichuan Opera, while Sheng (male actor), Dan (female actor), Jing (the actor with a painted face), Mo (the role of an old-aged male actor) and Chou (the role of a clown) are the five major roles. Several TV series were filmed at the Old Opera House, including *Master Haideng*, *China's Face-changing King*, and *Tea Houses in Sichuan*.

Lingguan Temple

Located at the eastern end of the town, Lingguan Temple was originally built in 1754, the 19th year under Emperor Qianlong's reign in the Qing Dynasty. Although it was rebuilt twice in

清真寺

　　古镇300多年来一直居住着汉、回两族人民。在清康熙、乾隆年间，先后有两批回族人民迁来罗城。罗城镇成为犍为县回族人聚居地，伊斯兰教随之传入。回族人民自发募集资金，于清雍正至同治年间在罗城先后修建了四座清真寺（北寺、东寺、南寺、西寺），作为回族人民及教民举行仪式、沐浴、主持婚丧、讲经说教之场所，现保留下来的清真寺即西寺，建于1876年。

清真寺

1859 and 1919, the temple has almost all its original features intact. With a dual structure, the temple consists of a Main Hall in the front and the Guanyin Hall at the back.

The West Mosque

The town has been inhabited for over 300 years by both Han and Hui people. During the Kangxi and Qianlong years of the Qing Dynasty, two groups of Hui people migrated to Luocheng and this town has since become a major Hui settlement in Qianwei County. With the quick spread of Islam, Hui people built four mosques (North Mosque, East Mosque, South Mosque, and West Mosque) during the Yongzheng (1723—1735) and Tongzhi years (1862—1874) of the Qing Dynasty. The mosques were places where Hui people and other Muslims held rituals, ceremonies and congregations. Only one mosque, the West Mosque built in 1876, has survived till today.

16. 西昌礼州古镇

Lizhou Ancient Town, Xichang City

礼州古镇简介

　　礼州古镇，位于西昌市西北部安宁河谷平原腹心，距西昌23千米。礼州历史悠久，始建于西汉元光年间，名为"苏亓"，东汉至蜀汉年间更名为"苏祁县"，后因"崇德尚礼"之意，改名为"礼州"。礼州现存古镇始建于明洪武年间，城池方正，东南西北各设四城门：新运门（原名迎晖门）、启文门、宝城门、迎恩门。镇内庙宇众多，现存文昌宫、西禅寺、南华宫、川主庙等。镇内现有七街八巷，传统民居规模较大，多为砖木或土木结构，具有鲜明的地域特征，体现出汉、白、彝族混合的风格。礼州古镇面积虽小，但其积淀厚重，在历史发展中扮演了不可或缺的角色。礼州曾是古代南丝绸之路上重要的牦牛古道驿站。1995年，经省政府批准，礼州镇被列为四川省级历史文化名镇。

—传奇故事—

修行得道：杨祖师传说

　　杨祖师（1748—1804），俗名杨学信，是西昌很有名的宗教偶像，法号悟真。他出生于书香门第，其祖超遵为雍正朝阁老。乾隆年间，其父官至翰林。然而，家境优越的他为何

A Brief Introduction to Lizhou Ancient Town

The Ancient Town of Lizhou, located in the heart of the Anning River Valley, is 23 kilometers northwest of Xichang, the capital of Liangshan Yi Autonomous Prefecture in Sichuan Province. It has a long history and was known as Suqi when it was originally built during the Yuanguang years (134 BC—129 BC) of the Western Han Dynasty (206 BC—AD 25). It was renamed as Suqi[①] County from the Eastern Han Dynasty to the Shu-Han Dynasty of the Three Kingdoms and later changed to its current name Lizhou, meaning upholding morality and honoring ritual. The existing town, originally built during the Hongwu years of the Ming Dynasty, is square in shape with four city gates standing erect at each of the four corners known as the Xinyun Gate (formerly known as Yinghui Gate), Qiwen Gate, Baocheng Gate and Ying'en Gate. The town was dotted with temples and the existing ones include Wenchang Hall which is also called the Palace of Literary Prosperity, Xichan Temple, Nanhua Hall, Chuanzhu Temple. Lizhou now has seven streets and eight lanes, lined with traditional residential houses, mostly brick or wood-and-earth structures, with distinct geographic features that combine Han, Bai and Yi ethnic styles. Compact as it is, Lizhou has played an indispensable role in history. It served as an important yak courier station in the ancient Southern Silk Road. In 1995, Lizhou was listed as one of Sichuan's Provincial Historical and Cultural Towns by the provincial government.

——Legendary Stories——

Becoming a Saint: The Legend of Master Yang

Master Yang (1748—1804), whose name is Yang Xuexin and whose Dharma name is Wuzhen, is a famous religious idol in Xichang. He was born into a scholarly family, and his forefather Chaozun was the grand secretary of the Grand Secretariat during the reign of Emperor Yongzheng. Xuexin's father was a member of the Imperial Academy during the reign of Emperor Qianlong. Yang Xuexin renounced the world even though he was from a well-to-do family. He had started to read Confucian classics in his childhood and was greatly influenced by

---

① The two names Suqi have the same pronunciation but different spellings.

遁入空门？杨学信自幼学习儒家经典，深受儒学影响。在父母安排下，他16岁便娶妻成家。成亲仅一年，妻子便撒手人寰。深受打击的杨学信便离家去云游四方。乾隆年间，杨学信云游至今德昌县内的紫微山"仙人洞"，正式皈依佛门，法名悟真，号普度。后来在华光长老和了妙大师的指点下，杨学信悟性顿开，佛法益增。1782年，即乾隆四十七年，杨学信来到冕宁灵山寺修行，广招弟子。杨祖师亦僧亦道。嘉庆九年（1804），其端坐圆寂于灵山寺，但圆寂时红光满面，并无离去之相。弟子见状便将其移至佛堂进行供奉，后来身体虽已枯干，但并未腐烂。1964年，其肉身被两位信徒盗至礼州，途中不幸被毁，但其遗骨生成的舍利子至今保存在礼州西禅寺后院的舍利塔中。

—民俗文化—

饮食文化：西禅寺素斋

礼州特色美食有西禅寺素斋、礼州挂面、礼州汤圆粉、王凉粉等。其中西禅寺的素斋是一大特色。素斋为寺庙提供。一般寺庙斋饭做法单一，口感清淡，但礼州的西禅寺的斋饭却大不相同，其特色和南方丝绸之路有密切关系。

礼州是南方丝绸之路上的重镇大驿。南来北往的商贾聚集此地，并在西禅寺用餐。由于南来北往，人口众多，口味不同，寺院为满足各地人的口味而变换做法，渐渐形成了西禅寺素斋品种多样、取材广泛、口味丰富的特点。形成了"烹、蒸、炒、烧、炖、卤、煮、拌、腌"等9种系列的素斋，菜品多达上百种。

茶文化

很多地方，人们打招呼喜欢问一句："吃饭了吗？"但在礼州，人们见面的寒暄为："吃茶不？"喝茶是礼州人的嗜好。传统的茶馆遍布礼州城，但这里的茶馆和别处不太一样。礼州茶馆有招待彝族人的，也有专门招待汉族人的。彝人茶客与汉人茶客的不同之处在于彝

Confucianism. His parents arranged for him to marry a girl when he was 16 years old. However, one year after the marriage, his wife passed away. He was severely shocked and left his home to roam about the world. During the period of Emperor Qianlong, he traveled to Xianren Dong or Fairy Cave at Ziwei Mountain which is located in present-day Dechang County. There he converted to Buddhism. He was given a Dharma name of Wuzhen and a courtesy name of Pudu. Under the guidance of Elder Huaguang and Master Liaomiao, he soon gained enlightenment and his knowledge of Dharma was greatly broadened. In 1782, the forty-seventh year of the reign of the Emperor Qianlong, he set off for Lingshan Temple in Mianling to continue his spiritual journey or *bhavana* and recruited a crew of disciples. He was both a Buddhist and a Taoist. In the ninth year during the reign of the Emperor Jiaqing (1804), he passed into parinirvana while seated at Lingshan Temple. He had such a radiant countenance without the typical features of death that his disciples moved his body to the Buddhist hall to have it enshrined. Although his body eventually shriveled, it did not fall into decay. In 1964, his corpse was stolen by two worshippers and taken to Lizhou. Unfortunately, the body was destroyed. However, the relics generated from the rudimentary bones that were found were then enshrined in a stupa in the backyard of Xichan Temple.

—Folk Culture—

Food Culture: Vegetarian Dishes at Xichan Temple

Lizhou cuisine specialties include vegetarian dishes served at the Xichan Temple. Some examples of the dishes include guamian or fine dried noodles, glutinous rice flour and Wang's Bean Jelly. The highlight is the vegetarian dishes prepared by the people at the Xichan Temple. Unlike the bland and insipid food typically served at temples, fasting food at the Xichan Temple was influenced by the Southern Silk Road.

As an important courier station along the Southern Silk Road, Lizhou was inundated with merchants from different regions of the country. To cater to their various tastes, people at the Xichan Temple experimented with different recipes and formed a culinary style that has a collection of over one hundred vegetarian dishes with a variety of ingredients and flavors. There have evolved nine series of vegetarian dishes cooked respectively by boiling, steaming, stir frying, roasting, stewing, post-stewing, cooking, mixing and marinating.

Tea Culture

In other parts of China, people greet each other with "have you eaten?", whereas in Lizhou people greet with "would you like tea?" Drinking tea is a ritual in this town which is jam-packed with teahouses. Teahouses in Lizhou serve exclusively the Yi or Han clientele. Different from

人茶客常自带酒壶，喝一口酒，饮一口茶。茶客们往茶馆一坐，然后就开始了传统项目：摆龙门阵。对于老茶客来说，吃茶不是关键，摆龙门阵才是要事。说客们端起茶杯，浅浅地喝一口，然后故作深沉，龙门阵开始。好的说客即便每天讲同样的故事，都能引得听客们忘了神。讲到关键部分，说客摆摆手，拿起茶杯大饮一口："要知后事如何，明天茶馆再见。"礼州的茶文化贵不在茶，而是其中的人文情怀。街上来来往往的人见面都能打一句招呼，问一声安，这样的地方，着实难能可贵。

—主要景点串游—

文昌宫

据《明史·礼志》记载："梓潼帝君，姓张，名亚子，巨蜀七曲山，仕晋战殁。"仙人张亚子坐化后被封为文昌帝君，又称梓潼帝君，其庙宇则为文昌宫。礼州文昌宫坐落于城外南街，是礼州保存最为完整、最为宏伟的古建筑群。文昌宫始建于1884年，即清朝光绪甲申年，坐东朝西，规模较大，直接望去给人肃穆之感，可见其势不凡。除此之外，文昌宫布局考究严谨，工艺精湛，纵横三院三排，红墙筒瓦，极具古韵。院子中间曾修建"拜阅台"，左面钟楼阁下是"诵经厅"，右面鼓楼下为"习作室"。清末时，这里曾开办过"亮善书院"。

西禅寺

西禅寺又名祖师庙，建造于明朝万历五年（1577），是古镇的最高点。西禅寺正殿天灯阁为两台楼阁，在顶阁屋脊置一盏灯阁。昔日，每至黄昏油灯就被点亮，为过往商贾指引方向。据说客商远距10千米外就能看见"天灯"光亮。

their Han compatriots, the Yi will bring their own wine pots to the teahouse and sip some wine before drinking their tea. As they drink their cups of tea, they talk about their daily lives and tell stories. A good storyteller could hold his listeners spellbound even if he told the same story every day. When the story reaches the climax, the storyteller would stop narrating the story and would wave his hand and take a gulp of tea. The conclusion would be disclosed the next day. The heart of tea culture here is not the tea itself, but the human interraction, which is not only felt in the teahouse, but also in the stone paths where passersby greet and salute each other.

─Main Tourist Attractions─

Wenchang Temple

According to the "Record of Rites" of the *History of the Ming*, "the Imperial Sovereign of Zitong, whose surname was Zhang and given name Yazi, lived on Mount Qiqu, and died in a war as a minister of the Jin Dynasty". He was then honored as the Imperial Sovereign of Wenchang or Imperial Sovereign of Zitong and enshrined at Wenchang Temple. Located on South Street outside the town, the temple is the most completely preserved and the most magnificent ancient architectural complex in Lizhou. It was originally built in 1884 during the Jiashen era of the Emperor Guangxu (1875—1908) and is reputed for its well-planned layout and exquisite craftsmanship. It sits east and faces west and consists of three rows and in each row sits three courtyards, with red walls and pantile roofs, presenting an air of majesty and solemnity. In the middle of the temple complex, there originally stood the Baiyue Terrace for classical learning; on the left under the Bell Tower stands the Chanting Hall; on the right under the Drum Tower is the Study Room which was once the Liangshan Academy during the late Qing Dynasty.

Xichan Temple

Founded in 1577 during the era of Wanli (1573—1619) in the Ming Dynasty, Xichan Temple, also known as the Temple of Patriarchs, occupies a commanding position in the town. The two-storey main hall, called the Sky Lantern Pavilion, is set with a lamp in the ridgepole of the upper level. As dusk approaches, the lamp is lit to serve as a guiding star for travelling merchants. It is said that this light can be seen from over 10 kilometers away.

17. 南充阆中古城

Langzhong Ancient City，Nanchong City

阆中古城简介

　　阆中古城位于四川盆地东北缘、嘉陵江中游，东枕巴山，西倚剑门，雄峙川北，坐卧阆中市城区南侧，总面积达4.59平方千米，呈带状分布。阆中别名"阆苑""琅環福地"。传说是西王母居住和天帝藏书的地方。古城已有2300多年的建城历史。它不仅是古代巴蜀军事重镇，也是四川省唯一完整保存下来的古城，为"中国四大古城"之首。阆中古城属于国家5A级旅游景区。有张飞庙、滕王阁、川北道贡院等8处全国重点文物保护单位及22处省级文物保护单位。2010年，阆中市被评为"中国春节文化之乡"。

—传奇故事—

学海无涯：状元轶事

　　阆中是一个人杰地灵的地方，曾出过四位状元，而且这四位状元分别是两对兄弟。一对是唐代的尹枢、尹极，另一对是宋代的陈尧叟、陈尧咨。71岁的尹枢于唐德宗贞元七年（791）中辛未科状元，成为全国年龄最大的"古稀状元"，也是四川寿命最长的"长寿状元"。

A Brief Introduction to Langzhong Ancient City

The Ancient City of Langzhong is located in the northeast margin of the Sichuan basin and the middle reaches of the Jialing River. It faces east of Mount Ba, and faces west of the Jianmen Pass. This city is in the south of Langzhong City and has an area of 4.59 square kilometers, which is shaped like a ribbon. Langzhong is also called "Lang Park" or "Langhuan Paradise", which means a place where immortals live. Langzhong is believed to be a fairyland where the Queen Mother of the West[①] lived and the Emperor of Heaven kept his books. With a history of more than 2,300 years, it was an important military town of the ancient Shu Kingdom. It is the only well-preserved ancient city in Sichuan Province. In addition, the city is ranked first on the list of China's Four Ancient Cities and is also listed as an AAAAA-national tourist scenic attraction. There are 22 provincial cultural heritage sites and eight national cultural heritage sites, including Zhang Fei Temple, Prince Teng Pavilion and the North Langzhong Examination House. Langzhong was listed as the Hometown of Chinese Spring Festival Culture in 2010.

──Legendary Stories──

Live to Learn: The Anecdote of Zhuangyuan

Langzhong, a city with outstanding scholars, has witnessed four special Zhuangyuan[②] who were two brothers each from two different families. They are Yin Shu and Yin Ji during the Tang Dynasty and Chen Yaosou and Chen Yaozi during the Song Dynasty. In 791, the 7th year of the Zhenyuan period (785—805) of the Tang Dynasty, Yin Shu, a 71-year-old man was selected as Zhuangyuan. He was known as the eldest and also the longest-living Zhuangyuan.

Yin Shu was over 70 years old when he participated in the imperial examination. In that exam, the chief examiner was Du Huangshang who is the chief examiner for the first time. Du was worried about how he would publish the list of successful examinees fairly. At the end of the third examination, he exclaimed, "All of you are talented, but no one can help me!" Over 500

---

① The Queen Mother of the West is a goddess in Chinese religion and mythology.

② Zhuangyuan, a title conferred on the one who came first in the highest imperial examination.

尹枢应试时已70多岁。当时的主考官杜黄裳第一次当主考，一直在想怎样才能做到公平公正地出榜。三场考试结束后，他对众举子说道："诸位学士都是当代才子，怎么就没有人帮我一把？"应试者总共有500多人，大家面面相觑，不知道考官是什么意思。这时尹枢独自上前问道："不知您有什么吩咐？"杜黄裳说："没有人写榜。"尹枢立即毛遂自荐，他拿起笔，逐一题名，唱名，自始至终，全场肃然，大家都觉得尹枢的做法很公平公正。最后发现唯独少了状头，杜考官问："写谁好呢？"尹枢毫无愧色地回答道："非老夫不可！"杜黄裳大吃一惊，但仔细一想确实非他莫属。此事传出，轰动朝野。

尹枢的弟弟尹极为唐宪宗元和八年（813）癸巳科状元。尹枢、尹极兄弟俩在22年中先后中状元，被称为"梧桐双凤"。后人为纪念他们，在家乡建庙，取名解元寺（因唐时举人、进士皆由地方解送入试，故称乡试第一名为解元），至今犹存。1951年至1992年此处设立过解元乡。

赤胆忠心：张飞故事

张飞与阆中有着一段很深的渊源。张飞英勇善战，身先士卒，生擒巴郡太守严颜。益州平定后，张飞被刘备任命为巴郡太守，镇守阆中达七年。相传张飞初到阆中时，发现这

里山川秀美，乡风淳朴，但人们的日子却过得艰苦。于是他亲自教当地人栽桑养蚕，发展农业和手工业。直到现在，阆中丝绸业发达，古城内仍保留着许多蚕丝手工作坊，所产蚕丝享誉中外。

张飞不但是一个会带兵打仗的英雄、猛将，而且还粗中有细，写得一手漂亮的好字。同时，他也是一位亲民

examinees looked at each other with confusion and did not understand what the examiner meant. Only Yin Shu stepped forward and asked, "What can I do for you, Sir?" Du Huangshang said: "No one can help me write the list." Yin Shu volunteered to write the list. Taking up a brush pen he wrote the names on the list one by one and then read the names out aloud. Everybody thought what he was doing was fair and showed their respect to him. However, the list omitted Zhuangyuan. Du asked, "Who should be the Zhuangyuan?" Confidently, Yin Shu replied, "It should be me!" Amazed, Du Huangshang thought carefully and agreed that only he could be the one. This story was spread widely, surprising the government and the public.

22 years later, Yin Shu's younger brother Yin Ji was selected as Zhuangyuan. These two brothers of the same family were selected as Zhuangyuan one after another and were thus regarded as two phoenixes[1] on sycamore tree. To commemorate them, their descendants built a temple named Jieyuan[2] Temple in their hometown. This temple is still standing there today. From 1951 to 1992, Jieyuan, a town was named after this story.

Devotion and Loyalty: A Story about Zhang Fei

There are many stories between Zhang Fei and Langzhong Ancient Town. Heroically, Zhang Fei led his men in a brave act, capturing Yan Yan who was the prefectural governor of Ba County. After the conquest of Yizhou (now Sichuan, Yunnan, Guizhou Provinces and most part of middle China), Zhang was assigned by Liu Bei the post of governor of Ba County, guarding Langzhong for seven years. It is said that when Zhang first came to Langzhong, he found the place beautiful in scenery and customs, but the residents here led a hard life. Therefore, he taught the local people to plant mulberries and breed silkworms, which boosted agriculture and manufacturing. To date, the silk industry has gained a reputation both at home and abroad.

As a gallant general, Zhang also had beautiful handwriting. Moreover, he was more than just a hardworking officer concerned about his people. He was also loved and respected by his people for what he had accomplished for them.

There is a legend that Zhang was killed by one of his subordinates, who betrayed Zhang and had planned to go to the Wu Kingdom with Zhang's head. Unfortunately, on the way to that kingdom, he heard that both the Shu and Wu Kingdoms had reconciled, so he gave up the plan and threw Zhang's head into a river. One day, a fisherman discovered the head floating upright with its eyes wide open. Frightened, the fisherman threw the head back into the river. That night, the fisherman dreamed of Zhang Fei. In this dream, Zhang Fei was afraid of his head drifting to the Wu Kingdom and begged the fisherman to save his head and bury it. The next day, the

---

① Phoenix here is a metaphor, referring to people who change their fate from humble to noble.

② Jieyuan ranks number one in the local examination.

爱民的地方官。他的为人处事，深受阆中人民爱戴。

传说张飞被他的部下杀死并割下了头颅。部下投奔东吴请赏，但途中听闻吴蜀讲和，便将头颅抛入江中。后来头颅被一打鱼人发现，捞起时双目圆睁，立着不倒，吓得打鱼人又将头颅重新丢回江中，晚上张飞托梦对他说："我是张飞，拜托您，将我的头捞起葬于此地。否则就要飘到吴国了。"第二天打鱼人就依张飞所嘱，将他的头颅捞起葬于云阳。

张飞死后谥为桓侯，阆中人民念及他的忠诚、仁义和爱心，建桓侯祠以祭祀。1000多年来，到阆中桓侯祠来祭祀张飞的人络绎不绝，既有文官又有武将，既有高人又有屠夫等寻常百姓。更有意思的是，据传张飞曾托梦给台北的屠夫们，祝他们生意兴隆。所以，凡是台湾的朋友到四川，一般都会来阆中祭拜张飞。由此可见张飞享有很高的威望。

功成身退：醋神传说

阆中民间，酿醋要供奉神明。相传，当年分封神位时，姜子牙主动向周武王讨了一个"醋炭神"，因为他知道，自己功高盖世，因此自甘人后，也算功成身退。据《保宁府制》记载：阆中清代曾有祭拜"醋炭神"姜子牙的习俗，与甘肃靖远一带祭拜方式相差无几。每年除夕，醋坊的工人从嘉陵江边捡回鹅卵石，用炭火烧得透红，放入盛有保宁醋的大铜勺或其他器皿中，一边摇动，一边在院中跑圈，边跑边唱《醋炭神》民谣："醋炭神，醋炭神，封神榜

上你为尊，今夜除夕来家内，驱逐邪魔离家门，一不打天，二不打地，三不打门臣户尉，四不打家神灶君，五不打吉庆财神，六不打福禄寿星，七不打三代祖考，八不打过路贵人，九不打平民百姓，十专打瘟魔疫君、泼神乱鬼。醋炭有灵，扫除疾病，保佑全家，如意吉庆。"

——民俗文化——

川北灯戏

川北灯戏，又称"鼓乐神"，是流行于川北一带历史悠久的汉族民间歌舞小戏。阆中是川北灯戏的故乡，每当农村收获季节，灯戏艺人在田头或院场点亮写有"五谷丰登""人寿年丰"等字样的大红灯笼。打起锣鼓，拉起胡琴，演起滑稽逗趣、热闹非凡的灯戏。农民

fisherman followed the instructions in his dream and buried the head in Yunyang City.

Hearing about the death of Zhang Fei, the Langzhong Town's people built Heng Hou Temple to commemorate Zhang for his loyalty, righteousness and benevolence. The temple was named after Zhang's posthumous title, Heng Hou (Marquis). For more than a thousand years, people have come in an endless stream to Heng Hou Temple to commemorate Zhang Fei. These include both civil and military officers, masters and ordinary people such as butchers. More interestingly, it was said that Zhang had blessed the butchers of Taipei in a dream. Consequently, when visiting Sichuan Province, the Taiwanese would often go to Langzhong to worship Zhang. Obviously, Zhang Fei has garnered high prestige among many people.

Retire when Mission Accomplished: The God of Vinegar

It is said that the citizens of Langzhong are supposed to worship God when they make vinegar. In ancient legends, Jiang Ziya[1] required his king to give him the position in charge of "vinegar and charcoal". He was a modest man. Although he made an incomparable contribution to his country, he was unwilling to be the top one on the awarding list when he retired. According to the local ancient annals, the custom of worshipping Jiang Ziya, the God of Vinegar can be dated back to the Qing Dynasty. This custom is quite like that of Jingyuan County, Gansu Province in northwest China. Every New Year's Eve, the workers in the vinegar workshop will bring back pebbles from Jialing River and heat them till they are hot. Then the workers put these hot pebbles into a large copper spoon or some other containers filled with vinegar. They shake these containers, and they run laps in the yard, singing a folk song called *Vinegar God*: "My God, you are respectful in the 'Legend of Deification' and tonight please come to exorcise evil spirits. Love your people and protect your people from pestilence. Drive diseases away and bless your people with happiness and luck."

—Folk Culture—

North Sichuan Lantern Opera

The North Sichuan Lantern Opera, also known as the "Happy Drum Musical", is a popular historical folk song and dance drama in northern Sichuan. Langzhong is the home of this lantern show. During the harvest seasons, performers will light big red lanterns written with characters which express best wishes for good harvests or good health. They play the gong, drum, er-hu, and perform an interesting and lively lantern show. The red lanterns which are hung high are a

---

[1] Jiang Ziya was a Chinese semi-mythological figure who resided next to the Weishui River about 3,000 years ago.

们看见红灯笼高挂，便打起灯笼火把，从四面八方赶去看灯戏。由于灯戏源自民间，反映了民众的人生理念和审美情趣，因而为山乡民众所喜闻乐见，被称为"农民戏""喜乐神"。2006年5月，川北灯戏被国务院授牌为首批"国家级非物质文化遗产"。

阆中傩戏

阆中傩戏又称川北傩戏，是古代一种驱除邪祟的仪式，世代沿袭，自成一格，很少受外来影响，至今保持着古朴、粗犷、原始的风格，被称为"戏曲活化石"。我国傩祭和傩戏历史悠久，据《汉书·艺文志》记载，汉朝时，每到元宵节，有人扮演成原始神灵，带领很多儿童，蹦蹦跳跳踏遍宫廷各个角落，将所谓的鬼祟赶到河里，以这种方式来驱除宫廷中的邪祟和不洁。后来这种仪式逐渐传到民间。民间仪式更侧重于祈雨求神，保佑风调雨顺、人畜平安、天下承平或者庆祝丰收。傩戏表演者按角色戴彩绘面具，俗称"脸子"，分为一末、二净、三生、四旦、五丑、六外、七贴旦、八小生。

饮食文化

阆中古城饮食文化远近闻名，堪称一绝。阆中名特小吃品种繁多，特色佳肴闻名遐迩，被中国食品工业协会命名为"中国名特食品小吃之乡"。

阆中有著名的"阆中四绝"：热凉面、白糖蒸馍、张飞牛肉和保宁醋，还有川北凉粉、牛羊杂碎面、油茶撒子等。阆中小吃既有四川小吃色、香、味俱全的特点，又有浓厚的地域特色，还有营养丰富、滋补益寿之效，令人望而生"味"，常食不厌，颇受中外食客喜

signal of the lantern show, thus at the sight of these lanterns, farmers from different places come at night, torches raised, to enjoy the lantern show. Greatly influenced by folklore, the show reflects the philosophy and aesthetic taste of the locals. Loved by the local residents, it is also called "Nongminxi, a local opera entertaining farmers" or "Xileshen, a local opera delighting gods". In May of 2006, the North Sichuan Lantern Show was listed on the first batch as a National Intangible Cultural Heritage by the State Council.

Langzhong Nuo Opera

Langzhong Nuo Opera, also called North Sichuan Nuo Opera is an exorcism ritual. The North Sichuan Nuo Opera, inherited from generation to generation, has its own unique style. Regarded as a living fossil of opera, Nuo Opera has a plain, straightforward and primitive style. The Nuo Festival and Opera have a long history. According to the *Book of Han* written during the Han Dynasty (206 BC-AD 220), people would dress like the early man and lead children to jump on the bodies of all the residents of the royal court to drive so-called evil spirits into rivers. This custom gradually spread to civilians. People mainly use this ritual to pray to the Rain God for good weather for the crops, security for both humans and livestock, for a good harvest and peace for the land. Outfitted with painted masks, the performers of Nuo Opera are divided into eight different characters, including Mo, Jing, Sheng, Dan, Chou, Wai, Tie Dan and Xiao Sheng[1].

Food Culture

The food culture of Langzhong enjoys a widespread reputation. Langzhong has various famous local snacks and specialties. Therefore, Langzhong became known as a Town of Special Chinese Food and Snacks by the China Food Industry Association.

Hot noodles with sesame sauce (beef noodles with sesame sauce), steamed buns with white sugar, Zhang Fei Beef and Baoning vinegar are known as the Four Langzhong Uniques. Additionally, North Sichuan Jelly, beef and mutton noodles and Camellia Sazi are also delicious. Langzhong special snacks share common features with Sichuan snacks in their unique color, aroma and taste. More importantly, these nutritious snacks embody the local flavors and style. Visitors from all over the world go to Langzhong to taste these special snacks.

In addition, folk snacks of this ancient town, including Baoning wine, preserved egg, noodles with Chinese sauerkraut and tofu pudding, crispy pancake and Lamian noodles with

---

[1] They are different roles in Chinese opera. Sheng refers to the male actor; Dan is the female actor; Jing is the actor with a painted face; Mo is the main male actor; Chou is the role of a clown; Tie Dan is the minor female actor; Xiao Sheng is the role of young men.

爱。此外，还有久负盛名的保宁压酒、松花皮蛋、酸菜豆花面、锭子锅盔、酥锅盔、吊汤扯面等充满古城民间韵味的饮食小吃，足以让人一饱口福。

—主要景点串游—

张飞庙

阆中桓侯祠为全国文物保护单位，俗称张飞庙，明代又称雄威庙。因张飞死后追谥为桓侯，故名。如今的桓侯祠为明清时重建的四合庭院式古建筑群，占地5000多平方米，规模恢宏，建造精美，由山门、敌万楼、左右牌坊、东西厢房、大殿、后殿、墓亭、墓冢组成，建筑面积达2400多平方米，为三国文化的一大胜迹。

川北道贡院

川北道贡院俗称清代考棚，现位于城内学道街，原由山门、廊道、考房、大殿、二殿、后殿和考生宿房组成。现仅存卷棚式廊道，纵横共长50多米，廊道两旁的木栏上带有飞仙椅。左右有两排考室，各室相隔，饰以雕花。至今保护较好，是全国仅存的两处考棚之一。

滕王阁

坐落于阆中城北的玉台山，同南昌滕王阁一样，是唐高祖李渊第二十二子滕王元婴建造。滕王于679年由寿州调隆州（阆中），嫌"衙役卑陋"，便在城中建"隆苑"，唐玄宗时

stock, have long enjoyed a good reputation. People can enjoy a real treat here.

—Main Tourist Attractions—

Zhang Fei Temple

Langzhong Huan Hou Temple, a national cultural heriatge site, is commonly known as Zhang Fei Temple and was called Xiongwei Temple during the Ming Dynasty. The name of the temple came from Zhang Fei's posthumous title, Huan Hou. The magnificent temple today is a quadrangle-courtyard-style building, which was reconstructed in the Ming and Qing dynasties. It covers over 5,000 square meters of land. The temple consists of the gate, memorial archway on the left and right sides, east and west wing rooms, main hall, back hall, tomb pavillion and tombs, with a construction area of more than 2,400 square meters. The temple is one of the major historical sites of the Three Kingdoms Culture.

North Sichuan Examination House

The North Sichuan Examination House, also named Langzhong Gongyuan[1] is located in Xuedao Street and was reconstructed during the reign of Emperor Jiaqing[2]. It was originally composed of a gate, corridor, examination room, main hall, the second hall, back hall and the examinees' room. Today, there is only a corridor which is 50 meters long. There are feixian chairs (flying fairy chairs)[3] on both sides of the wooden banister of the corridor. On both the left and right sides of Gongyuan, there are two rows of examination rooms decorated with carvings, each of which allows only one examinee each time. Nowadays, there are only two well-preserved examination halls in China and Langzhong Gongyuan is one of them.

Prince Teng Pavilion

Lying on Mount Yutai in the north of Langzhong, the Prince Teng Pavilion, like the Pavilion in Nanchang, was built by Prince Teng, the 22nd son of Li Yuan, the Emperor Gaozu[4] of Tang Dynasty. Prince Teng officially transferred to Longzhou (the ancient name of Langzhong) from Shouzhou in 679. The Prince thought his government office was not adequate, and therefore decided to build another one. Thus, a new pavilion named Long Park was built. Later, it was

---

[1] Gongyuan refers to the examination hall in feudal China.

[2] Emperor Jiaqing (1796—1820) is the 7th emperor of Qing Dynasty.

[3] Feixian chair refers to a type of Chinese armchair decorated with beautiful patterns like flying fairies.

[4] Tang Gaozu (618—626) is the 1st emperor of Tang Dynasty.

改称"阆苑"，又在玉台山建玉台观和滕王阁，供其游乐，杜甫有诗《滕王亭子二首》为证。

大佛寺

大佛寺又名大像寺，为四川省文物保护单位。大佛有三重檐楼遮护。其大佛为释迦牟尼坐像，高9.88米，头有螺髻，左手半置膝上，右手上屈作施无畏手印状。脚踏莲花皆着地。佛身衣纹为凸纹，佛像端庄。佛头后有火焰纹背光。五代隆德元年（921），佛龛内刻小佛4万余尊，高10厘米左右，排列整齐，工艺精细，为全国罕见。

山上现存唐、宋、元、明、清碑刻30余处，石刻造像五尊，并有宋徽宗崇宁年间摩岩楷书"虎溪"二字，字径逾5米。传说唐代著名医学家孙思邈曾来此采药，在状元山崖上流下的一条小溪旁，路遇一负伤猛虎。药王将之治愈，虎为感恩，遂化为药王坐骑，随药王而去。此后，这条山溪遂名"虎溪"，也喻佛家虎啸唤人猛醒之意。

renamed Lang Park during the reign of Emperor Xuanzong[1] to avoid the resemblance of the pronunciation the emperor's name. In addition, Prince Teng also built Yutai Temple and Prince Teng Pavilion on Mount Yutai for entertainment purposes. All these events are recorded in Du Fu's[2] poem "Two Poems on the Pavilion of Prince Teng".

Giant Buddhist Temple

The Giant Buddhist Temple, also known as the Giant Statue Temple, is one of Sichuan's provincial cultural heritage sites. There are triple eaves covering the statue of the giant Buddha. The Buddha is the statue of Sakyamuni and is 9.88 meters in height. The Buddha's hair is styled in a chignon that has a whirlpool pattern. In this statue, Buddha places his left hand on his knee and lifts his right hand to his chest demonstrating a gesture of soothing troubled souls. He is also stepping on a lotus flower. The Buddha looks dignified surrounded by a flower of a flame pattern flammule behind his head. In 921, there were more than 40,000 small Buddha statuettes carved in Buddha shrines, each with a height of about ten centimeters or so. These were arranged neatly and are considered to be very rare nationwide.

Today, there are still more than 30 stone tablets with inscriptions and five stone statues from five dynasties, including Tang, Song, Yuan, Ming and Qing dynasties. In addition, there are two characters written in the style of regular script that say "虎溪" (means Tiger Creek), which were carved during the reign of Emperor Huizong[3] of the Song Dynasty. There is a tale that Sun Simiao, a famous physician during the Tang Dynasty, arrived here to collect medicinal herbs. He came across an injured tiger lying beside a creek which flowed from Zhuangyuan Cliff. Sun healed the tiger. To express its gratitude, the tiger became Sun's mount. Since then, the creek is named "Tiger Creek", which also has a religious connotation that when the tiger roars it will awaken people from ignorance.

---

① Tang Xuanzong (712—755) is the 9th emperor of Tang Dynasty.

② Du Fu (712—770) is a great realistic poet in Tang Dynasty.

③ Huizong (1101—1125) is the 8th emperor of Song Dynasty.

18. 广元昭化古镇

Zhaohua Ancient Town, Guangyuan City

昭化古镇简介

　　昭化古镇位于川北广元市的南郊，古称"葭萌"。明洪武十年（1377），更名为昭化，意为"昭示帝德，化育人心"。古镇距今已有2300多年的建镇史和2244年连续建县史，是国家重点风景名胜区——剑门蜀道风景名胜区，全国重点文物保护单位剑门蜀道遗址群的重要组成部分，同时也是迄今为止国内唯一一座保存完好的三国古镇。历史上有"蜀汉兴于昭化，亡于剑门"之说，其地理位置很重要，历来为兵家必争之地。昭化依山傍水，人杰地灵，风貌保存完好，历史文化底蕴丰厚，素有"天下第一山水太极自然奇观"之美誉和"巴蜀第一县，蜀国第二都"之嘉称。2008年被评为中国第四批历史文化名镇。

—传奇故事—

双雄对决：张飞夜战马超

　　古镇西南角的临清门前有一个坝子叫"战胜坝"，因三国名将张飞、马超曾在此"挑灯夜战"而闻名。当时诸侯割据，汉宁太守张鲁命马超攻葭萌关。葭萌关由蜀将霍峻驻守，

A Brief Introduction to Zhaohua Ancient Town

The Ancient Town of Zhaohua is located in the southern suburbs of Guangyuan City in northern Sichuan. It was known as Jiameng in ancient times. In 1377, the 10th year of the reign of Hongwu (1368—1398) in the Ming Dynasty, the name was changed to Zhaohua, to declare the merit of the emperor and his influence on educating the people. With a history of more than 2,300 years, the town is now a famous national tourist attraction, boasting the Jianmen Pass Scenic Spot and Ancient Shu Road Ruins. Zhaohua is the only ancient town of the Three Kingdoms[1] that is well-preserved in China. As the proverb goes, the rise of the Shu Han Kingdom began in Zhaohua and its fall was in Jianmen. The unique geographical location of Zhaohua has made it a place of military and strategic importance in the history of Sichuan Province. Surrounded by mountains and rivers, it has produced outstanding people. At the confluence of the three rivers[2] in this area, one can see the natural shape of Tai Chi (a natural diagram of the universe), which is an unrivalled wonder in the world. With its well-preserved historical sites and fascinating cultural heritage, Zhaohua has earned its reputation as "the top one county in Ba Shu[3] and the second capital of the Kingdom of Shu". In 2008, it was on the list of Famous Historical and Cultural Towns in China (the fourth batch).

—Legendary Storiese—

Dueling Between Two Heros: Zhang Fei Fighting versus Ma Chao Overnight

Near the southwest gate of the town lies a dam called Victory Dam where Zhang Fei, a valiant general of the Kingdom of Shu had fought overnight with Ma Chao, an excellent general serving for another lord. At that time, there was chaos because of the warlords. Zhang Lu,

---

[1] The Three Kingdoms (220—280) was a period in history when China was divided among the states of Wei, Shu and Wu.

[2] The three rivers here refer to Bailong River, Jialing River and Qingjiang River.

[3] Ba Shu also called Shu, is the ancient name of Sichuan. Shu is one of the states in the Three Kingdoms.

刘备担心其失守而受到两面夹击，找军师诸葛亮商议。诸葛亮献计命魏延率兵先行，张飞紧跟其后，刘备最后压阵率大军到达葭萌关。魏延为抢头功，首位出战。打败对方大将杨柏后乘势追赶，但见前有一路人马，马岱为首。魏延误以为是马超，挥刀而上，战了十八回合，马岱败下，在魏延乘胜追击之时，却被马岱回身一箭射中左臂，魏延只好返回，但马岱复又返追。危急之时，张飞赶来救下魏延。张飞与马岱激战十多个回合，马岱败走，张飞欲追，刘备赶到，叫回张飞，当日休战。

第二日天刚亮，葭萌关下鼓声阵阵，原是马超请战。刘备爱才，站在关上感叹道："人称锦马超，名不虚传！"此时张飞要求出战，但刘备不允，欲避其锐气。而张飞热血沸腾，意欲即刻杀马超，被刘备挡下。

午后，刘备见马超人马均已疲倦，遂精选五百人马，与张飞一齐出关迎战。张、马二人战过一百多回合，不分胜负。刘备担忧张飞有失，即刻要其收兵。张飞回营休息片刻，复出战与马超厮杀，又战了一百多回合，仍不分胜负。这时天色已晚，刘备又鸣金收兵。张飞当时战意正酣，哪肯罢战，马超也不示弱。于是张飞请求安排夜战，刘备应允，一时两军点燃千万火把，将战场照得如同白昼。马超也换马出阵，两将又展开鏖战，仍不分胜负，各自收兵回营，准备次日再战。

此时，诸葛亮赶来，要求停战。诸葛亮对刘备说："张飞和马超俱是忠勇虎将，如再战，必有一伤，有损将才，实乃可惜！我能施计收降马超。"后来，诸葛亮当真用离间计收服了马超，为己所用。

女中豪杰：鲍三娘传说

鲍三娘是蜀汉女英雄，关羽之子关索的夫人。相传鲍三娘是夔州鲍家庄鲍员外的小女

the mayor of Hanning[①] County, ordered Ma Chao to attack Jiameng Pass where Huo Jun, a general of the Kingdom of Shu was garrisoned. Liu Bei, the king of the Shu, was afraid of being attacked on two sides and counseled his military counsellor Zhuge Liang. The wise counselor suggested that General Wei Yan lead the troops first, followed by Zhang Fei, and lastly by Liu Bei with his big army. General Wei Yan volunteered to meet the enemy first, hoping to gain the highest respect. After defeating Yang Bo, a general from the enemy side, he tried to pursue the retreating enemy. On the way he encountered troops led by Ma Dai, but Wei mistook him for Ma Chao. He held his sword at Ma Dai, dueling with him for dozens of rounds. Defeated by Wei, Ma attempted to flee. Wei Yan pushed his advantage and kept chasing him. Ma Dai turned around suddenly and shot Wei in the left arm. Wei tried to retreat. However, this time Ma Dai began to chase him with a sword. At this critical moment General Zhang Fei came and saved Wei. Zhang ran swiftly like the wind and had a fierce fight with Ma Dai for dozens of rounds. Ma Dai was finally defeated and tried to flee. Zhang wanted to keep chasing him, but Liu Bei arrived and stopped him. Finally, they held a truce for the rest of the day.

Early next morning, near the Jiameng Pass came the sound of drums. It was the real Ma Chao, a young general with a graceful appearance. He was requesting a battle. Standing on the gate tower, Liu Bei who appreciated excellent swordsmanship observed him carefully, exclaiming that Ma was worthy of the reputation "perfect Mao Chao". Zhang Fei was very excited at the sight of his rival and volunteered to fight Ma to death, but Liu Bei stopped the rash general and commanded him to wait with the intention of depleting the energy of the enemy.

In the late afternoon, noticing that the soldiers in Ma's army had become tired and their morale low, Liu Bei, together with Zhang Fei and five hundred selective brave soldiers went out and accepted Ma's challenge. Ma and Zhang fought for a long time but neither side could gain any advantage. Liu Bei was worried that Zhang might lose the battle and immediately asked for a temporary truce. After a short rest, Zhang went out again, fighting against Ma for another hundred rounds. There was still no winner. As it was getting dark, Liu had to order Zhang to return. However, neither one of them was willing to call it a truce. Finally, Zhang Fei requested another fight at night and received approval from Liu. At night, the two sides lit thousands of torches to illuminate the dam. While Ma Chao rode a new horse out of his camp, another fierce fight started. However, nobody gained advantage. Eventually, they had to withdraw their troops, and get ready to fight the next morning.

---

① Hanning is in Hunan Province now.

儿，自小聪明伶俐，深受大家的喜爱。有一日，关羽的三儿子关索来到此地，发现街头乱哄哄的。原来一位山匪头目看上了貌美的鲍三娘，上门求亲。这山匪鼠目獐头，鲍小姐自然看不上。土匪求亲不成，便欲抢亲，关索听说此事，便拔刀相助，英雄救美。美人也爱上了英雄，顺理成章结为连理。关羽也非常疼爱这个儿媳妇，甚至亲自传授鲍三娘武艺，因此也造就了她的文武双全。

关羽荆州失守后，关索逃难到鲍家庄养病，病愈后听说东吴仇人已死，就和鲍三娘回归蜀国，并随诸葛亮征讨蜀西南部落。平定蜀西南部落后，夫妻二人一直在此替诸葛亮镇守着南中。建兴五年（227），鲍三娘随夫屯兵汉寿（今昭化古镇）。炎兴元年（263），曹魏以三路大军十五万之众讨伐蜀国，兵临葭萌关下。面对来势汹汹的曹军和敌众我寡的形势，蜀军五万将士奋勇抵抗。交战中，关索被庞会打下江去，溺水身亡。鲍三娘来不及悲痛，手持两把大刀，表现得异常勇猛，在土基坝与魏军展开血战，刀光剑影，厮杀声响彻云霄，大战几百回合。然而，面对众敌，她最终难以抗御。姜维领军前来救援，却未成功。最后，鲍三娘战死疆场，是三国时期为数不多的巾帼英雄，为后人所敬仰。鲍三娘死后葬在距昭化古镇北5千米处白龙江畔的曲回坝。

—民俗文化—

建筑文化

古镇建筑群布局合理，现存的四条大街、五条小巷由青石板铺砌而成，为三横两纵、中间高两侧低的瓦背风格。街巷间"T"字相连，具有"道路交错相通，城门不相对"的军事防御特色。古街两侧古朴的川北风味民居保留着完整的明清建筑，多为穿斗式木架结构和小青瓦。石砌的古城墙，虽断断续续，但至今仍保留着三座城门，完好如故。

The next moment, Zhuge Liang arrived and suggested that they end the battle. Zhuge told Liu that both Ma and Zhang were excellent generals, brave and loyal. If they kept fighting, inevitably one or other would get injured, which would be a great loss. Later, Zhuge Liang outwitted Ma with the strategy of "setting one against another", and finally persuaded him to serve the Kingdom of Shu.

An Excellent Heroine: The Legend of Bao Sanniang

Bao Sanniang, the wife of Guansuo and daughter-in-law of General Guan Yu, was a great heroine of Shu Han Kingdom. According to a legend, Bao Sanniang was the third daughter of Lord Bao, a rich landowner in the village of Bao in Kuizhou[1] County. She had gained popularity for her cleverness and beauty. One day, Guan Suo, the third son of General Guan Yu[2] came to the village. The noise in a crowded street caught his attention and he saw a young girl being bullied by an ugly and fierce-looking man. He inquired about the situation and discovered that the bandit wanted to force the girl to marry him even though he had failed to win her affection. Hearing this, Guan became angry and tried to rescue the girl. Thereafter, the girl fell in love with the hero and they got married. Guan Yu, the father of Guan Suo became fond of his daughter-in-law and spent time teaching her martial arts.

After the fall of Jingzhou[3] where Guan Yu was stationed, Guan Suo was wounded in battle and fled to Bao Village to heal his wounds. When he had recovered, he found out about the death of his foe in the Wu Kingdom and returned to Shu with his wife. The couple followed Zhuge Liang to pacify the tribes in southwestern Shu. Later, they were given the mission of guarding the garrison of Nanzhong[4]. In 227, the 5th year of the reign of Jian Xing (223—237), the couple was ordered to station troops at Hanshou (present-day Zhaohua). In 263, the first year of Yan Xing[5], an army of three divisions with a hundred and fifty thousand soldiers led by Cao Cao[6] marched to Shu and approached the Jiameng Pass.

---

① Kuizhou is today's Fengjie County of Chongqing Municipality.

② See foot note ④ on page 55.

③ Jingzhou is in Hubei Province now.

④ Nanzhong covered the places of present-day Yunnan, Guizhou and Sichuan Provinces.

⑤ Yan Xing is the title of Liu Shan, King of Shu Han Kingdom. The reign of Yan Xing lasted only four months in 263.

⑥ Cao Cao (155—220) was a Chinese warlord and the penultimate Chancellor of the Eastern Han Dynasty who rose to great power in the final years of the Dynasty.

饮食文化

昭化古镇位于白龙江、嘉陵江、清江三江汇合处。嘉陵江的鱼肉质鲜嫩，慕名前来的食客络绎不绝，最为流行的吃法为嘉陵江河鲜汤锅。

当地流行一种说法："不吃'剑门豆腐'，枉游天下雄关。"剑门豆腐是蜀道剑门关一带所产的豆腐，由当地优质的黄豆和纯净水制作而成。采用炒、炸、熘、烧、炖、蒸、氽、凉拌等烹调方法，可制作出上百种菜肴。据说其制作方法始于三国时期。当时蜀汉大将军姜维

Outnumbered by the enemy, the soldiers of Shu resisted bravely. Unfortunately, during combat, Guan Suo died by accidentally drowning in a river. Burying the sorrow in her heart, Bao Sanniang held two broad swords in her hands and fought vigorously against the enemy in the Tuji Dam. She kept fighting for hundreds of rounds. However, she exhausted all her strength and was finally outnumbered. Later General Jiang Wei came to rescue her but failed to do so. Bao fought and fought until her last breath. She died for Shu Han, and was regarded as a rare heroine in the period of Three Kingdoms and admired by her descendants. Bao was buried at the Quhui Dam near the Bailong River, which is five kilometers away from the north of the Zhaohua.

—Folk Culture—

Architecture Culture

The layout of the town is carefully planned. The four main existing streets as well as five alleys are all bluestone-slate-paved, with three slates paved horizontally and two vertically with tile roofs which are high in the middle and low on the two edges. Where the main streets and alleys meet is the T-shape. Crossed roads and asymmetrical gates were designed for military defense. The old streets are lined with wooden primitive and simple houses which were well-kept structures of the Ming and Qing dynasties. There are still three well-preserved gates in the ancient town despite the disconnected stone-built walls.

Food Culture

The town is rich in fish because Bailong River, Jialing River and Qingjiang River merge in Zhaohua. Tourists flock to taste the fresh and tender fish which are caught from the Jialing River. Hot pot is the most popular way to cook Jialing River fish.

As the proverb goes, "a man who never tastes Jianmen Tofu hasn't really visited the Jianmen Pass." Jianmen Tofu is made from local soybeans of high quality and purified water. There are various methods of cooking tofu including stir-frying, stewing, boiling, steaming. Hundreds of dishes can be made of it. It is said that the custom dates back to the period of Three Kingdoms when General Jiang Wei was defeated and withdrew his exhausted troops to the Jianmen Pass. A local official suggested to the general that it be wise for the Shu army to stop fighting and have a rest for three days. During this period, each family at Jianmen made tofu to feed the soldiers and the residue was used for feeding the horses. Jiang took his advice and three days later, Jiang, together with his five-thousand cavalry, won a great victory over Cao Cao and forced the enemy to retreat dozens of miles. From then on, the custom of tofu cooking has been passed on.

兵败，退到剑门关内，兵疲马乏，不能续战。剑门地方官向姜维献计："闭关三日不战，今百姓家家磨豆做豆腐，以养士兵，把豆渣喂战马，待兵马体力恢复后再战。"三日后，姜维以五千奇兵获得大胜，迫使魏军退却数十里。从此，做豆腐的习俗得以流传。

女皇蒸凉面是昭化特色小吃之一，有酸、甜、麻、辣、香五味。蒸凉面选用上等大米，淘洗干净后，用清水浸泡一天，再加十分之一的大米饭，磨成适度稀浆。放入蒸笼蒸熟后，冷却切成细丝即成。这道小吃的得名与唐朝女皇武则天相关。广元是武则天的家乡，她非常喜欢这道美食。后来当了女皇，每逢生日，即命御厨做一碗，以寄托怀念家乡之情。

—主要景点串游—

昭化考棚

昭化考棚是为本县及邻县学子应试岁考和科举而设，始建于清同治年间（1856—1875），因年久失修，大部分毁损，2008年修复。昭化考棚可供322名考生同时考试，考棚内设有听事房、管房、考舍、致公堂等。

费祎墓

费祎曾是诸葛亮出师前为后主刘禅推荐的贤臣之一。他擅长外交，常被派往东吴，执行联吴抗魏的使命。费祎墓位于昭化古城外一农舍旁，历代屡有增建。明代已规模宏伟，有围墙、牌坊、碑亭、费公祠、草堂等。现仅存高约3米的封土，另有清光绪时立的墓碑，写着"蜀汉大将军录尚书事成乡侯费祎之墓"，供人凭吊。

Empress steamed cold rice noodle is one of the local snacks of Zhaohua. It has various flavors like sour, sweet, spicy, hot and savory. The noodle is not made of wheat flour but high-quality rice. The procedure is as follows. First, wash the rice and soak it for one day. Then, mix this with one tenth of amount of cooked rice and grind it into a thick liquid. Finally, put the liquid into a steamer until it is cooked. Slice when cool. It is said that the fame of the snack is owed to Empress Wu Zetian[1] in the Tang Dynasty because Guangyuan was her birth place. The Empress was fond of these noodles since her childhood. After she took the throne, the Empress missed eating these noodles and would always request her cook to make the snack on her birthday.

—Main Tourist Attractions—

Zhaohua Kaopeng

In ancient times, Zhaohua Kaopeng was a place where the imperial exam was held for candidates from Zhaohua and its neighboring counties. It was founded in the reign of Emperor Tongzhi (1856—1875) in the Qing Dynasty. Most of the buildings had fallen into disrepair however they were renovated in 2008. Zhaohua Kaopeng had a capacity for 322 examinees to unite their exams at the same time. It also has rooms for duty officers, candidates, files, examiners, and raters, etc.

Fei Yi Tomb

Fei Yi, a talented politician, was recommended to be the minister for King Liu Shan[2] by Zhuge Liang before the war against the Wei Kingdom stalled. Good at diplomacy, Fei was sent on a special mission to create allies between the Shu Kingdom and the Wu Kingdom in order to go to war the Wei Kingdom. After his death, he was buried near a farmhouse outside the town. In the Ming Dynasty, his tomb was expanded with walls, memorial gateway, pavilion, memorial hall and thatched cottage, etc. The existing tomb is only three meters high with a tombstone built in the Guangxu period (1875—1908) of the Qing Dynasty. On the tombstone are carved the words "Grand General Fei Yi of the Shu Kingdom".

---

① Wu Zetian was a Chinese sovereign who ruled unofficially as empress consort and later officially as empress regnant during the brief Zhou Dynasty (690—704), which interrupted the Tang Dynasty.

② Liu Shan is the son of Liu Bei, King of Shu Han Kingdom in the period of Three Kingdoms.

牛头山

牛头山位于昭化城西7千米处，清江河南岸，嘉陵江西岸。系剑门山的东支，海拔1214米。它是一座巨石耸立的大山，远远望去，俨然似牛立头，故得此名。山腰，有天雄关险隘；山脚，有昭化古镇衬托，清江、嘉陵江、白龙江三江蜿蜒其周。山里有一口神奇的井，名为姜维井。据传，三国时蜀汉大将姜维屯兵牛头山，三万士兵被困山上，因无水源而军心纷乱，士气低落。诸葛亮托梦设坛拜水而解了困，此后便留下了久雨不溢、大旱不涸的拜水池：姜维井。

Niutou Mountain

With an altitude of 1,214 meters, Niutou Mountain, the eastern branch of the Jianmen Mountain, is located seven kilometers west of Zhaohua. Rising south of the Qingjiang River and west of Jialing River, it looks like the head of a cow from a distance. Surrounded by three rivers, Mount Niutou is remarkable for its scenery with a magnificent mountainside pass and an ancient town at the foot. There is a magic well named Jiangwei Well. As the story goes, General Jiang Wei and his thirty thousand soldiers were once trapped on the mountain. Short of water, the soldiers were in very low spirits. Zhuge Liang helped Jiang in a dream, suggesting him to dig a well and build a sacrificial altar to pray for water. After he had completed his prayers, a miracle occurred. Water gushed out of the well. From then on, the well was named Jiangwei Well and it is said to never run dry.

19. 德阳孝泉古镇

Xiaoquan Ancient Town, Deyang City

孝泉古镇简介

孝泉镇地处川西平原，位于全国重工业基地德阳市西北20千米处，距离成都75千米。孝泉古镇素以"德""孝"闻名，已有2000余年历史。我国著名的孝文化中心"中国德孝城"便坐落其中。镇内三孝园建以祭祀中国"二十四孝"中的"一门三孝"，即孝子姜诗、庞三春及其儿子安安。镇内有包括姜孝祠、姜公坟等在内的众多文人遗址及文墨真迹，十分珍贵。古镇还是多元文化融合之地，道教的道场、佛教的寺庙、儒家的祠堂、伊斯兰教的清真寺等，在这里各显风貌，交融成趣。

——传奇故事——

孝道感天：涌泉跃鲤

东汉雒县（今四川广汉市）汛乡（今孝泉）有个叫姜诗的人。他母亲患有眼疾，得知临江河水可以医治眼病，便很喜欢喝江里的水。姜妻庞氏每天走单程7里山路去挑江水给婆婆喝，为婆婆洗眼。姜母又特别爱吃鱼，姜诗夫妇就常常做鱼给母亲吃。姜母不愿意独自吃，他们又请来邻居老婆婆一起吃。一次因风大，庞氏取水晚归，姜诗怀疑她怠慢母亲，加之婆婆又听信别人的挑唆，说缸里的水是野男人帮庞氏挑的，于是将庞氏逐出了家门。庞氏离家后虽寄居破庙，仍然用柴换鱼托人送给婆婆吃。最后，其孝行感天动地，庞氏被姜诗请回家，当天在姜家房舍的旁边忽然喷涌出泉水，泉水的味道就如江水一样，而且每天还跃出两条鲤鱼来供庞氏侍奉婆婆。这就是中国历史上"二十四孝"之一"涌泉跃鲤"的来历。

A Brief Introduction to Xiaoquan Ancient Town

The Ancient Town of Xiaoquan is situated on the western Sichuan plain, 20 kilometers northwest of Deyang City, an industrial base and 75 kilometers away from the provincial capital Chengdu. With a history of over 2,000 years, the town is famous for "morality" and "filial piety". China's filial piety cultural center is located here. There is a Sanxiao[①] Garden, which is in commemoration of three filial people: Jiang Shi, his wife Pang Sanchun and his son An'an. There are also numerous precious calligraphy and cultural ruins such as Jiangxiao Temple and Jianggong Tomb. In addition, it is a place where cultural diversity is in full display. Taoist temples, Buddhist temples, Confucian ancestral halls and Islam mosques exist charmingly side by side.

—Legendary Stories—

Filial Piety Touching the God: Spring Bursting and Carp Jumping

During the Eastern Han Dynasty (25—220), there was a man called Jiang Shi in Xunxiang Town (the ancient name of Xiaoquan Town) in Luo County (the ancient name of Guanghan City). His mother suffered from an eye disease. Hearing that water in Linjiang River was effective in curing any eye diseases, she wanted to give it a try. Thus, Jiang Shi's wife Pang trekked over mountain trails every day to fetch water from the river for her mother-in-law. She kept on cleansing her mother-in-law's eyes with the water every day. The old lady also liked eating fish, so the couple cooked fish dishes for her. Knowing that she did not want to eat alone, they invited an old woman nearby to have dinner with her. One day, Pang came home late from fetching the water. Jiang Shi was upset with her for neglecting his mother. Coupled with the mother's gossip that another man was helping Pang to fetch water, Jiang Shi got angry and forced Pang to leave this family. However, Pang was wronged. Instead she sought refuge at a dilapidated temple and continued to send fish every day to her mother-in-law by bartering firewood for fish. Finally, her filial piety touched the God, and she was invited back by her husband. On that day, spring water

---

① Sanxiao refers to three filial persons.

223

母慈子孝：安安送米

姜诗夫妇生有一子名安安，安安得知母亲庞氏被休，日夜思念非常伤心。后来从邻居那得知母亲迁居白衣庵。安安觉得母亲孤身一人，生活清苦，便决定给母亲送米，让她吃顿饱饭。安安在塾馆念书，每天都要带上米在塾馆里吃一顿午饭。上学途中，路过土地庙，安安就抓上一把米，放入口袋，磕个头，藏在土地爷爷背后。几个月后，安安看米存得不少了，就偷偷到白衣庵看母亲，母子相见很是高兴。安安把米掏出来，但母亲突然脸色沉重，说："安安，我们家里的人，历来不偷人家的东西。人穷要穷得有志气，我宁愿饿死，也不吃人家的米。"安安忙把事情从头到尾告诉了母亲，母亲听后，悲喜交集，高兴的是有这么一个孝顺懂事的孩子，悲的是安安为了给自己送米，每天少吃一把米，已经饿得瘦了，就抱住安安大哭了一场。这段佳话人称"安安送米"。

—民俗文化—

建筑文化

孝泉古镇的建筑集中反映了川西民居朴实淡雅的特色，其建筑以庭院式为主，基本组合单位为"院"，由一正两厢一下房组成，平面和立体都布局灵活，对称要求并不严格。同时，其建筑色彩以冷色调为主，青瓦白墙，门窗多为棕色。孝泉古镇著名的半边街，除了川西民居特色明显，还有部分伊斯兰风格建筑。据史料记载，自康熙年间，有来自甘、陕两地回族人民迁徙至此，因此，其建筑汉、回特色兼而有之。

饮食文化

果汁牛肉是孝泉最出名的特色食品，已有近百年历史，被载入《中国土特名产词典》一书，其特色是麻、辣、香、酥，清香味美，入口即化。它的名称"果汁"实为"裹汁（子）"之意，是指用腌制、卤煮、油炸等工艺加工牛肉时，在肉的表面裹上一层特制的调味汁水，使其味道香醇。

在广为流传的"涌泉跃鲤"故事中，姜诗之妻庞三春常常烹制鲤鱼孝敬婆婆。如今家常鲤鱼成为孝泉当地一道特色菜。常用泡菜坛里的酸姜、酸辣椒，配上芹菜、大蒜，用油炒过后，

burst forth near their cottage. The taste of the water was just the same as that in the Linjiang River. To everyone's surprise, every day two carp would jump out from the spring, which were prepared and cooked for Pang's mother-in-law. This is the story of "Spring Bursting and Carp Jumping" among the stories of "Twenty-Four Filial Pieties" in China.

Affectionate Mother and Filial Son: An'an Sending Rice

Jiang Shi and his wife had a son called An'an. Knowing that his mother had been driven out of the family, An'an was extremely sad. From his neighbors, he knew that his mother had moved to Baiyi Nunnery. Feeling that his mother must be lonely and impoverished, he decided to send some rice to help his mother. An'an studied at a private school, and every school-day he would take some rice for his lunch at school. On the way to school, there was an Earth-god Temple. Each time he passed this temple, he would secretly put a handful of rice into a small bag which was hidden behind the Earth God. Several months later, it had become quite an accumulation. One day, he visited his mother at the Baiyi Nunnery with the rice. Pang was so happy to see her son, but she felt upset when she saw An'an opening the rice bag. She said, "An'an, there is no thief in our family. Poor as we are, we should also hold our heads high. Even if I were starving to death, I would never eat the stolen rice." An'an then told her how he had collected the rice. After hearing that, his mother had mixed feelings. She felt happy because her son was such a faithful and considerate boy. She also felt guilty because of her son's sacrifice and he had lost a lot of weight. Pang hugged her son and cried. This is the story of "An'an Sending Rice".

—Folk Culture—

Architecture Culture

Buildings in Xiaoquan Ancient Town reflect the simple and elegant characteristics of civil residences in western Sichuan. They are courtyard-style buildings, each of which is composed of one main room, two wing rooms and one lesser room. They are arranged flexibly and are not strictly symmetrical. The buildings are in cooler color tones, with grey tiles, white walls, and brown windows and doors. There are also some Islamic-style buildings along the famous Banbian Street (also called Half Street). According to historical records, during the reign of Emperor Kangxi (1661—1722), Hui people migrated here from Gansu and Shaanxi Provinces in northwestern China. Thus, the buildings are characterized by both Han and Hui architecture styles.

加水制成汤料，再放入鱼肉，待肉熟后加米酒、红糖勾芡，起锅时放入葱花、茴香、花椒面，色香味俱全。鱼肉吃完，剩下汤汁可做卤，做一份鱼香面，余味无穷。

庙会文化

上九，即正月初九，是汉族岁时习俗。自明清时期，每年从农历正月初七到初九，孝泉古镇都会举行传统的"上九会"，宣传孝道文化。"上九会"期间，各类民俗文化活动如民俗巡游、文艺表演、猜灯谜、赏幽兰等，热闹非凡。此外，每年农历五月初四开始，古镇会举办为期一周的特色庙会，皮影戏、被单戏、打道筒、唱围鼓等

表演悉数登场。农历十月初八，古镇还有高僧念经、祭塔等大型仪式，重现元朝五龙护塔的盛况。游古镇、逛庙会、观民俗成为孝泉古镇庙会文化的一大特色。

—主要景点串游—

三孝园

三孝园的大门在形制上仿照原有的姜孝祠，横额上的"三孝园"三个隶书体字一跃眼前。两旁各有一副歌咏姜家孝事和孝泉风土的楹联。门楣上装饰有彩色泥塑，四周风景秀丽，环境清幽。进入大门，首先映入眼帘的是姜公殿，接着是"一门三孝"的塑像，儿子安安在正中，两旁是姜诗

Food Culture

Guozhi Beef is a specialty in Xiaoquan and has a history of nearly a hundred years. This food dish has been written into the book *China's Famous Local Specialties Dictionary*. Guozhi Beef is very tender and delicious and tastes spicy, hot, fragrant and crisp. Guozhi means "wrapped with seasoning juice". In the processes of pickling, stewing and deep-frying the beef, the seasoning juice, which is used to wrap the beef, renders a special mellow and savory flavor.

In the widely-circulated story "Spring Bursting and Carp Jumping", Pang Sanchun, the wife of Jiang Shi, often cooked carp for her mother-in-law, demonstrating filial piety. Nowadays, Home-style Carp has become a local specialty. To make such a dish, first, mix pickled ginger and peppers, celery and garlic together and fry them with cooking oil. Next, put the fish into the pan and when the fish is done, pour some rice wine. Add brown sugar before turning off the heat and sprinkle chopped green onions, fennel and pepper powder on the surface. These ingredients make the fish rich in color, flavor and taste. After the fish is eaten, the gravy can be used for cooking noodles. The taste will linger on your palate after finishing the noodles.

Temple Fair Culture

Shangjiu, the 9th day of the first month of the Chinese lunar year, is a special occasion among Spring Festivals for the Han people. Since the Ming and Qing dynasties, from the 7th to the 9th day of the 1st lunar month, many folklore activities including parades, performances, guessing lantern riddles, orchid appreciation, etc. are organized to promulgate filial piety. In addition, every year, starting from the 4th day of the 5th lunar month, the town holds a week-long temple fair with local features, including shadow plays, sheet plays, drum singing and so on. On the 8th day of the 10th lunar month, there are grand ceremonies such as eminent monks chanting scriptures and pagoda worshipping where there's a re-enacting of the scene of five dragons guarding the pagoda in the Yuan Dynasty (1271—1368). It is a great experience to tour around the ancient town, visit the temple and experience the folk ambiance during the temple fair.

—Main Tourist Attractions—

Sanxiao Garden

The gate of Sanxiao Garden is similar to that of Jiangxiao Temple in shape, with clerical-script Chinese characters "三孝园" (means Sanxiao Garden) on the plaque and a pair of couplets depicting the filial piety of the Jiang family and the customs of Xiaoquan respectively on two sides. The lintel on the gate is decorated with colorful clay sculptures. The surroundings of the garden are quiet and beautiful. As they enter into this garden, people will first see Jianggong Hall and then the three statues. The statue of An'an (the son) is in the middle of the statues with his

和姜妻庞氏。右廊里有八组彩色泥塑，讲述了三孝故事。左边是"涌泉跃鲤"池，池边矗立着藏龙井亭，亭内有一仿古大钟。池周杨柳吐翠，假山、盆景相依相衬，十分幽雅。

藏经楼

藏经楼始建于明朝，经楼有两座，一左一右，经楼间原本有经堂，经堂里有八道扁额。20世纪六七十年代，经楼大面积毁坏，木板壁上原镌有的字画木刻，几乎有半数被人挖取，现残存的21块上刻着佛家偈语，其中包括书法家谢无量的书刻，尤为珍贵。

舍利塔

古镇上的舍利塔，又称"龙护舍利琉璃宝塔"。"龙护"，寓意有两条龙相护，"舍利"由梵文音译而来，原指释迦牟尼遗骨，意为建塔供奉佛骨。始建于汉代，最初为木塔，后被火焚，仅有塔基尚存。元顺帝至正二年（1342），安西府人赵文德发愿修成砖塔，修至7层中止，他的弟弟赵文礼续修6层，至正十三年（1353）竣工。明正德十三年（1481）又改置塔尖为琉璃宝顶，该塔有13层，高37米，为纺锤形砖塔，塔檐四角挂有铜铃，塔内有阶梯盘旋而上，可登至11层。孝泉舍利塔是四川省唯一尚存的元代砖塔，对研究四川砖塔演变过程具有重要的意义与价值。

father Jiang Shi and his mother Pang on each side. There are eight sets of clay sculptures inside the right corridor depicting their filial piety stories. To the left, there is a pool in commemoration of the story "Spring Bursting and Carp Jumping". The Dragon-hidden Pavilion, with a big bell inside, stands beside the pool. Willow trees, a rockery, and miniature trees are nearby, constituting a peaceful and elegant landscape.

Buddhist Sutra Mansions

There are two Buddhist sutra mansions built during the Ming Dynasty which were originally connected by a sutra hall with eight horizontal inscribed boards inside. During the 1960s, the mansions were heavily damaged; almost half of the calligraphy, paintings and wooden engravings on boarded partitions were dug out. There are only twenty-one pieces left, carved with Buddhist quotes, including those written by a calligrapher Xie Wuliang, which are especially valuable.

Stupa

The stupa (Sheli pagoda) of the town is also called Longhu Stupa, meaning "protected by two dragons". The Chinese characters "舍利" pronounced "Sheli" is a translation from the original Sanskrit language, meaning the "relics of Buddha". A stupa is used to preserve the remains of the Buddha. Built during the Han Dynasty (206 BC—AD 220), it was originally a wooden pagoda. Unfortunately, it was burnt down by a fire, and only the base survived. In 1342, the 2th year of Zhizheg period in Yuan Dynasty, Zhao Wende, a man from An'xi (in Gansu Province now), initiated the rebuilding effort. It was re-made into a seven-storey brick pagoda. His younger brother Zhao Wenli continued building another six storeys until 1353. In 1481, the 13th year of Zhengde period in Ming Dynasty, the spire of the pagoda was reconstructed with a glazed tile roof. The pagoda has thirteen storeys and is 37 meters high. It is spindle-shaped and has brass bells hung on the four corners of the pagoda. Inside the pagoda, there is a staircase spiraling up to the eleventh floor. The stupa is the only extant Yuan-Dynasty brick pagoda in Sichuan Province. Thus, it holds great value and importance on research on transformation of brick pagodas in Sichuan.

20. 达州石桥古镇

Shiqiao Ancient Town, Dazhou City

石桥古镇简介

石桥镇位于川东北的达州市境内，距城区61千米。因镇内有条河，河上建有众多石桥，故得此名。石桥镇与渠县、营山、平昌三县接壤，"巴彭"省道穿镇而过，素有达川"西大门"之美誉。全镇面积56.33平方千米，总人口7万。古镇风光秀美，植被繁茂，具有悠久的历史文化和纯厚的民俗风情。镇内古老院落众多，拥有省市重点文物保护对象。

—传奇故事—

烧龙祈雨：烧火龙传说

石桥镇"烧火龙"的来历与"雨"息息相关。相传，古时石桥附近连年闹旱灾，民不聊生。有一年正值元宵佳节，一位老道士云游至石桥，听闻该镇情况后，很想帮助当地人渡过难关。于是老道士让每家每户准备好香、烛、鞭炮和烟花等，然后他来到场镇旁的挑水

河边施法术。随着法术的施展，人们突然听到一声嚎叫，惊天动地，响彻云霄。霎时间，河水倒流，水位猛涨，一根巨大的水柱从河中喷涌而出。接着，东边天空突然闪烁起耀眼的光，这些光浮动着，仿佛快要从四周流泻下来。忽然又从半空中飞来一条威风凛凛的金黄色的火龙，口吐祥云。当天空被祥云完全覆盖，倾盆大雨瞬间席卷而至，并持续下了好几天。大雨的来临把人们从旱灾中解救了出来，人们笑逐颜开，载歌载舞地度过了旱灾后的第一个元宵节。石桥人十分感激老道士和火龙，所以每年正月十一到正月十五都会组织烧火龙的庆祝活动，巡街游巷，模仿火龙兴云降雨的场景。

A Brief Introduction to Shiqiao Ancient Town

The Ancient Town of Shiqiao is located in Dazhou City in the northeast part of Sichuan Province. It is about 61 kilometers away from the city of Dazhou. The name Shiqiao which means stone bridges in Chinese derives from the fact that there are many stone bridges that cross the river of the town. The town is bounded by three counties, Quxian, Yingshan and Pingchang. With the Bazhong-Pengshui[1] provincial highway passing through the town, Shiqiao is regarded as the "west gate" of Dazhou City. The town covers an area of 56.33 square kilometers and has a population of 70,000. Shiqiao Town is famous for its scenic beauty, abundant vegetation, splendid culture as well as rich folklore. There are numerous ancient courtyards in the town, which are listed as provincial cultural heritage sites.

—Legendary Stories—

Burning Dragon for the Pray of Rain: The Legend of Burning Fiery-dragon

The origin of Burning Fiery-dragon is closely related to the rain. In ancient times, the town was said to suffer from drought for many years, causing people to live on the edge of starvation. One Lantern Festival, a Taoist wandered to the town. After learning about the situation, he decided to help the people there. The Taoist asked every family to get joss sticks, candles, firecrackers and fireworks ready and then he went to the riverside of Tiaoshui River. The Taoist cast spells and people suddenly heard a loud roar, shaking both heaven and earth, resounding through the sky. At that moment, the river flowed back. The water soared, and a huge water column gushed out of the river. Then, a dazzling array of lights suddenly flashed in the sky. These lights which seemed to pour down from the sky moved around. Suddenly, a golden majestic-looking dragon flew from the sky, with his mouth spewing auspicious clouds. When the sky was completely covered by the clouds, rain poured down immediately and lasted for several days. The rain rescued people from the drought. Singing and dancing, people spent the first Lantern Festival happily in this previously long drought-stricken area. People were very grateful to the Taoist and the Fiery-dragon, so from the 11th to the 15th of the first month of the lunar

---

[1] Bazhong is a city in Sichuan Province and Pengshui is a county in Chongqing Municipality.

——民俗文化——

石桥有众多颇具地方特色的民间传统文艺，其中"烧火龙"和"翻山铰子"被列为省重点非物质文化遗产。

烧火龙

古石桥人为求国泰民安，风调雨顺，防止火灾，减少瘟疫，逐渐形成了耍火龙的习俗。据石桥镇的老人们介绍，神龙共九节，分龙宝、龙头、龙身、龙尾四部分。龙头、龙身、龙尾由麻布连接，长12尺[①]，代表一年的12个月。"烧火龙"有一系列的仪式。神龙制作好后，首先要请当地有声望的老人主持"请龙"仪式。"请龙"仪式后，就要为龙点睛，伴随着锣鼓、爆竹声，人们在河边为龙"请水"。接着从正月十一到十五晚上，人们便走街串巷烧火龙。烧火龙期间，九名青壮年汉子裸露上身，只穿一条短裤，各举一节火龙，伴随着锣鼓声在石桥的大街小巷穿梭。街民沿路用硝磺、柴炭、铁屑等配制的烟花，对火龙进行燃放。霎时烟花四溅，人们喝彩不绝。直到正月十六下午，人们再次来到河畔，用火点燃神龙，举行"送龙"仪式。

翻山铰子

翻山铰子是一种汉族民间舞蹈，由清朝咸丰年间石桥镇一位民间艺人冯白仁所创。翻山铰子通常由单人或多人组成方阵表演。伴随着唢呐和锣鼓声，表演者合着节

拍，双手挥动铰子（一种汉族打击乐器，又称为镲或小钹），放长或收短铰子上所系的绳子，或甩过头顶或绕过腰腿敲击双铰，展现舞姿。舞蹈动作由打、擦、翻、转4种方式组成。其特点为欢快热烈，刚健粗犷。常用于当地民间婚嫁仪式，现已被列为国家级非物质文化遗产。

---

① 1尺≈0.3333米。

year, the ceremonies of the Burning Fiery-dragon or parading on the streets are held to reproduce the scene of rain brought by the Fiery-dragon.

——Folk Culture——

There are many traditional folk arts with local features, including the Burning Fiery-dragon and the Fanshanjiaozi Dance which are on the list of the Provincial Intangible Cultural Heritage.

Burning Fiery-dragon

For peace and prosperity, ancient people in the town gradually formed a custom of burning a fiery dragon to prevent fire disasters and reduce the occurrence of plague. It is said that the dragon has a total long piece of nine joints including a dragon ball, head, body and tail. Each of them is connected by a piece of linen, and the whole dragon is twelve foots long, representing the twelve months of a year. There are a series of ceremonies for burning the fiery dragon. When a fiery dragon has been made, the first thing to do is to invite a prestigious elderly man to preside over the ceremony of "inviting the dragon from the heaven". After that, it is essential to paint eyes on the dragon. With drums and firecrackers, people fetch water in the river for the dragon. On the nights between the 11th to the 15th in the first month of the lunar year, people go out on the streets to burn the fiery dragon. During this process, nine young men, each wearing only a pair of shorts leaving the upper body bare, will hold only one joint of the dragon while running on the streets and lanes back and forth accompanied by the sound of gongs and drums. Local residents scatter fireworks which are made of sulfur, charcoal, and scrap iron over the dragon so that the dragon will burn. As this is happening, people applaud and cheer. On the 16th of the first lunar month, people go to the local riverside to light the dragon for the ceremony "seeing the dragon off".

Fanshanjiaozi Dance

The Fanshanjiaozi[①] Dance is a Han folk dance, created by a folk artist named Feng Bairen who lived during the Emperor Xianfeng's reign (1851—1861) in the Qing Dynasty. The dance is usually performed by one or more men. With the sound of trumpets and drums, performers dance to the beat, waving Jiaozi (an instrument of Han, also known as cymbals or small cymbals). They clash the Jiaozi over their heads or around their waist by adjusting the length of the strings on the Jiaozi. The performance of the dance often consists of hitting, rubbing, turning and shifting the Jiaozi, which is frequently seen in local wedding ceremonies for its cheerful, warm, and vigorous styles. Now it is listed as a national intangible cultural heritage.

---

① Fanshan means crossing the mountain and jiaozi refers to a musical instrument.

一主要景点串游一

民居

石桥古镇完好保存了传统街巷套四合院的格局，全镇以列宁街为主体，街面均为斜坡青石板，整齐划一地排列着。街边有走廊可供人行走。石桥古镇民居建筑多为穿斗式结构，空枋逗榫为主，小青瓦盖顶。临街一楼为门面，配置吊脚木质柜台。二楼为阁楼，屋檐下建有吊脚木楼，古风犹存。

庙宇

石桥镇属移民聚居之地，各地移民都十分重视传统礼教和建筑风格，因而古镇里建了不少庙宇。镇管辖范围内有27座寺庙，但由于历史原因，大部分被毁。街道上分布有四宫、四庙、一馆、一堂。此外，距场镇3千米处的"三教寺"有大量摩崖造像，于清代凿于高8.5米，宽13米，距地面2米的岩壁上。现存佛像260余尊。

节孝牌坊

石桥老街中心，有四座令人赞叹不已的"节""孝"牌坊，分别建于嘉庆二十一年（1816），同治八年、九年（1869、1870）及光绪二十六年（1900）。四座牌坊均由青石制作而成，造型敦厚朴实，形制各有异同。每坊上端必作"五龙捧圣"，其他各层雕刻"八仙过海""普陀岩""桃园结义""二十四孝"等历史戏曲故事，或以花卉、动物、棋琴书画等各种吉祥图案作为装饰，运筹巧思，别出心裁。

—Main Tourist Attractions—

Dwellings

Shiqiao is well preserved with a street that resembles a traditional style and is lined with courtyards. The main street is Liening Street, which is regularly paved with slant bluestone slates. There are corridors on the roadsides for people to walk on. The structures of the civil residences are in a vertical truss style, which adopt empty tiebeams, tenons, and gray tile on the roof. The first floors along the street are used as facades of shops that have a suspended wooden counter. The second floors are lofts under whose eaves are wooden buildings with ancient characteristics.

Temples

Shiqiao was inhabited by many migrants who attached great importance to traditional ethics and the architectural style of the town. That is why there are quite a few temples here. Originally there were 27 temples in the town, but most of them were destroyed. The street is lined with four palaces, four temples, one guild hall and one church. In addition, the Temple of Three Religions is located 3 kilometers away from the town. There, on the surface of the rocks are carved many statues which have existed from the Qing Dynasty. They are about 8.5 meters high, 13 meters wide and 2 meters above the ground. Today, there are around 260 Buddha statues.

"Jie" and "Xiao" Memorial Archway

There are four "Jie[①]" and "Xiao[②]" memorial archways in the center of the old street. They were respectively built in 1816, 1869, 1870 and 1900[③]. Four memorial archways made by blue stones are plain and simple in model and vary in shape. The upper end of each archway is carved with "five loyal ministers protecting the emperor" and the other layers are carved with opera tales, including "the Eight Immortals Crossing the Sea" and "Potalaka Temple", "the Story of Sworn Brothers in Peach Garden", and "24 Ancient Examples of Showing Filial Pieties" or with auspicious patterns like flowers, animals, lyre-playing, chess, calligraphy and painting, etc. as decorations.

---

① Jie in Chinese refers to integrity or chastity.

② Xiao in Chinese refers to filial piety.

③ The four years respectively refer to the 21st year in the reign of Emperor Jiaqing, 8th and 9th year in the reign of Emperor Tongzhi and the 26th year in the reign of Emperor Guangxu.

参考文献

陈可石,王波,焦杰. 城市设计与古镇复兴——成都洛带古镇整体设计和建设工程简述 [M]. 北京:中国水利水电出版社,2006.

陈中东,王海文. 泡在成都:解码中国第四城的优雅闲适[M]. 广州:广东旅游出版社, 2007.

丁浩. 时光影像36个四川古镇的瞬间记忆[M]. 成都:四川科学技术出版社,2006.

董谊思. 洪雅县志[M]. 北京:方志出版社,2007.

冯松. 浦江县志[M]. 北京:方志出版社,2011.

黄新初. 阿坝文化史[M]. 成都:四川民族出版社,2006.

焦虎三. 素面朝天福宝镇[J]. 民族论坛,2006(3):50-51.

赖武. 巴蜀古镇[M]. 成都:四川人民出版社,2003.

赖武,喻磊. 四川古镇[M]. 成都:四川人民出版社,2010.

李万斌,董立,孙亮亮 川东地区民间舞龙文化特色与价值研究[J]. 中华文化论坛.2011(3) 48-53.

凌立. 丹巴嘉绒藏族的民俗文化概述[J]. 西北民族学院学报(哲学社会科学版),2000(4): 77-85.

刘乾坤. 藏羚羊:四川重庆——特立独行自助旅行手册[M]. 3版. 桂林:广西师范大学出 版社,2007.

潘家德. 近代四川民俗变化研究[M]. 成都:四川大学出版社,2017.

《亲历者》编辑部. 亲历者旅行指南:中国古镇游[M]. 北京:中国铁道出版社,2011.

秦俭. 古镇川行[M]. 北京:中国旅游出版社,2004.

阮仪三. 遗珠拾粹——中国古城古镇古村踏察(一)[M]. 上海:东方出版中心,2013.

四川省旅游协会. 四川红色旅游景区导游词[M]. 北京:中国旅游出版社,2005.

乌丙安. 民俗学原理[M]. 长春:长春出版社,2014.

吴波. 石桥烧火龙的起源、现状及价值初探[M]. 中国民间文化艺术之乡建设与发展初 探. 北京:中国民族摄影艺术出版社,2010.

肖天清. 图说四川古镇[M]. 成都:西南交通大学出版社,2007.

谢智源. 古镇孝泉[M]. 北京:中国文史出版社,2008.

辛玉昌. 甘孜史话[M]. 兰州:甘肃文化出版社,2012.

藏羚羊旅行指南编辑部. 中国最美的100个古村古镇[M]. 北京:人民邮电出版社,2014.

中国地方志集成编委会. 中国地方志集成：四川府县志［M］. 成都：巴蜀书社，2017.

《中国古镇古村游》编写组. 中国古镇古村游［M］. 4版. 北京：中国旅游出版社，2012.

《中国古镇游》编辑部. 中国古镇游［M］. 西安：陕西师范大学出版社，2010.

《中国古镇游》编辑部. 中国古镇游6：四川［M］. 西安：陕西师范大学出版社，2005.

棕榈树编辑部. 2013中国古镇游［M］. 上海：龙门书局，2013.

附 录

附录1 自然景观中英对照表
Appendix 1 A List for the Natural Landscape

中文 Chinese	英文 English	所属古镇 Town
白龙江	Bailong River	昭化古镇
白沫江	Baimo River	平落古镇
白马泉	Baima Spring/ White Horse Spring	上里古镇
大渡河	Dadu River	丹巴古镇
大漕河	Dacao River	昭化古镇
凤栖山	Fengqi Mountain	街子古镇
府河	Fuhe River	黄龙溪古镇
贡嘎山	Gongga Mountain	丹巴古镇 磨西古镇
黄水河	Huangshui River	五凤溪古镇
葫芦海	Hulu Lake	丹巴古镇
黑岩坪	Mount Heiyanping	上里古镇
花溪河	Huaxi River	柳江古镇
九龙山	Jiulong Mountain	街子古镇
嘉陵江	Jialing River	昭化古镇
龙泉山	Longquan Mountain	洛带古镇
鹿溪河	Luxi River	黄龙溪古镇
临溪河	Linxi River	西来古镇
陇西河	Longxi River	上里古镇
墨尔多山	Moerduo Mountain	丹巴古镇

中文 Chinese	英文 English	所属古镇 Town
牦牛谷	Yak Valley	丹巴古镇
牛头山	Niutou Mountain	昭化古镇
青城后山	Qingcheng Back Mountain	街子古镇
骑龙山	Qilong Mountain	平落古镇
清江	Qingjiang River	昭化古镇
石城寺山	Shichengsi Mountain	五凤溪古镇
沱江	Tuojiang River	五凤溪古镇
味江	Weijiang River	五凤溪古镇
小云顶山	Little Yunding Mountain	五凤溪古镇
杨村河	Yangcun River	柳江古镇
鹧鸪山	Zhegu Mountain	丹巴古镇
杂谷脑河	Zagunao River	桃坪羌寨

附录2 文化景观中英对照表
Appendix 2 A List for the Cultural Landscape

中文 Chinese	英文 English	所属古镇 Town
安乐堰	Anle Weir/ Happy Weir	平落古镇
半边街	Banbian Street/ Half Street	五凤溪古镇 孝泉古镇
白衣庵	Baiyi Nunnery	孝泉古镇
丙灵殿	Bing Ling Hall	李庄古镇
常乐庵	Changle Monastery	街子古镇
潮音寺	Chaoyin Temple	黄龙溪古镇
陈家羌碉	Chen's Diaolou	桃坪羌寨
藏经楼	Buddhist sutra mansions	孝泉古镇
川北道贡院	North Sichuan Examination House	阆中古城
船形街	Boat-shaped Street	罗城古镇
川主庙	Chuanzhu Temple	礼州古镇
大山门	Mountain Gate	李庄古镇
大佛寺	Giant Buddhist Temple	阆中古城
岱宗殿	Daizong Hall	李庄古镇
东岳庙	Dongyue Temple	李庄古镇
吊脚楼	Stilted House	五凤溪古镇 平落古镇 柳江古镇 福宝古镇
二仙桥	Er-xian Bridge	上里古镇
费祎墓	Fei Yi Tomb	昭化古镇
高桥	Gaoqiao Bridge	上里古镇
古龙寺	Gulong Temple	黄龙溪古镇
关帝庙	Guandi Temple	西来古镇

中文 Chinese	英文 English	所属古镇 Town
关圣宫	Guansheng Hall	五凤溪古镇
光严禅院	Guangyan Temple	街子古镇
韩家大院	Han's Grand Courtyard	上里古镇
贺麟故居	He Lin's Former Residence	五凤溪古镇
黑风寺	Heifeng Temple	五凤溪古镇
会馆	Guild Hall	洛带古镇
回龙街	Huilong Street	福宝古镇
惠远寺	Huiyuan Temple	丹巴古镇
黄金堰	Huangjin Weir / Gold Weir	平落古镇
葭萌关	Jiameng Pass	昭化古镇
甲居藏寨	Jiaju Tibetan Village	丹巴古镇
建川博物馆	Jianchuan Museum	安仁古镇
姜维井	Jiangwei Well	昭化古镇
姜公坟	Jianggong Tomb	孝泉古镇
姜孝祠	Jiangxiao Temple	孝泉古镇
金花寺	Jinhua Temple	磨西古镇
九世石牌坊	Jiushi Stone Paifang / Nine-generation Stone Paifang	上里古镇
奎星阁	Kuixing Pavilion	李庄古镇
乐善桥	Leshan Bridge	平落古镇
凉厅街	Liangting Street/ Cool Hall Street	罗城古镇
灵官庙	Lingguan Temple	罗城古镇
刘氏庄园	Liu's Manor	安仁古镇
泸定桥	Luding Bridge	磨西古镇
民国风情街区	Block with the Style of the Republic of China	安仁古镇

中文 Chinese	英文 English	所属古镇 Town
南华宫	Nanhua Hall	洛带古镇 五凤溪古镇 礼州古镇
袍哥楼	Paoge Building	安仁古镇
唐公祠	Tanggong Temple	街子古镇
滕王阁	Prince Teng Pavilion	阆中古城
字库塔	Ziku Pagoda	街子古镇 上里古镇
巫氏大夫第	Lord Wu's Residence	洛带古镇
禹王宫	King Yu's Palace	洛带古镇
燃灯寺	Randeng Temple	洛带古镇
三圣宫	Sansheng Hall/ Hall of Three Saints	五凤溪古镇
三孝园	Sanxiao Garden	孝泉古镇
移民广场	Migrant Square	五凤溪古镇
镇江寺	Zhenjiang Temple	黄龙溪古镇
舍利塔	Stupa / Sheli Pagoda	孝泉古镇
十二殿	Twelve Hall	李庄古镇
唐家酒坊	Tang's Wine Workshop	黄龙溪古镇
文昌宫	Wenchang Temple/ Wenchang Hall	李庄古镇 罗城古镇 礼州古镇
文峰塔	Wenfeng Pagoda	西来古镇 上里古镇
西禅寺	Xichan Temple	礼州古镇
西林寺	Xilin Temple	西来古镇
惜字宫 / 惜字亭	Xizi Pagoda	西来古镇 福宝古镇
席子巷	Mats Lane	李庄古镇
解元寺	Jieyuan Temple	阆中古城

天府文化之旅：四川古镇文化双语读本

中文 Chinese	英文 English	所属古镇 Town
旋螺殿	Gyraulus Temple	李庄古镇
杨家大院	Yang's Grand Courtyard	桃坪羌寨
玉皇楼	Yuhuang Pavillion	李庄古镇
禹王庙九龙碑	The Nine-dragon Stele in King Yu's Temple	李庄古镇
战胜坝	Victory Dam	昭化古镇
张飞庙 / 桓侯祠	Zhang Fei Temple/ Huan Hou Temple	阆中古城
张家祠堂	The Zhangs' Ancestral Temple	李庄古镇
昭化考棚	Zhaohua Kaopeng	昭化古镇
曾家园	Zeng's Courtyard	柳江古镇

附录3　地方美食中英对照表
Appendix 3　A List for the Local Food

中文 Chinese	英文 English	所属古镇 Town
钵钵鸡	Benben Chicken/ Bobo Chicken	五凤溪古镇 柳江古镇
保宁醋	Baoning vinegar	阆中古城
白糖蒸馍	Steamed Bun with White Sugar	阆中古城
陈烧腊	Chen Roasted Meat	五凤溪古镇
川北凉粉	North Sichuan Bean Jelly	阆中古城
豆腐干	Dried Tofu	洛带古镇
豆花	bean curd pudding/ tofu pudding	平落古镇 西来古镇
蛋裹圆	Danguoyan/ Omelet Stuffed with Minced Pork	柳江古镇
锭子锅盔	crispy pancake	阆中古城
挞挞面	Tata Noodles	上里古镇
果汁牛肉	Guozi Beef	孝泉古镇
黄辣丁	Yellow Catfish	黄龙溪古镇 李庄古镇
剑门豆腐	Jianmen Tofu	昭化古镇
九斗碗	Hakka Jiudouwan	洛带古镇
礼州挂面	Lizhou Guamian / fine dried noodles	礼州古镇
李庄白肉	Sliced Boiled Pork with Garlic Sauce	李庄古镇
猫猫鱼	Maomao Fish	黄龙溪古镇
毛血旺	Maoxuewang / Duck Blood in Chili Sauce	西来古镇
面片汤	noodle soup	洛带古镇
奶汤面	Naitang Noodles	平落古镇

天府文化之旅：四川古镇文化双语读本

续　表

中文 Chinese	英文 English	所属古镇 Town
酿豆腐	Yong Tau Foo/ Hakka-style stuffed tofu	洛带古镇
牛羊杂碎面	beef and mutton noodles	阆中古城
女皇蒸凉面	Empress steamed cold rice noodle	昭化古镇
热凉面	hot noodles with sesame sauce	阆中古城
伤心凉粉	Sad Bean Jelly	洛带古镇
酥油千层饼	Multi-layered Pancake/ crispy pancake	柳江古镇
汤麻饼	Tang's Sesame Pastry	街子古镇
天主堂鸡片	Tianzhutang Sliced Chicken	街子古镇
坨坨肉	Tuotuo Meat/ lump pork	桃坪羌寨
王凉粉	Wang's Liangten / Wang's bean jelly	礼州古镇
西禅寺素斋	vegetarian dishes served at Xichan Temple	礼州古镇
盐卤鸡	salted pot-stewed chicken	洛带古镇
油烫鹅	fire-cured goose	洛带古镇
油茶撒子	Camellia Sazi	阆中古城
张飞牛肉	Zhang Fei Beef	阆中古城
芝麻糕	Sesame Cake	黄龙溪古镇

附录4　民风民俗中英对照表
Appendix 4　A List for the Folklore

中文 Chinese	英文 English	所属古镇 Town
川北灯戏	North Sichuan Lantern Show	阆中古城
翻山铰子	Fanshanjiaozi Dance	石桥古镇
放龙灯	Dragon Lantern Play	李庄古镇
福宝贯打唢呐	Fubao Guanda Suona Horn	福宝古镇
合江傩戏	Hejiang Nuo Opera	福宝古镇
划花船	Flower Boat Race	李庄古镇
火龙灯舞	Fiery Dragon Lantern Dance	黄龙溪古镇
街子兰花会	Jiezi Orchid Exhibition	街子古镇
客家山歌	Hakka folk songs	洛带古镇
阆中傩戏	Langzhong Nuo Opera	阆中古城
洛带水龙节	Luodai Water-dragon Dance Festival	洛带古镇
麒麟灯	Kylin Lantern Dance	罗城古镇
烧火龙	Burning Fiery-dragon	石桥古镇
舞草龙	Straw-dragon Dance	李庄古镇

附录5　民间技艺中英对照表
Appendix 5　A List for the Folk Crafts

中文 Chinese	英文 English	所属古镇 Town
巴惹	Ba-re	丹巴古镇
擦尔瓦	Chalva	磨西古镇
瓷胎竹编	Porcelain-bodied Bambooware	平落古镇
面人 / 面塑	Dough Figurine	安仁古镇
羌绣	Qiang embroidery	桃坪羌寨
藤编	rattan knitting	街子古镇
棕编	palm knitting	街子古镇
竹编	bamboo knitting	街子古镇 平落古镇

附录6　神话人物中英对照表
Appendix 6　A List for the Mythological Figures

中文 Chinese	英文 English	所属古镇 Town
白石神	White Stone God	桃坪羌寨
东岳大帝	Dongyue God	李庄古镇
醋炭神	God of Vinegar	阆中古镇
二郎神	Er-lang God	黄龙溪古镇
灌口神	Guankou God	福宝古镇
观世音大士 / 观世音菩萨	Merciful Buddha	黄龙溪古镇
灵官菩萨	God Lingguan	罗城古镇
弥勒佛	Maitreya Buddha	黄龙溪古镇
燃灯铁佛	Dipankara Buddha	洛带古镇
释迦牟尼	Sakyamuni	阆中古城
睡观音	Sleeping Guanyin/ Reclining Guanyin	洛带古镇
西王母	Queen Mother of the West	五凤溪古镇
镇江王爷	Lord Zhenjiang	黄龙溪古镇

附录7　古镇旧称中英对照表

Appendix 7　A Comparative Name List for the Ancient Towns

古镇名中文 The Present Name in Chinese	古镇名英文 The Present Name in English	古镇旧称中文 The Old Name in Chinese	古镇旧称英文 The Old Name in English
街子古镇	Jiezi	横渠镇	Hengqu Town
洛带古镇	Luodai	甄子场	Zengzi Town
黄龙溪古镇	Huanglongxi	赤水	Chishui Town
西来古镇	Xilai	临溪场	Linxi Town
上里古镇	Shangli	罗绳	Luosheng Town
桃坪羌寨	Taoping	赤溪寨	Chixi Village
丹巴古镇	Danba	诺米章谷	Nuo Mi Zhang Gu
昭化古镇	Zhaohua	葭萌	Jiameng
磨西古镇	Moxi	磨西面	Moximian/ Moxi Facet
柳江古镇	Liujiang	明月镇	Mingyue Town
福宝古镇	Fubao	佛保场	Fobao Town
礼州古镇	Lizhou	苏亓	Suqi
孝泉古镇	Xiaoquan	汛乡	Xunxiang Town

后 记

  成都理工大学文化价值观译介科研创新团队自2015年初成立以来一直围绕"中国文化价值观英译"展开研究工作。随着研究的不断深入，我们发现四川古镇文化资源特别丰富。据统计，省内现存1400多座古城镇，其中24座被评为国家级历史文化名镇，列入由建设部、国家文物局联合评选的中国历史文化名镇名单（第1～6批）。然而，令人惊讶的是目前对古镇的研究大多侧重于遗产保护与旅游开发，有关四川古镇文化译介的研究却非常少。市面上有关古镇的书籍大多以旅行指南的形式出现，对古镇文化的深度关注还不够。于是，我们便萌生了结合团队所长，为四川古镇文化外宣实践做出一点贡献的念头。团队成员群策群力，尝试对有关四川古镇文化的材料进行整理及编译，力图深度挖掘古镇背后的文化故事，讲好蕴含中国区域文化及价值观的古镇故事，希冀借助中英双语叙述的形式，带领读者开始一场天府文化之旅。

  本书依据古镇的知名度，遴选出川东、川南、川西、川北等不同方位合计20座知名古镇。每个古镇分四大板块进行编译：首先对古镇进行概述，让读者对该镇有一个整体认知；其次，讲述古镇背后的传奇故事，力图展示蕴藏其中的中国传统文化及其价值观；随后，从经济、社会、游艺、信仰等方面呈现颇具特色的民俗文化，带领读者领略当地的民俗风貌；最后，着眼于古镇较为著名的自然、人文景观，以客观的笔触展现其真实风貌。

  我们深感本书的编译过程也是一次文化审视之旅及语言赏析之旅。我们根据古镇特色，力图通过小小的传奇故事，讲述蕴藏其中的文化故事，以期回望中国传统文化。比如，街子古镇的"一瓢诗人"唐求的故事彰显出其淡泊名利、潜心诗作的品质，在当今社会显得难能可贵。罗城古镇灵官庙菩萨显灵的传说反映出古代人们对正义与社会良知的期盼。孝泉古镇"安安送米"的故事则体现了尊老爱幼的孝文化。无疑，移植到当下的语境中，该故事对读者仍具有现实意义，母慈子孝既是家庭和睦的保障，更是国家和谐的基石。我们希望通过这种小故事大道理的叙述方式，帮助读者走进古镇文化深处，引起心中的情感、伦理、道德共鸣。

  古镇上各式各样的建筑并非冷冷冰冰木石结构的物质，而是一个个有温度、鲜活的文化符号，通过时空的跨越传递出中国古人的智慧与信仰。比如，享有"中国西部客家第一镇"之称的洛带古镇建筑呈"一街七巷子"的封闭式布局，民居多为单进四合院式围拢屋。其建筑理念源自客家人的文化心理：由于家里男子常年在外谋生，出于对家里妇幼老人安全性的考虑，其房屋建筑特别注重防御功能。又如，我们发现许多古镇都建有字库塔或称文峰塔、惜字亭，其存在的本身则折射出中国古代文人对文字敬畏与珍惜的思想。由此，期盼重述建筑背后惜字积福的小故事，唤起人们敬惜字纸、爱护环境的生态意识。通过这种对建筑等物质形态的文化解读，希望能帮助读者形成一种敏锐的文化观察力，让古镇游变成一场更有意义的深度文化游。

编译与审校的过程同样也是一场语言赏析之旅。在编译过程中，我们尽量遵循文化传真的原则，即从文化角度准确再现源语传达的意义、方式和风格，对文字进行推敲，确保准确传递其文化含义，深有"两句三年得，一吟双泪流"之感。

对文化信息丰富的语段，以传递意义为主，采取了意译法，比如有一段对大佛的描述："其大佛为释迦牟尼坐像，……左手半置膝上，右手上屈作施无畏手印状。"初稿中"施无畏手印状"翻译成了 fearless fingerprint，译文为直译，显得有些生硬，导致阅读者不解其意。经过仔细审校及大量查阅相关资料后，对译文不妥之处进行了修改。佛教中不同手印代表了不同的寓意。无畏印为右手前臂上举于胸前，与身体略成直角，手指自然向上舒展，手心向外。其含义为使众生心安，无所畏怖。于是根据其意修改为"demonstrating a gesture of soothing troubled souls"，通过意译法传递出源文实际所指。

在地名、人名、美食名等文化信息不对等的翻译中，采用音译或音译＋注释的方式，比如"半边街"译为 Banbian Street，同时进行注释，说明中文 Banbian 的语义为英语中的 Half。在民谣等反映游艺民俗的翻译上，尽量考虑源文音韵等文体特征，以便传真源文风格，如有一小段关于当地美食的民谣"陈烧腊，摆上摊，小街上下香气窜，花钱买个鸡爪爪，翻来覆去啃半天"。译文为："Chen Roasted Meat, on a market stall. Aroma pervades the air in the street. If you buy a chicken paw, you can't help biting it all." 在翻译的时候尽量考虑到尾韵一致，尽可能地传真出中文民谣的音韵特点。

书稿历经两年多时间，从构思、设计、整理、编译、审校，到今天的成书，着实不易。参与书稿整理、编译、审校的同仁们自身也有着比较繁重的教学、管理等工作。大家均是利用宝贵的空余时间，不辞辛苦地对相关材料进行整理、编译，并对书稿中的历史、文化事实进行一一查证，确保表述的真实、准确性。在此对为本书付出努力的全体成员表示衷心的感谢。

此外，还要特别感谢加拿大里贾纳大学博士生导师 Fatima Pirbhai-Illich 教授对本书英文部分的校阅，她严谨谦逊的治学态度让我们非常感动。

本书部分图片来自编写人员的拍摄，部分来自互联网。来自互联网的照片由于未能联系到原作者，没有一一注明作者与出处。在此对相关作者表示歉意，并表示真诚的感谢。

另外，还要由衷感谢浙江大学出版社各级领导及编辑们的大力支持，感谢他们的理解、耐心和支持，使本书得以顺利出版。特别要感谢编辑李晨女士，她非常耐心细致地为我们解答了许多版式设计方面的困惑，让书稿以最恰当的方式呈现在读者面前。

最后，真心感谢成都理工大学各级领导对团队的关心、鼓励与支持，使得团队研究工作得以顺利推进，让研究成果能回馈社会。

文化价值观译介团队

2018年8月8日　成都

图书在版编目(CIP)数据

天府文化之旅：四川古镇文化双语读本：汉英对照 /
段成，董勋主编 . —杭州：浙江大学出版社，2019.9
ISBN 978-7-308-19322-1

Ⅰ . ①天… Ⅱ . ①段… ②董… Ⅲ . ①乡镇—文化史—
四川—汉、英 Ⅳ . ① K297.15

中国版本图书馆 CIP 数据核字（2019 ）第 143421 号

天府文化之旅：四川古镇文化双语读本

主 编 段 成 董 勋

责任编辑 李 晨

责任校对 郑成业

封面设计 春天书装

出版发行 浙江大学出版社
（杭州市天目山路148号 邮政编码310007）
（网址:http://www.zjupress.com）

排 版 杭州朝曦图文设计有限公司

印 刷 杭州杭新印务有限公司

开 本 787mm×1092mm 1/16

印 张 16.5

字 数 480千

版 印 次 2019年9月第1版 2019年9月第1次印刷

书 号 ISBN 978-7-308-19322-1

定 价 68.00元